D0215803

Basic NEC
with Broadcast
Applications

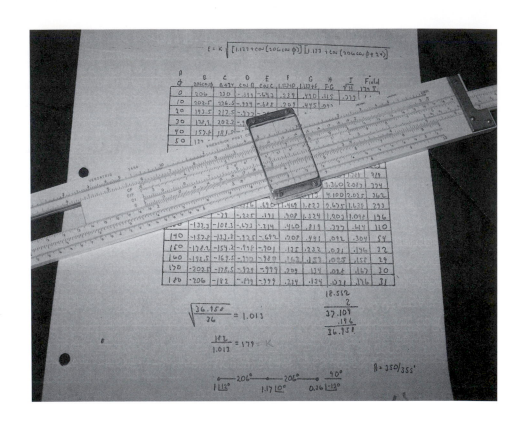

THE PURPOSE OF COMPUTING IS INSIGHT,
NOT NUMBERS
- *R.W. Hamming*

Basic NEC
with Broadcast
Applications

J.L. Smith, PE

ELSEVIER

AMSTERDAM • BOSTON • HEIDELBERG • LONDON NEW YORK • OXFORD
PARIS • SAN DIEGO • SAN FRANCISCO • SINGAPORE • SYDNEY • TOKYO
Focal Press is an imprint of Elsevier

Acquisitions Editor: Angelina Ward
Publishing Services Manager: George Morrison
Project Manager: Marilyn E Rash
Assistant Editor: Kathryn Spencer
Marketing Manager: Christine Degon Veroulis
Design Direction: Joanne Blank
Cover Design: Gary Ragaglia
Cover Images © J.L. Smith
Text Printer: Sheridan Books
Cover Printer: Phoenix Color Corp.

Focal Press is an imprint of Elsevier
30 Corporate Drive, Suite 400, Burlington, MA 01803, USA
Linacre House, Jordan Hill, Oxford OX2 8DP, UK

Copyright © 2008, Elsevier Inc. All rights reserved.

No part of this publication may be reproduced, stored in a retrieval system, or transmitted
in any form or by any means, electronic, mechanical, photocopying, recording, or otherwise,
without the prior written permission of the publisher.

Permissions may be sought directly from Elsevier's Science & Technology Rights Department
in Oxford, UK: phone: (+44) 1865 843830, fax: (+44) 1865 853333, E-mail: permissions@elsevier.com.
You may also complete your request on-line via the Elsevier homepage (*http://elsevier.com*), by
selecting "Support & Contact" then "Copyright and Permission" and then "Obtaining Permissions."

Library of Congress Cataloging-in-Publication Data
Smith, J.L.
  Basic NEC with broadcast applications / J.L. Smith.
      p.   cm.
Includes index.
ISBN 978-0-240-81073-7 (alk. paper)
1. Antenna arrays. 2. Radio—Transmitters and transmission. 3. Transmitters and transmission.
    I. Title.
TK7871.6.S566 2008
621.384'135—dc22   2008004493

British Library Cataloguing-in-Publication Data
A catalogue record for this book is available from the British Library.

For information on all Focal Press publications
visit our website at *www.books.elsevier.com*

08 09 10 11 12   5 4 3 2 1

Printed in the United States of America

Working together to grow
libraries in developing countries

www.elsevier.com | www.bookaid.org | www.sabre.org

ELSEVIER   BOOK AID
             International   Sabre Foundation

To my lovely wife, Marguerite,

who has been in my corner for 63 years.

She assures me that I'm the Champ,

she tells me that I'm winning,

and she pushes me back into the ring

to fight another round.

Contents

Foreword

The development of computer programs for modeling antennas began in the 1960s when main-frame computers were making advancements. Modeling codes that could run on desktop computers made their appearance in the early 1980s. The design of directional antenna arrays for medium-frequency (MF) broadcasting stations has a much longer history, however, reaching back to the mid-1930s when computations were done using a slide rule.

In the early years, methods involving approximations (such as the assumption of sinusoidal current distributions on the radiators) were developed and broadcasters have used them with reasonable success up to the present day. For the most part, however, to do that work the broadcaster's use of the computer has been relegated primarily to arithmetical operations rather than to actual modeling of the antenna. The success of simple design methods, and the fact that the general-purpose modeling codes and broadcast antenna engineers sometimes seem to "speak a different language," may account for the somewhat slow adoption of computer modeling by the broadcast community.

J.L. Smith has extensive experience in directional antenna design, which began long before the development of computer modeling. In *Basic NEC with Broadcast Applications*, he describes methods he has developed to use the public domain NEC-2 modeling code to design and tune MF directional antenna arrays. Some of the methods parallel the techniques developed by the navy's antenna designers by starting with simplified models and sometimes adjusting the models to match measurements. By using these methods, model parameters can be varied or features can be added to study effects.

In teaching courses on antenna modeling, we have found that new users often start by trying to model with too much detail. As a result, they run into problems with code limitations and eventually produce a large model that takes a long time to run and makes it difficult to try variations. Smith shows how to start with simple models, how to allow for code limitations and still get the important information. He illustrates the effectiveness of his methods by eventually comparing model results to measurements.

This book should be useful for both the beginning student and the working broadcast engineer. Beyond learning the methods described, you will be encouraged to see that it is possible for an ordinary user to get valuable results from the free public domain NEC-2 computer code.

Jerry Burke
Livermore, California

Preface

The Numerical Electromagnetics Code version 2 (NEC-2) is a public domain computer program that eliminates most of the shortcomings inherent in the conventional design methods for medium-frequency (MF) broadcast directional antennas. It is most useful for the increasingly complex arrays, and it yields parameter settings that greatly aid the initial adjustment of a new array.

NEC-2 was developed at Lawrence Livermore National Laboratories by G. J. Burke and A. J. Poggio in 1981 as a general-purpose tool for the design and analysis of antennas in general. For the most part, its published applications deal only with antennas that have a single drive source such as those found on dipoles, yagis, rhombics, and so on. Broadcast applications, on the other hand, use multiple sources to individually drive the separate elements of a multi-element array, with each source having a unique magnitude and phase so as to create a particular radiation pattern.

NEC-2 is not necessarily user-friendly to the broadcaster. From the very beginning, it gives the broadcaster a swift kick in the shin when it calls for defined source voltages as the inputs to initiate a given antenna analysis, whereas broadcasters have conventionally started their design with a given set of field ratios. Then among other complications, NEC-2 uses the coordinate system common to mathematics, whereas broadcasters have traditionally used the geographical coordinate system. Then NEC-2 deals with peak values, not RMS, as does the broadcaster.

Thus, while NEC-2 is indeed a magnificent tool, it is not at all directed to broadcast use. As a result, when NEC-2 first made its appearance, it was not immediately accepted by the broadcast community and only a few broadcast engineers even attempted to use it.

In time, however, broadcast engineers with various levels of expertise studied the use of NEC-2 and each developed their own postprocessing software to read data from the standard output file and to use that data to perform the various tasks necessary for broadcast work. Such studies have been carried on rather independently, and somewhat privately, however, and some engineers even consider their work proprietary. Unfortunately, little of the work has been published to enjoy peer review or to serve as tutorials for those seeking entry into the profession.

In recent years, some engineers have written software to make the moment method programs more user-friendly to the broadcaster, and some of the more developed efforts have been packaged as commercial products for sale to the broadcast community. The consensus is, however, that the commercial products all use the same basic moment method engine and that they differ mainly in the user interface with, perhaps, some special features added.

Because there has been such a diversity in the development of the procedures for applying NEC-2 calculations to broadcast arrays, there may be multiple approaches to accomplish a given analysis, and each approach possesses merit. Therefore, as you study NEC-2 from this book and other sources, you might find additional and even contradicting methods of analysis; in that case, I encourage you to weigh the merits of each and to exercise your judgment as to the best use of available methods.

At the present time, there is no modern and comprehensive tutorial available to a person desiring to enter the field of MF directional antenna design, and the few remaining people who are knowledgeable of the science are becoming older and, unfortunately, fewer. This regrettable circumstance occurs at a time when we are on the brink of a resurgence of need as new forms of modulation make their way into the MF band. Digital modulation methods make it necessary to renew our interest in directional antenna systems as we study bandwidth requirements and learn new implementation schemes to accommodate the more sophisticated application. At the same time, 5000 existing directional antenna systems continue to demand maintenance, and the need for replacement grows as they come to their life's end at the rate of approximately 100 per year.

Basic NEC with Broadcast Applications was written to show how the features of NEC-2 can be accommodated in the design and analysis of MF broadcast directional antennas. I also envision this book as a depository where one may come to learn modern basics of the science; in so doing, the book will assist younger people who wish to enter the field. This book also serves as a useful desk reference that can remind the professional user of the many details encountered while using NEC-2 to analyze and design modern MF directional antenna arrays.

Finally, a somewhat lofty goal is that others more skilled in the science than I will see this book as an incentive to make their own contributions to publicly documenting the use of NEC for broadcast applications.

Acknowledgments

Someone once said, "We see the future by standing upon the shoulders of those who have gone before us." While I don't mean to imply that the following persons have preceded me in time (for I'm much too old for that), I do want to acknowledge that they have preceded me in knowledge and that they have given of that knowledge generously to make this book possible.

My sincere appreciation goes to the many people who have contributed to this book, but I am especially indebted to:

- Gerald J. (Jerry) Burke, of Lawrence Livermore National Laboratory and cocreator of NEC-2, who gave so generously of his time to review this manuscript and to make many valuable suggestions.

- Jack Sellmeyer, Sellmeyer Engineering, McKinney, TX, and former coworker at Collins Radio Company, whose contributions and patience through the years have provided the practical experience necessary to bring realism to theory.

- Paul Carlier, FanField, Ltd., UK, for his contribution to, and review of, that portion of the manuscript pertaining to measured data.

And for years of discussions and the sharing of practical experience, I express my sincere appreciation to my long-time friend, Paul Cram, Broadcast Technical Services, Mansfield, GA, who started working with directional antennas when the concept first appeared in 1935. Now in his nineties, Paul is still in the profession and aggressively applying NEC-2 to broadcast directional antennas.

About the Author

J.L. Smith received a B.S. degree in physics from the University of Houston in 1956 and an M.S. degree in engineering from Southern Methodist University in 1959. He began his career in broadcasting at KTRH in Houston in 1946. In 1956, he joined Collins Radio Company where he held the usual positions in research and development culminating in head of the Department of Research and Development. He served as the manager of Broadcast Systems Engineering at Collins Radio Company during the 1960s. While there he directed the development of a complete catalog of new broadcast products.

Mr. Smith has been active in FCC matters, having filed the first petition advocating automatic unattended operation of FM broadcast transmitters. He participated in the coordination of international broadcasting through his service on CCIR Study Group 10 and has participated in various national and international symposia. J.L. Smith has authored approximately 50 technical papers and has published two other books—*Basic Mathematics with Electronics Applications* (Macmillan, 1972) and *Intermodulation Prediction and Control* (Interference Control Technologies, 1993).

He is now retired in Covington, Louisiana, where he devotes much of his time to analytical research pertaining to AM directional antennas.

The Array Adjustment Process

1.1 The Nature of NEC-2

It is important to recognize that the Numerical Electromagnetics Code (NEC) is no magic tool—it does some things very well but it cannot do other things. In spite of this, it is a valuable tool that makes a significant contribution to easing the design and adjustment of medium-frequency (MF) broadcast directional antennas.

The user of NEC-2 should have realistic expectations, and recognize from the outset, that the results of a NEC-2 analysis are, at best, an approximation, and they are not necessarily exact answers. Fortunately, however, the results of a NEC-2 analysis need not be precise to be beneficial.

1.2 The Directional Antenna Adjusting Process

The process of physically adjusting the network components of an array to achieve a desired pattern is very similar to that of mathematically synthesizing a radiation pattern using computerized optimizing methods. Both processes start with a given pattern, compare it to a target, determine an error, and then make parameter adjustments in an attempt to reduce the error. In the physical adjustment process, the pattern error is a matter of human opinion; in the case of computerized pattern synthesis, the error is defined mathematically.

The mathematical synthesis process and the physical adjustment process possess the same significant limitation in that neither can know when the minimum error has actually been reached. Therefore, in both cases the usual practice is to test a potential error minimum by changing a parameter value and noting the effect on the error. If the error increases, then the parameter is returned to its original value and another parameter value is changed. If all the parameter values are changed in turn and none reduces the error, then it is often assumed that the error is at a minimum.

The task does not end there, however. The error may indeed be at a minimum, but it may not be at the *absolute* minimum. There may be another set of parameters that will create an even smaller error. That concept can be better understood by considering the following analogy.

1.3 Local and Global Minima

The pattern error can be envisioned as an $N + 1$ dimension surface where N is the number of variables.

Figure 1-1 shows a three-dimensional error surface of two variables, arbitrarily called Field Ratio and Phase for example purposes. Point S in Figure 1-1 is taken as an arbitrary starting point from which we

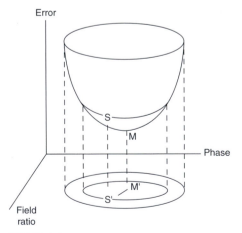

FIGURE 1-1

Error surface of two variables.

will make a search in an effort to find point M, which is the point on the surface representing the values of Field Ratio and Phase where the error is least.

The object is to change the values of Field Ratio and Phase so as to move from point S to point M. That is not necessarily a simple task, especially if there are more than two variables. One must know not only which variable to change, but also the direction of the change and how much change is required. Ultimately, however, after a number of changes, a point will be reached where an additional change of either variable will cause the error to increase. It might then be concluded that point M has been reached.

Only the simplest arrays have smooth error surfaces, as shown in Figure 1-1. The more complex arrays are pock-marked with variations that may be viewed as downward-pointing dimples in the surface. These dimples press the surface down for a range then allow it to rise again. Figure 1-2 shows such a dimple but, for the sake of simplicity, only a one-variable error curve is shown.

Again point S is the starting point in the search for the minimum at point M. Notice, however, that to follow the curve from point S to point M, one must go through point D. While point D suggests that it is the minimum (i.e., at point D the error increases if the variable is varied in either direction), the reduced error at point D is larger than the error at point M. Point M is unique; that is, there can be only one point of least error, so point M is called the *global* minimum. Point D, on the other hand, is not unique because there can be several points of this type. Therefore, points such as D are called *local* minima. When adjusting a

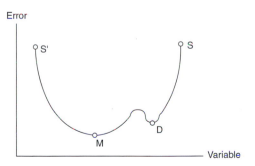

FIGURE 1-2

Single-variable error curve containing a local minimum.

directional array to a target pattern, then in essence, one must journey along the error surface attempting to reach the global minimum. If the error surface does not continuously increase or decrease but instead has a number of dimples, then one may well fall into a dimple and be in a local minimum. Unfortunately, it is not possible to know that it is a local minimum, nor is there a way to determine that it is a local minimum.

Usually, if the error in a minimum is tolerable, then the adjustment process will be stopped, notwithstanding whether the minimum is local or global. This happens more often than not when physically adjusting a complex array.

If the error in the local minimum is intolerable, however, then a new starting point must be chosen and a new adjustment process started from there, hoping to bypass any local minima. For example, if the starting point in Figure 1-2 is changed from point S to point S', it is obvious that the journey along the curve to point M will occur without complications.

1.4 The Role of NEC-2

The idea to convey here is that if the array is simple, then the error surface is likely to be smooth and the probability of reaching the global minimum is high. If the array is complex, however, then the error surface may contain several local minima and the probability of reaching the target without falling into a local minimum is practically zero; so the search process must be repeated over and over ... *unless the starting point is initially chosen to be very near the global minimum.* This is where NEC-2 makes its contribution.

In most cases, a NEC-2 analysis will define a set of starting parameter values that, although they may not necessarily be exact, they are sufficiently accurate to be near enough to the global minimum to avoid most local minima. Therefore, the engineer can initially set the array component values to those determined by a NEC-2 calculation then manually adjust the array to the global minimum without being trapped by a local minimum. This benefit of knowing where to set the parameters in preparation for an initial start-up of a new array can save thousands of dollars in fieldwork. The case histories in later chapters of this book give vivid demonstrations of this benefit.

1.5 Analysis Overview

Unless the reader has previous knowledge of the use of NEC-2, it is not likely that the following steps for NEC-2 analysis will be self-explanatory. Nevertheless, the procedure is presented here as an overview to let the reader know what to expect and what the explanations that follow are seeking to accomplish. So if questions remain after finishing this section, be patient; more detail will be revealed in later chapters.

When using the public domain software furnished on the CD included with this book, it is necessary to make three separate NEC-2 runs to arrive at the NEC-2 output file that yields the final analysis. Fortunately, this is not difficult; nor is it excessively time consuming and the results are just as valuable as those obtained with any commercial software that might have a more user-friendly interface. The NEC-2 computations are made using a slightly modified version of the public domain NEC-2 program called bnec.exe (included on the CD with this book).

The sequence leading to a NEC-2 analysis proceeds according to the following steps.

1. Create a NEC-2 unity drive input file that excites each tower individually with $1.0 + j0$ volts while the companion towers are grounded. Using that unity drive file as the input file, run bnec.exe.

2. Using the NEC-2 output file created by step 1, run the NecDrv.exe computer program included on the associated disk to determine the normalized base drive voltages corresponding to the target field ratios.

3. Create a NEC-2 normalized drive input file that excites the towers simultaneously with the normalized base drive voltages determined in step 2. Run bnec.exe with that normalized drive file as the input file.

4. Using the NEC-2 output file created by step 3, run the NecMom.exe program included on the associated disk to confirm that the normalized base drive voltages do, in fact, create the target field ratios.

5. Scale the normalized base drive voltages determined in step 2 to the full power level (described in Chapter 6 of this book) to generate the desired power output.

6. Create a NEC-2 full-power drive input file that excites the towers simultaneously with the full-power base drive voltages determined in step 5. Using that full-power drive file as the input file, run bnec.exe.

7. The NEC-2 output file created by step 6 contains the final data for analysis.

Later chapters in this book will show how to interpret the output file to learn the peak values of voltages and current at significant points in the system plus how to read the operating drive point impedance of each tower. Armed with this information, the engineer may calculate the antenna-matching networks and set the individual network component values to a reasonable starting value in preparation for the initial turn-on of the array.

Perhaps the most beneficial result of a NEC-2 analysis is the current distribution listing for each tower of the array. From these current distribution listings, the designer can determine at what height to position the antenna monitor sampling loops such that the antenna monitor will give indications that closely correspond to the associated far-field ratios. He can also determine the base voltage ratios corresponding to the target field ratios if his antenna monitor samples those voltages.

If the sample loops are not positioned at the optimum height, or if current transformers are used to sample the tower current, then the NEC-2 current distribution listing can be used to determine the monitor reading that corresponds to the desired far-field ratio.

Thus, with some indication of the radiated far-field ratios at hand during the initial adjustment process, the array networks can be adjusted to very near their final values without the benefit of distant-field strength measurements and without being plagued by falling into a local minimum.

1.6 Additional NEC-2 Benefits

In addition to defining a suitable set of starting parameters, later chapters will show that the NEC-2 analysis serves several other useful purposes.

First, a NEC-2 analysis allows the engineer to explore physical arrangements that are not practical using hardware—the effects of different tower heights, for example. In addition, the engineer is able to examine the impact of unused towers and other structures in the vicinity of the array. He or she is able to study the effects of top loading and tower skirts, as well as shunting reactance at the tower insulator. NEC-2 also gives good indications of power budget, currents, impedances, and so on.

In summary, the results obtained from the NEC-2 analysis may not be exact, but they still provide the engineer with an insight into array performance that minimizes the "cut-and-try" effort so common to array adjustment.

1.7 Software Requirements

Antenna analysis software sells for as much as $2000 or more and many of the commercial computer programs being sold for that purpose use the basic NEC-2 or NEC-4 engine. They differ, for the most part, only in the way they present a convenient or novel user interface.

Therefore, in the interest of economy, this book uses the NEC-2 public domain software that can be downloaded from the Internet free of charge. The human interface with the public domain software may not be as elegant as some of the purchased products, and the public domain software may not be as user-friendly, but the results are just as useful and just as rewarding, and the time spent in learning to use it is indeed invested wisely.

If, however, the reader already possesses commercial software, then in most cases the commercial software can be used in lieu of the public domain software. The concepts presented in this book are valid independently of the software used. And while the postprocessing programs furnished on the associated disk may not be compatible with the output format of the commercial software, sufficient information is furnished in the book to allow one to write simple postprocessing programs that are compatible with the output files at hand.

NEC-2 Fundamentals

2

2.1 Scope

As the name implies, this book covers only the basic application of NEC-2 to the design and analysis of MF directional antennas. The essentials are described in sufficient detail to teach the useful design and analysis of medium-frequency (MF) broadcast antenna arrays, but some refinements of NEC-2 are not specifically described in this text or they are given only cursory mention. Some of these refinements include the use of symmetry and reflection to simplify the input file, wire arcs, dimension scaling, and multiple structures. Only a cursory explanation of the use of Numerical Green's Function and the Sommerfeld/Norton finite-ground method is given in the last chapter so more study will be needed to fully exploit those topics.

In addition, NEC-2 has some capabilities that are not usually associated directly with broadcasting; therefore, those topics are not included in this text. These include the ability to model helix and cylindrical structures, surface patches, and circular and elliptical polarization.

However, to augment the material in the text, Appendix A includes the complete catalog of NEC-2 commands. They are described in sufficient detail in the appendix to permit the reader to individually extend study to any capability of NEC-2.

2.2 The NEC-2 Engine

The Numerical Electromagnetics Code was written in 1977 by G. J. Burke and A. J. Poggio at Lawrence Livermore National Laboratory under contract to the U.S. Navy. The code was originally known as the Numerical Electromagnetics Code (NEC). As the code was improved over time, it was renamed NEC-2 in 1980, NEC-3 in 1983, and ultimately NEC-4 in 1990. NEC-2 has been declared public domain, NEC-3 no longer exists, and the distribution of NEC-4 is controlled by licensing through the Industrial Partnership and Commercialization Office at Lawrence Livermore National Laboratory.

The NEC-4 source code is an extensive revision of the NEC-2 code that makes more use of the Fortran 77 constructs and is more modular and easier to understand and maintain. Additional features and capability were added in the revision process. For example, NEC-2 models wire structures both in free space and over a ground plane. The ground plane may be either perfectly conducting or have finite ground characteristics. NEC-4 possesses the same abilities as NEC-2 in this regard plus it is able to model wire structures buried in the ground or passing through the air/ground interface.

NEC-4 also carries revisions of the NEC-2 code that reduce the loss of precision when modeling tightly coupled wires and electrically small structures. In addition, NEC-4 has been changed to be more accurate than NEC-2 when treating models containing stepped-radius wires or junctions of wires of differing radius. NEC-4 can also accommodate the effects of insulated wires, whereas NEC-2 has no such provision.

Thus, while NEC-4 is, indeed, considered the most accurate, NEC-2 is quite adequate for most broadcast applications. Therefore, because NEC-2 is in the public domain and available at no charge, it was selected to be the code used in this book.

Both the executable and source code for NEC-2 are widely distributed on the Internet and the code has been liberally modified by various users. The NEC-2 computer program used in this book is a modified version of NEC2dxs.zip. At the time of this writing, NEC2dxs.zip can be downloaded free of charge from the Internet: *http://www.si-list. net/swindex.html*.

The unzipped version has been included on the disk that accompanies this book. What's there has been modified and renamed bnec. exe but will be referred to henceforth by the general term NEC-2. The program bnec.exe is a Win 95/98/Me/NT4/2000/XP 32 bit Windows application that works from a DOS console window. It has been modified slightly to make the GM command input format more useful to the broadcaster and to dimension the arrays to accommodate a 120 wire ground screen. It has also been changed to protect the input file from accidental erasure. Please be aware that the GM command (described in Chapter 3) has been modified. It is compatible with bnec.exe, but the modified version is not compatible with the usual NEC2dxs programs. The GM command used here is, however, compatible with the NEC-4 file format. Therefore, the input files generated during the study of this book are, for the most part, usable with both bnec.exe and NEC-4.

2.3 NEC-2 Operation

In perhaps an oversimplified explanation, the antenna to be analyzed is modeled by a series of wires and voltage sources as described to NEC-2 in an input file furnished by the user. When run, NEC-2 divides each wire into the number of segments specified by the user. It then calculates the current on each segment and finally sums the effects of all segments to get a final result. NEC-2 stores its output in a file that it places in the computer's currently active folder. The user must recall the output file to read, print, or otherwise use it.

2.4 Creating the Input File

To use NEC-2, the user must generate an input file that describes the antenna geometry and operating parameters in a defined format. This is done using any convenient text editor and saving the file in text form. When NEC-2 is run, it issues a call for the path and name of the input file plus the name that the user wishes to assign to the output file. There are no other communications with the user while NEC-2 runs.

2.4.1 Naming the Files

During the course of conducting a directional array analysis, it is necessary to make several NEC-2 runs and to generate several NEC-2 input and output files. To conveniently keep track of the various files, a naming convention is recommended. The convention used in this book is defined as we go along and the reader is encouraged to follow that convention to avoid confusion.

In that regard, it is sufficient to say at this time that all files may be named with the call letters of the station using the antenna array. For some discussions in this book, CALL will represent a generic station call being used for illustration purposes. All input files will carry the extension .NEC. Thus, the input file will be named CALL.NEC. The output file generated by NEC-2 when CALL.NEC is the input file can be named anything but it is highly recommended that it be named CALL.OUT.

2.4.2 Data Commands

The original NEC-2 computer program used punched cards to input the data that describes an antenna and to request computation of antenna characteristics. But, as mentioned earlier, modern NEC-2 now uses an input text file with the format of the data within that file being similar to that of the punched card set. Each line in the input file is a separate command and each command carries the data that initially appeared on a single punched card. Instead of the data being written into positional fields, however, modern NEC-2 files use data fields delimited by commas or spaces. Because of the similarity to a punched card set, and of course the inertia of habit, each data statement command in the input file is sometimes referred to as a "card." However, in an attempt to be more descriptive, this book follows the precedent set by the documentation of NEC-4 and uses the word "command" rather than the word "card" when referring to the statements in the input file.

A typical data command is:

RP 0, 1, 361, 1001, 90., 0., 0., 1., 1609., 0.

The commands in an input file must be written in ASCII text and they must begin in column 1 of line 1. Each successive command must then begin in column 1. Do not indent the commands or use spaces at the beginning of the commands and do not use blank lines.

Every data command begins with a two-letter alphabetic code in columns 1 and 2 to identify the command to the program. There are 34 two-letter command codes in the NEC-2 vocabulary and all of them are given in Appendix A. However, only about 20 of these codes are normally used in broadcast calculations. The simple example that follows later uses only 9 of the command codes and those are probably the most common command codes used by broadcasters.

All commands having numeric data are written in a similar format, with fields for integer numbers first, followed by fields for real numbers. Integer numbers are written with no decimal point. Real numbers are written as a string of digits and may contain a decimal point. Real numbers may also be written as a string of digits containing a decimal point followed by an exponent of 10 in the form $1.234E^{\pm6}$. This is interpreted as multiplying the number 1.234 by $10^{\pm6}$.

2.4.3 Data Command Types

The input file for a single NEC-2 run must contain at least one of each of the three types of command.

1. The input file must begin with one or more comment commands that can contain any type of information but they usually provide a description of the NEC-2 run. This information is printed at the start of the output file as a label.

2. The comments are followed by geometry commands, which describe the antenna system. The geometry commands have two fields for integer numbers followed by real-number fields as necessary.

3. Finally, a number of program control commands specify electrical parameters such as frequency, loading, and excitation. Commands of this type also request the execution of the .NEC file. The program control commands have four integer fields followed by real-number fields.

2.4.4 An Input File Illustration

The following illustration is included here to stimulate the reader's interest before we embark upon a series of long explanations. A single tower is used in this example because it is the simplest representation. Of course, a broadcast array will have multiple towers. The object of this one-tower calculation might be to determine the driving point impedance of the tower, although enough data is included in the output file to enable one to plot the current distribution on the tower and to view the antenna radiation pattern.

Remember that the data commands in an input file must begin in column 1 of line 1. Each successive command must then begin in column 1. Do not indent the commands or use spaces at the beginning of the commands and do not use blank lines.

The example input file listed here contains three comment commands (CM, CM, CE), two geometry commands (GW, GE), and five program control commands (GN, FR, EX, RP, EN). A full explanation of all the input commands is given in Appendix A. As each command code is addressed in the paragraphs that follow, the reader is encouraged to read the full description of that command code as it appears in Appendix A.

The commands in Listing 2-1 make up the sample input file.

Comment Commands

Every input file must contain at least one comment command and if there is only one comment command, it must be the CE command. Any other comment commands must precede the CE command and must be identified as CM commands. In the preceding example. CM and CE are comment commands.

Geometry Commands

Several types of geometry command can be used to describe the wires in an antenna but the GW is the most used for broadcast work. The

Listing 2-1

```
CM This is a comment line – usually shows the file name, CALL.NEC
CM The comment lines will be printed in the Output file.
CE The last comment line must use the CE designation.
GW, 101, 20, 0., 0., 0., 0., 0., 115., 0.5
GE,1
GN,1
FR, 0, 1, 0, 0, 1.5, 0.
EX, 0, 101, 1, 00, 1266.084, 0.
RP, 0, 1, 9, 1001, 90., 0., 0., 45., 1609., 0.
EN
```

GW command describes a straight wire located in an XYZ coordinate system where lengths are measured in meters. For our broadcast work, towers are considered to be wires or to be made up of a group of wires. The simplest description of an antenna tower is a single vertical wire of defined radius, as represented in the GW command of Listing 2-1.

The position of each wire must be specified and the number of segments into which the wire is to be divided must also be specified. The position of a wire is defined by showing the coordinates of each end, as presented in the XYZ coordinate system. While you must specify the number of segments, it is not necessary to define the position of each segment because NEC-2 does this routinely. While only one wire is used in the simple example above, multiple wires can be used to describe a single tower and, of course, multiple wires are used to describe a multi-tower directional array.

Referring to the GW wire in Listing 2-1, the number 101 is the wire tag number assigned to identify this wire. By broadcast convention, the 100 tag series (101, 102, 103, etc.) is used to identify wires associated with tower 1. The 200 series (201, 202, 203, etc.) identifies wires associated with tower 2; the 300 series, tower 3, and so on. Be sure to get into the habit of using this convention because some postprocessing programs take advantage of this convention to identify towers and to determine the number of towers in an array.

In Listing 2-1, the wire tag 101 in the GW command shows that this is wire 1 of tower 1. Next, the digits 20 show that we have elected to divide the wire into 20 segments. The next three fields show that the first end of the wire is located at X = 0 meters, Y = 0 meters, and Z = 0 meters (ground level at the origin). The following three fields show that the second end of the wire is located at X = 0 meters, Y = 0 meters, Z = 115 meters. This describes a vertical tower (wire) located at the origin and 115 meters high. The last field of the GW command shows that the effective radius of the tower is defined to be 0.5 meters.

Next is the GE command, which is mandatory and indicates the end of the geometry description. The GE command also signals whether the antenna is in free space or whether it is operating over a ground plane. GE with no following digit, or with the digit 0 following, indicates free space operation, whereas GE with the digit 1 following is used when a ground plane is present. The GE command does not specify the characteristics of the ground plane; it only readies NEC-2 to accept the ground-plane parameters from a following command. If a ground plane is present, then in addition to the GE command, the GN command must be included to define the characteristics of that ground plane. Please read the full description of the GE command and the GN command in Appendix A.

Program Control Commands

The GN command is a program control command and shows the characteristics of the ground in the immediate vicinity of the antenna. Appendix A explains that the digit 1 following GN shows that the ground plane is perfectly conducting. A zero or 2 following GN indicates a finitely conducting ground, which must be defined in the remaining fields of the GN command. The finitely conducting ground is used only in calculating radiated fields. The NEC-2 calculated value for the self-impedance of the tower will be the same whether using a perfecting conducting ground or a ground with finite constants. Please refer to appendix A for more details on the GN command.

The FR command sets the frequency to 1.5 MHz, although it is capable of doing more. See Appendix A for a full description of the use of the FR command.

The first zero on the EX command shows we are exciting the wire with a voltage source. The following two data fields showing wire tag 101 and segment 1 place the excitation on wire 1 of tower 1 using segment 1. The excitation is defined to be 1266.084 + j0 volts by the last two fields of the EX command. Notice that the excitation voltage is a complex number expressed by its real and imaginary parts; thus, it has both magnitude and phase.

It is important to say here that modeling voltage sources is a critical step in the analysis of broadcast antennas. NEC-2 offers two models for voltage sources, the applied-field source and the bicone source. The applied-field source ($I1 = 0$ on the EX command) is most appropriate for broadcast work. See the EX command in Appendix A for a full explanation.

The RP command tells NEC-2 to calculate the radiated pattern. This command is also an automatic execute command. The XQ command can also be used to cause execution but it is not necessary when preceded by the RP command, although no error is caused if the XQ command is included. Again, refer to Appendix A to read the full description of each of these commands.

As an exercise, type the input file commands given as Listing 2-1 in Section 2.4.4 into a file and save it as a text file with the name CALL.NEC. Any convenient text editor may be used—the EDIT command in Windows works fine, as does WordPad and Notepad. If WordPad or Notepad is used, be sure to save the work as a text file.

2.5 Reading the Output File

To run the CALL.NEC input file using bnec.exe, place CALL.NEC and bnec.exe in the same folder, then run bnec.exe. The bnec.exe will ask for the name of the input file, which is CALL.NEC. It will then ask for the name that you wish to assign to the output file, and an appropriate response is CALL.OUT. When bnec.exe finishes its run, it will leave the output file (CALL.OUT) in the currently active folder.

If your input file contains an error, NEC-2 does not signal that error during the run time. Instead, it records the error in the output file and aborts the run if it is a fatal error. Therefore, you must examine the output file to identify an error. A brief description of the error will appear at the place in the output file where the error occurred. More error descriptions are given in general in Appendix B.

The output file can be quite long and it contains some lines longer than 100 characters; thus, it is difficult to read in a DOS window. The output file is most conveniently viewed using WordPad and called by a batch file whose location is included in the PATH variable of the AUTOEXEC.BAT file. While on this subject, it is recommended that you also include bnec.exe and a viewing program (described in Appendix C) called NVCOMP.EXE in the PATH variable of the AUTOEXEC.BAT file. This will make it more convenient for you to make calculations from any folder.

A satisfactory hard copy of the output file can be printed in the portrait orientation by changing the font of the entire file to size 6. The font can be changed to size 8 if the file is printed in the landscape orientation. (Listings and outputs are shown in 8.5 point Trade Gothic font throughout this book.)

Portions of the file CALL.OUT are displayed next with commentary. Please refer to your own printout if you have made one.

2.5.1 The Header

The header and comment lines are displayed at the start of the output file. See Output 2-1.

2.5.2 Structure Specifications

The wire geometry commands are listed under the heading - STRUCTURE SPECIFICATION -, as shown in Output 2-2.

Only one wire has been used in this example. Had additional wires been used, they would have been shown as additional printed lines in the output file and would be numbered under the heading WIRE NO.. For verification purposes, the X1, Y1, and Z1 headings show the coordinates of wire end 1. The coordinates of wire end 2 are X2, Y2, and Z2 and the wire radius is listed. The number of segments on the wire is shown, as well as the identifying numbers for those segments and the associated wire tag number.

The presence of a ground plane is verified, as is the ground image. A table of multiple-wire junctions listing any junctions at which three or more wires join is shown next, although this example has none. When multiple-wire junctions are present, the number of each segment connecting to the junction are printed, as a positive number if the reference direction of the segment is into the junction or a negative number if the reference direction is out of the junction.

2.5.3 Segmentation Data

Segment data is printed as shown in Output 2-3 (see page 20) under the heading- SEGMENTATION DATA - together with the angles ALPHA and BETA.

The angle Alpha is the vertical angle of the wire segment relative to the horizon. Zero degrees is horizontal and 90° is vertical. The angle alpha is used when calculating current moments in later chapters. Beta is the azimuth angle the wire makes relative to the coordinate system and is not currently used in any of the referenced postprocessing programs.

Output 2-1

```
*************************************************
                the ARRAY DESIGN system
                   NEC-2dxs (mod)
*************************************************
```

- - - - COMMENTS - - - -

This is a comment line - usually shows the file name, CALL.nec
The comment lines will be printed in the Output file
The last comment line must use the CE designation

Output 2-2

- - - STRUCTURE SPECIFICATION - - -

COORDINATES MUST BE INPUT IN
METERS OR BE SCALED TO METERS
BEFORE STRUCTURE INPUT IS ENDED

WIRE NO.	X1	Y1	Z1	X2	Y2	Z2	RADIUS	NO. OF SEG.	FIRST SEG.	LAST SEG.	TAG NO.
1	0.00000	0.00000	0.00000	0.00000	0.00000	115.00000	0.50000	20	1	20	101

GROUND PLANE SPECIFIED.

WHERE WIRE ENDS TOUCH GROUND, CURRENT WILL BE INTERPOLATED TO IMAGE IN GROUND PLANE.

TOTAL SEGMENTS USED= 20   NO. SEG. IN A SYMMETRIC CELL= 20   SYMMETRY FLAG= 0

- MULTIPLE WIRE JUNCTIONS -
JUNCTION   SEGMENTS   (- FOR END 1, + FOR END 2)
  NONE

Within the subheading CONNECTION DATA the numbers under I−
and I+ indicate the conditions at the first and second ends of segment number I, respectively. Segments connected at a junction can be
located by tracing connection numbers through the table. After the
sign is dropped, the connection number under I− or I+ is the number
of the segment connecting to the end of segment I. If the sign of the
connection number is positive, the segment reference directions are
aligned (end 1 to end 2 or vice versa); if the number is negative, the

Output 2-3

- - - - SEGMENTATION DATA - - - -

COORDINATES IN METERS
I+ AND I- INDICATE THE SEGMENTS BEFORE AND AFTER I

SEG. NO.	COORDINATES OF SEG. CENTER			SEG. LENGTH	ORIENTATION ANGLES		WIRE RADIUS	CONNECTION DATA			TAG NO.
	X	Y	Z		ALPHA	BETA		I-	I	I+	
1	0.00000	0.00000	2.87500	5.75000	90.00000	0.00000	0.50000	1	1	2	101
2	0.00000	0.00000	8.62500	5.75000	90.00000	0.00000	0.50000	1	2	3	101
3	0.00000	0.00000	14.37500	5.75000	90.00000	0.00000	0.50000	2	3	4	101
4	0.00000	0.00000	20.12500	5.75000	90.00000	0.00000	0.50000	3	4	5	101
5	0.00000	0.00000	25.87500	5.75000	90.00000	0.00000	0.50000	4	5	6	101
6	0.00000	0.00000	31.62500	5.75000	90.00000	0.00000	0.50000	5	6	7	101
7	0.00000	0.00000	37.37500	5.75000	90.00000	0.00000	0.50000	6	7	8	101
8	0.00000	0.00000	43.12500	5.75000	90.00000	0.00000	0.50000	7	8	9	101
9	0.00000	0.00000	48.87500	5.75000	90.00000	0.00000	0.50000	8	9	10	101
10	0.00000	0.00000	54.62500	5.75000	90.00000	0.00000	0.50000	9	10	11	101
11	0.00000	0.00000	60.37500	5.75000	90.00000	0.00000	0.50000	10	11	12	101
12	0.00000	0.00000	66.12500	5.75000	90.00000	0.00000	0.50000	11	12	13	101
13	0.00000	0.00000	71.87500	5.75000	90.00000	0.00000	0.50000	12	13	14	101
14	0.00000	0.00000	77.62500	5.75000	90.00000	0.00000	0.50000	13	14	15	101
15	0.00000	0.00000	83.37500	5.75000	90.00000	0.00000	0.50000	14	15	16	101
16	0.00000	0.00000	89.12500	5.75000	90.00000	0.00000	0.50000	15	16	17	101
17	0.00000	0.00000	94.87500	5.75000	90.00000	0.00000	0.50000	16	17	18	101
18	0.00000	0.00000	100.62500	5.75000	90.00000	0.00000	0.50000	17	18	19	101
19	0.00000	0.00000	106.37500	5.75000	90.00000	0.00000	0.50000	18	19	20	101
20	0.00000	0.00000	112.12500	5.75000	90.00000	0.00000	0.50000	19	20	0	101

reference directions are opposed (end 1 to end 1 or end 2 to end 2). When more than one segment connects to a segment end, the connection number gives the next connected segment in the sequence of segments, searching cyclically through the list.

At a free end where the segment ends connects to nothing, the connection number is equal to zero.

One way of viewing the connection data is to recognize that the middle column is the segment of interest. To its right (I+) is the number of the next segment to which it connects. To its left (I−) is the number of the previous segment to which it is connected.

For example, notice the first entry, it is segment 1. To the right, it connects to segment 2. To its left, it connects to itself (segment 1) because the tower in this example is mounted over a perfectly conducting ground plane. Thus, the tower is connected to an image of itself in the ground.

Look now at the last entry in Output 2-3. It is segment 20. To the left of 20 is 19, which shows that the previous segment is 19. To the right is a zero, so segment 20 is open at that end.

Although it is not used very much in broadcast work, the utility of this listing will be more apparent when a more complex structure is displayed.

While the preceding may assist in confirming the correctness of the antenna geometry, there are several public domain programs available that will graphically display the antenna model. The program NVCOMP. EXE is one of these and is included on the disk associated with this book. Its use is covered in more detail in Appendix C.

2.5.4 Data Commands, Frequency, Loading, and Environment Data

Output 2-4 shows that the program control commands are listed in the output file for verification; the frequency and wavelength are stated;

Output 2-4

```
DATA CARD NO. 1 GN 1    0 0     0 0.0000E+00 0.0000E+00 0.0000E+00 0.0000E+00 0.0000E+00 0.0000E+00
DATA CARD NO. 2 FR 0    1 0     0 1.5000E+00 0.0000E+00 0.0000E+00 0.0000E+00 0.0000E+00 0.0000E+00
DATA CARD NO. 3 EX 0 101 1     0 1.2661E+03 0.0000E+00 0.0000E+00 0.0000E+00 0.0000E+00 0.0000E+00
DATA CARD NO. 4 RP 0    1 9 1001 9.000E+01   0.0000E+00 0.0000E+00 4.5000E+01 1.6090E+03 0.0000E+00
```

- - - - - - FREQUENCY - - - - - -

FREQUENCY= 1.5000E+00 MHZ
WAVELENGTH= 1.9987E+02 METERS

APPROXIMATE INTEGRATION EMPLOYED FOR SEGMENTS MORE THAN 1.000 WAVELENGTHS APART

- - - STRUCTURE IMPEDANCE LOADING - - -

THIS STRUCTURE IS NOT LOADED

- - - ANTENNA ENVIRONMENT - - -

PERFECT GROUND

- - - MATRIX TIMING - - -

FILL= 0.000 SEC.,   FACTOR= 0.000 SEC.

Output 2-5

- - - ANTENNA INPUT PARAMETERS - - -

TAG	SEG.	VOLTAGE (VOLTS)		CURRENT (AMPS)		IMPEDANCE (OHMS)		ADMITTANCE (MHOS)		POWER
NO.	NO.	REAL	IMAG.	REAL	IMAG.	REAL	IMAG.	REAL	IMAG.	WATTS
101	1	1.2661E+3	0.00E+0	1.5797E+0	3.6541E+0	1.2620E+2	−2.9193E+2	1.2477E−3	2.8861E−3	1.000E+3

and if any segments had been impedance loaded (as is covered in Chapter 5), the loading will be listed for verification. The ground conditions are also shown together with some timing information.

2.5.5 Antenna Input Parameters

The data in Output 2-5 is very important to the broadcaster because it shows the drive point impedance of the antenna elements plus the power to each element. If more than one voltage source is used (as is the case in a directional array), each voltage source is shown as a separate line under the heading - ANTENNA INPUT PARAMETERS -. *It is very important to remember that NEC-2 always works with PEAK values, not RMS.* Both voltage and current values are peak values when read in the output file and also when specified in the input file.

The voltage listing is the voltage at the feed point of that tower. The power shown on a particular line is the power to that particular tower. In this example, the base voltage is shown as 1266.1 + j0.0 volts *peak*, the base current is 1.5797 + j3.6541 amp *peak*, the drive point impedance is 126.20 − j291.93, and the power into the tower is 1000 watts.

2.5.6 Currents and Location

Output 2-6 shows the data under the heading - CURRENTS AND LOCATIONS -, which include the coordinates and length of each segment and the current in that segment. From these listings, the current distribution on the tower can be determined and the current moments for each tower will be calculated. These listings are also used to determine the indications to be expected on the antenna monitor when the array is correctly adjusted. They are also used to determine the correct height on the tower at which to mount the antenna monitor's sample

Output 2-6

- - - CURRENTS AND LOCATION - - -

DISTANCES IN WAVELENGTHS

SEG. NO.	TAG NO.	COORD. OF SEG. CENTER X	Y	Z	SEG. LENGTH	- - - CURRENT (AMPS) - - - REAL	IMAG.	MAG.	PHASE
1	101	0.0000	0.0000	0.0144	0.02877	1.5797E+00	3.6541E+00	3.9809E+00	66.621
2	101	0.0000	0.0000	0.0432	0.02877	1.5547E+00	2.3646E+00	2.8299E+00	56.676
3	101	0.0000	0.0000	0.0719	0.02877	1.5054E+00	1.1252E+00	1.8794E+00	36.775
4	101	0.0000	0.0000	0.1007	0.02877	1.4334E+00	−2.0305E−02	1.4335E+00	−0.812
5	101	0.0000	0.0000	0.1295	0.02877	1.3409E+00	−1.1052E+00	1.7376E+00	−39.498
6	101	0.0000	0.0000	0.1582	0.02877	1.2306E+00	−2.1179E+00	2.4495E+00	−59.841
7	101	0.0000	0.0000	0.1870	0.02877	1.1061E+00	−3.0390E+00	3.2340E+00	−70.001
8	101	0.0000	0.0000	0.2158	0.02877	9.7100E−01	−3.8472E+00	3.9678E+00	−75.835
9	101	0.0000	0.0000	0.2445	0.02877	8.2950E−01	−4.5220E+00	4.5975E+00	−79.605
10	101	0.0000	0.0000	0.2733	0.02877	6.8588E−01	−5.0456E+00	5.0920E+00	−82.259
11	101	0.0000	0.0000	0.3021	0.02877	5.4445E−01	−5.4035E+00	5.4309E+00	−84.246
12	101	0.0000	0.0000	0.3308	0.02877	4.0946E−01	−5.5857E+00	5.6007E+00	−85.807
13	101	0.0000	0.0000	0.3596	0.02877	2.8494E−01	−5.5866E+00	5.5939E+00	−87.080
14	101	0.0000	0.0000	0.3884	0.02877	1.7458E−01	−5.4056E+00	5.4084E+00	−88.150
15	101	0.0000	0.0000	0.4172	0.02877	8.1625E−02	−5.0467E+00	5.0473E+00	−89.073
16	101	0.0000	0.0000	0.4459	0.02877	8.8452E−03	−4.5182E+00	4.5182E+00	−89.888
17	101	0.0000	0.0000	0.4747	0.02877	−4.1540E−02	−3.8318E+00	3.8320E+00	−90.621
18	101	0.0000	0.0000	0.5035	0.02877	−6.7768E−02	−3.0000E+00	3.0007E+00	−91.294
19	101	0.0000	0.0000	0.5322	0.02877	−6.8279E−02	−2.0317E+00	2.0329E+00	−91.925
20	101	0.0000	0.0000	0.5610	0.02877	−3.8004E−02	−8.6589E−01	8.6673E−01	−92.513

loop so that the antenna monitor will give indications closely representative of the corresponding far-field ratio.

It is important to recognize that the distances shown in this listing is given in units of wavelengths. This is done to make it easier for the reader to confirm that the segment lengths are reasonable. The segment lengths in meters can be found under the SEGMENTATION DATA heading or they can be easily calculated. In this example, the segments are all of the same length and are shown as 0.02877 λ, where λ is given under the FREQUENCY heading as 199.87 meters. Each segment is then 0.02877 × 199.87 = 5.75 meters.

2.5.7 Current Moments

An interesting aside here is to take a cursory (and perhaps oversimplified) look at the definition of a current moment as the term is used in this book. In mechanics, by definition a moment is the product of a quantity times a distance. A familiar moment in mechanics is torque, which is the product of a force, perhaps measured in pounds, times a distance, perhaps measured in feet. In that instance, the units of the moment torque would be foot-pounds. In a similar but simplified manner, a current moment is the product of a current, perhaps measured in amperes, and the distance over which that current flows, perhaps measured in meters. The units of current moment then are ampere-meters.

As shown in Output 2-6, the current flowing in each segment appears under the – CURRENT AND LOCATION – heading in the output file. Real/Imaginary notation is shown as well as the Magnitude/Phase. The length of each segment is also shown so the current moment can be calculated. For example, the current moment of segment 1 is (1.5797 + j3.6541)5.75 = 9.08 + j21.01, or 22.89 @ 66.62° amp-meters. In a similar manner, the current moment of segment 20 is calculated to be only −0.22 − j4.98, or 4.98 @ −92.51° amp-meters.

The total current moment of the tower is the vector sum of the individual current moments of all 20 segments.

2.5.8 Power Budget

The input power, shown under the heading - POWER BUDGET - in Output 2-7 is the total power, summed from all towers and losses of the system. No losses have been included in this simple example so the efficiency is 100 percent. The radiated power is the input power less the power losses.

2.5.9 Radiation Pattern

The listings under - RADIATION PATTERNS - in Output 2-8 show the vertical angle, theta, at which the pattern is calculated versus the azimuth angle, phi.

These angles are explained in more detail in the Geometry section but it is necessary to explain now that the vertical angle, Theta, is

Output 2-7

```
                           - - - POWER BUDGET - - -

               INPUT POWER      =   1.0000E+03 WATTS
               RADIATED POWER   =   1.0000E+03 WATTS
               STRUCTURE LOSS   =   0.0000E+00 WATTS
               NETWORK LOSS     =   0.0000E+00 WATTS
               EFFICIENCY       =   100.00 PERCENT
```

Output 2-8

```
                     - - - RADIATION PATTERNS - - -
                      RANGE = 1.609000E+03 METERS
                      EXP(–JKR)/R = 6.21504E–04 AT PHASE –18.13 DEGREES
```

- - ANGLES - -		- POWER GAINS -			- - POLARIZATION - -			- - E(THETA) - -		- - E(PHI) - -	
THETA	PHI	VERT.	HOR.	TOTAL	AXIAL	TILT v	SENSE	MAGNITUDE	PHASE	MAGNITUDE	PHASE
DEG	DEG	DB	DB	DB	RATIO	DEG		VOLTS/M	DEG	VOLTS/M	DEG
90.00	0.00	7.80	–999.99	7.80	0.00	0.00	LINEAR	3.734E–01	–4.01	0.00E+00	–18.13
90.00	45.00	7.80	–999.99	7.80	0.00	0.00	LINEAR	3.734E–01	–4.01	0.00E+00	–18.13
90.00	90.00	7.80	–999.99	7.80	0.00	0.00	LINEAR	3.734E–01	–4.01	0.00E+00	–18.13
90.00	135.00	7.80	–999.99	7.80	0.00	0.00	LINEAR	3.734E–01	–4.01	0.00E+00	–18.13
90.00	180.00	7.80	–999.99	7.80	0.00	0.00	LINEAR	3.734E–01	–4.01	0.00E+00	–18.13
90.00	225.00	7.80	–999.99	7.80	0.00	0.00	LINEAR	3.734E–01	–4.01	0.00E+00	–18.13
90.00	270.00	7.80	–999.99	7.80	0.00	0.00	LINEAR	3.734E–01	–4.01	0.00E+00	–18.13
90.00	315.00	7.80	–999.99	7.80	0.00	0.00	LINEAR	3.734E–01	–4.01	0.00E+00	–18.13
90.00	360.00	7.80	–999.99	7.80	0.00	0.00	LINEAR	3.734E–01	–4.01	0.00E+00	–18.13

```
***** DATA CARD NO. 5 XQ 0 0 0 0 0.00E+00 0.00E+00 0.00E+00 0.00E+00 0.00E+00 0.00E+00
***** DATA CARD NO. 6 EN 0 0 0 0 0.00E+00 0.00E+00 0.00E+00 0.00E+00 0.00E+00 0.00E+00

RUN TIME =    0.000
```

measured from the zenith overhead as 0°, making the horizon 90°. Thus a horizontal pattern is calculated with a value of theta = 90°, not 0°. The field shown as E(THETA) is the vertically polarized component of radiation and E(PHI) is the horizontally polarized component.

Because the radiation is from a single vertical tower, the horizontally polarized component, E(PHI), is zero and the magnitude of the vertically polarized component, E(THETA), is the same at all azimuth angles, phi.

2.6 Exercises

2-1. Do a bnec.exe run using the example code given in Section 2.4.4, Listing 2-1 as the input file and record the drive point impedance.

2-2. The example code given in Section 2.4.4 as Listing 2-1 specifies a drive voltage of 1266.084 volts at 0°. Modify the Listing 2-1 code to specify the drive voltage as 1266.084 volts at an angle of 60°. Do a bnec.exe run using the modified code as the input file and compare the modified code drive point impedance with the original drive point impedance obtained in exercise 2-1. Explain the comparison.

2-3. Using the data given in the output file created by the modified listing in exercise 2-2, calculate the total current moment for the tower. How does this current moment compare with that determined from the output data of exercise 2-1? Why?

Modeling the Radiator

3.1 Modeling Guidelines

Towers are modeled with short, straight wire segments. The antenna towers and any other conducting objects in the vicinity that affect its performance must be included in the model. Although one might be inclined to duplicate the physical detail of the antenna as closely as possible, it must be kept in mind that NEC-2 has significant limitations concerning radius changes, segment lengths, spacing, and so on that sometimes make an exact physical duplication yield inaccurate NEC-2 responses. Therefore, the suggestion offered here is that you use the simplest model that conforms to the rules and produces a reasonably close approximation to measured data. Although a model configuration is recommended here, guidelines and experience gained by using the code will aid the user in developing a satisfactory model to suit individual need.

In the sections that follow, a number of requirements are suggested concerning the layout and physical size of the radiator's conductors and segments. However, it is important to realize that, for the most part, these suggestions are general and do not constitute exact, fixed requirements that cannot be varied. The requirements are indeed meaningful and should be kept in mind and followed as guidelines when it is practical to do so. On the other hand, considerable latitude exists in modeling radiators for broadcast applications.

When modeling the radiator, the main electrical consideration is segment length, Δ, relative to the wavelength, λ. The size of the segments

27

determines the resolution in solving for the current on the model since the current is computed at the center of each segment. Generally, Δ should be less than about 0.05λ at the desired frequency although somewhat longer segments may be acceptable on long wires with no abrupt changes, such as a tower radiator. However, extremely short segments, less than about $10^{-3}\lambda$, should be avoided to prevent numerical inaccuracy.

The wire radius, a, relative to λ is limited by the approximations used in the NEC-2 code. The acceptability of these approximations depends on the value of a/λ, which should be chosen such that $2\pi a/\lambda$ is much less than 1.

The accuracy of the numerical solution also depends on Δ/a. Studies of the computed field on a segment due to its own current have shown that Δ/a must be greater than about 8 for errors of less than 1 percent. When the EK command is used, Δ/a may be as small as 2 for the same accuracy.

Segments with small Δ/a should be avoided at bends. If at a bend, the center of one segment falls within the radius of the other segment, severe error will occur.

Segments must not intersect other than at their ends, and segments that are electrically connected must have coincident end points. However, segments will be treated as connected if the separation of their ends is less than about 10^{-3} times the length of the shorter segment. When possible, however, identical coordinates should be used for connected segment ends.

Failure to observe this requirement may appear when modeling ground screens. Since NEC-2 cannot model wires underground, the ground screen must be modeled as being slightly above ground. If it is modeled too close to the ground, this requirement will be violated. NEC-2 will usually show an error and tell you if this occurs, however.

The angle of the intersection of wire segments in NEC-2 is not particularly restricted, although the acute angle should not be so small as to place the observation point on one wire segment within the volume of another wire segment. Thus, as a minimum, one must ensure that the angle is large enough to prevent overlaps.

3.2 Guideline Summary

Generally speaking, specifying 20 segments on a broadcast tower will produce segment lengths that satisfy the modeling requirements. When specifying connecting wires, however, shorter segments can be used since the connecting wires usually have a smaller radius.

3.2.1 Modeling the Radiator

In general, the following guidelines should be followed in modeling the radiator proper.

- Segment length, Δ, should be less than about $0.05\,\lambda$ and longer than $10^{-3}\,\lambda$ at the desired frequency.
- Extremely short segments (less than about $10^{-3}\lambda$) should be avoided.
- The wire radius, a, should be such that λ/a is greater than 30 and $2\pi(a/\lambda)$ is much less than 1.
- The ratio Δ/a must be greater than about 8. When the EK command is used, Δ/a may be as small as 2.
- Segments with small Δ/a should be avoided at bends.
- The angle of the intersection of wire segments should not be so small as to place the center point on one wire segment within the volume of another wire segment.
- Segments may not overlap.
- Radius changes between connected segments decrease accuracy, particularly with small Δ/a.
- The ratio of larger segment length to smaller segment length should not exceed 5.
- When wires are parallel and close together, the segments should be aligned.
- Wires should be separated by a distance of several radii.

3.2.2 Modeling the Voltage Source

The applied-field voltage source (I1 = 0 on the EX command) is the most appropriate for broadcast work.

When defining a voltage source, keep the following points in mind:

- A segment is required at each point where a network connection or voltage source will be located because networks and voltage sources appear in the center of a segment.
- The segments on each side of a voltage source segment should be parallel and have nearly the same length and radius as the voltage source segment.
- If the source is on a segment connected to a ground plane, the segment should be vertical.
- When multiple wires are connected to the ends of the voltage source segment, the length of each segment at the junction should be made equal to that of the source segment.

3.3 Tower Configurations

Generally speaking, tower models fall into two categories: thick-wire models and lattice models. Thick wires are simply a single conductor with a rather large radius of 0.5 meter or so. Lattice models represent the tower using a leg and crossbar structure very much like the construction of the actual tower. A triangular tower might be modeled with three legs interconnected with multiple horizontal ring girths at intermediate heights. In Figure 3-1, parts (a), (b), and (c) represent thick-wire models and parts (d) and (e) represent lattice models.

It appears that every NEC-2 user has an idea of the best tower model configuration. It is important, however, to recognize that the limitations of NEC-2 sometimes prevent a direct physical replication

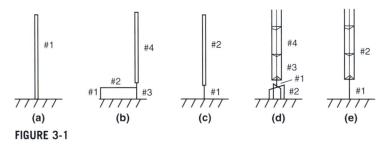

FIGURE 3-1

Tower configurations.

from yielding accurate self-impedance data on a single tower. When used in an array, however, the final result is determined more by the effects of mutual coupling between towers than it is by the features of the individual towers. This reduces the importance of which tower model configuration has been used and leads one to use the simplest configuration.

The sections that follow describe some common configurations of tower models.

3.3.1 Single-Wire Configuration

The most simple of all tower configurations is a single wire with a radius equal to the equivalent radius of the tower. See Figure 3-1(a). This configurations finds many applications, especially where detail is not required, for example, in evaluating the parasitic effect of a distant unused tower.

There is no rigorous method to determine the equivalent radius of a noncircular tower. Several methods have been mentioned such as the radius of the inscribed or circumscribed circle, the radius that yields an equivalent inductance, and so on. This book follows the lead given in Morecroft's *Principles of Radio Communication* and defines the equivalent radius of a noncircular tower as the radius of a circle whose circumference equals the perimeter of the noncircular tower. For a three-leg tower with a face equal to F, the equivalent radius, a, is taken to be

$$a = 3F/2\pi. \tag{1}$$

The radius is sometimes adjusted to other values in the attempt to match calculated and measured impedances, however.

3.3.2 Four-Wire Configuration

The most obvious model for a tower is shown in Figure 3-1(b). Here the wire labeled 1 represents the tuning network cabinet and its connection to ground. The wire labeled 2 is the connecting lead from the network cabinet to the tower base and might contain the inductance of the single-turn lightning-arrestor choke. Wire 3 has been assigned to the tower base insulator including the tower base pedestal. A series capacitor is usually placed in this wire to represent the base insulator capacity. If no insulator capacity is to be included, this wire must be omitted to prevent shorting the base to ground. Finally, the radiating tower proper is assigned wire 4.

Unfortunately, the error generated by the approximations used in NEC-2 often causes unsatisfactory results when using this configuration. The failure to accurately handle junctions of wires with differing radii and adjacent wire segments of unequal length, and the difficulty in modeling small loops, are some of the NEC-2 shortcomings that often cause unsatisfactory results using this configuration.

3.3.3 Two-Wire Configuration

The two-wire configuration shown in Figure 3-1(c) is a modified representation of the four-wire configuration. Wires 1, 2, and 3 of Figure 3-1(b) have been combined into a single vertical feed wire in Figure 3-1(c). The length and equivalent radius of this wire can be used as an adjustment parameter to match calculated and measured impedance. The logic here is that the equivalent radius of the ground connections to the tuning network cabinet as well as that of the base insulator and pedestal are unknown and probably large, so some license can be taken in setting a value for them. This is the model preferred by this writer when using the thick-wire category.

3.3.4 Lattice Configuration

The lattice configuration appears to be useful for instances that prefer all wires to be of the same or nearly the same radius. Some examples of this are antennas employing skirts, folded monopoles, and top-loaded antennas.

The lattice configuration can be generated with reasonable ease by using the move command, GM, in NEC-2 to stack identical sections vertically. Please read the description of the GM card in Appendix A. The configuration shown in Figure 3-1(d) will be used to illustrate a method of writing such an input file.

Coding the Lattice Configuration

Assuming a triangular tower with 24-inch face and 90° height at the frequency of 1500 kHz, the tower height, G, is 49.9675 meters. The tower legs radius, a, is 0.0191 meters.

A good starting place in coding the tower is the feed wire, which is also the wire carrying the base insulator. In this case, the insulator, including flanges, is arbitrarily assigned 1 meter in height with the bottom being 1 meter above ground. This assembly includes the spider connections necessary to connect the feed wire to the tower legs and a ring girth around that spider.

We must know the coordinates of each corner of the tower in order to define the spider and ring girth. The coordinates of the corners can be calculated as follows.

The triangular tower in this example has a 24-inch face (F = 24″). If we set the tower such that it is centered on the origin with one corner pointing north, the X-Y coordinates of the north corner are calculated by recognizing that the north corner of the tower is located on the +X axis at a distance equal to the radius of a circumscribed circle about the tower or

$$X_1 = F(\text{cosec } 60°)/2.$$

The Y coordinate, Y_1, of this corner is, of course, zero.

The X coordinate of the lower right corner is the negative of the radius of a circle inscribed within the tower or

$$X_2 = -F(\cot 60°)/2.$$

The Y coordinate, Y_2, of this corner is simply F/2.

Finally, the X coordinate of the third corner, X_3, is the same as that of the second corner so $X_3 = X_2$ and the Y coordinate of the third corner is the negative of that of the second corner so $Y_3 = -Y_2$.

The results are shown in Table 3-1. It is important to remember that although the tower face dimension is usually expressed in inches, NEC-2 requires that the corner coordinates be in meters.

Enough information exists now to start writing the commands to create the lattice tower. If the concrete base is defined to be 1 meter high, then the drive wire runs vertically from 1 meter to 2 meters. The

Table 3-1 Lattice Tower Leg Coordinates

Formula		24-inch Triangular Tower	
X	Y	X (meters)	Y (meters)
$X_1 = 0.5774F$	$Y_1 = 0.0$	0.3520	0.0
$X_2 = -0.2887F$	$Y_2 = F/2$	-0.1760	0.3048
$X_3 = -0.2887F$	$Y_3 = -F/2$	-0.1760	-0.3048

GW command defining the drive wire (wire 1) to which we have assigned 1 segment and set the radius to be 0.0191 meter is

```
GW, 101, 1, 0., 0., 1.0, 0., 0., 2.0, .0191
```

At the top of the drive wire is the spider assembly, which runs from the drive wire to each leg and is used to connect the drive wire the tower legs. Using one segment on each spider leg, the code for the spider is:

```
GW, 101, 1, 0., 0., 2.0, 0.352, 0., 2.0, .0191
GW, 101, 1,0., 0., 2.0, –0.176, 0.3048, 2.0, .0191
GW, 101, 1,0., 0., 2.0, –0.176, –0.3048, 2.0, .0191
```

A ring girth surrounds the spider to tie the ends of the spider together. Again using one segment on each wire, its code is:

```
GW, 101, 1, 0.352, 0., 2.0, –0.176, 0.3048, 2.0, .0191
GW, 101, 1, –0.176, 0.3048, 2.0, –0.176, –0.3048, 2.0, .0191
GW, 101, 1, –0.176, –0.3048, 2.0, 0.352, 0., 2.0, .0191
```

This completes the drive wire and its top portions.

There is no defined routine to follow in coding a tower, so the tower wires can be defined in any order. In this case, the four grounding straps (defined collectively as wire 2) running down the concrete base pedestal will be considered next. The four grounding straps run horizontally from the bottom of the drive wire to the edge of the concrete base pedestal, which in this example has been chosen to be 36 inches in diameter. From the pedestal edge, the straps then run downward to the ground system.

The equivalent radius of a flat strap is commonly taken to be one-fourth the strap width. Assuming a 4-inch strap, this would be (0.25 × 4) inches × 0.0254 meters/inch = 0.0254 meters as the equivalent radius of the ground straps.

The four straps with two wires each and one segment on each wire are coded using eight lines, as follows:

```
GW, 102, 1,0., 0., 1.0, 0.4572, 0., 1.0, .0254
GW, 102, 1,0. 4572, 0., 1.0, 0.4572, 0., 0., .0254
GW, 102, 1,0., 0., 1.0, 0., 0.4572, 1.0, .0254
GW, 102, 1,0., 0.4572, 1.0, 0., 0.4572, 0., .0254
GW, 102, 1,0., 0., 1.0, –0.457 2,0., 1.0, .0254
GW, 102, 1, –0.4572, 0., 1.0, –0.4572, 0., 0., .0254
GW, 102, 1, 0., 0., 1.0, 0., –0.4572, 1.0, .0254
GW, 102, 1, 0., –0.4572, 1.0, 0., –0.4572, 0., .0254
```

The main radiator is considered next. It stacks on top of the drive wire spider, whose height is 2.0 meters (Z = 2.0 meters). The total height of the tower (defined collectively as wire 4) is required to be 49.9675 meters, so 47.9675 meters must be added above the spider. If we arbitrarily elect to divide the tower into segments that are 10 feet long (Δ = 3.048 meters), then there will be 47.9675/3.048 = 15.7374 segments on the tower. One of those segments will be allocated as the standard to govern the stacking process, leaving a remainder of 14.7374 segments to be stacked. Since only an integer number of segments (14) can be stacked, the remainder (0.7374 × 3.048 = 2.2475 meters) will be included as a height adjuster section (collectively called wire 3) taking the height to Z = 4.2475 meters.

The code for the height adjuster section (which consists of three legs and a top ring girth) is:

```
GW, 103, 1, 0.352, 0., 2.0, 0.352, 0., 4.2475, .0191
GW, 103, 1, –0.176, 0.3048, 2.0, –0.176, 0.3048, 4.2475, .0191
GW, 103, 1, –0.176, –0.3048, 2.0, –0.176, –0.3048, 4.2475, .0191
GW, 103, 1, 0.352, 0., 4.2475, –0.176, 0.3048, 4.2475, 0.0191
GW, 103, 1, –0.176, 0.3048, 4.2475, -0.176, –0.3048, 4.2475, 0.0191
GW, 103, 1, –0.176, –0.3048, 4.2475, 0.352, 0., 4.2475, 0.0191
```

Next comes the standard tower section (a component of wire 4), which is very similar to the height adjuster section. It differs only in that it is a full segment ($\Delta = 3.048$ meters) in height. The bottom of the standard tower section is at $Z = 4.2475$ meters and the top is at $Z = 7.2955$ meters so the code for the standard tower section is:

```
GW, 104, 1, 0.352, 0., 4.2475, 0.352, 0., 7.2955, .0191
GW, 104, 1, –0.176, 0.3048, 4.2475, –0.176, 0.3048, 7.2955, .0191
GW, 104, 1, –0.176, –0.3048, 4.2475, –0.176, –0.3048, 7.2955, .0191
GW, 104, 1, 0.352, 0., 7.2955, –0.176, 0.3048, 7.2955, 0.0191
GW, 104, 1, –0.176, 0.3048, 7.2955, –0.176, –0.3048, 7.2955, 0.0191
GW, 104, 1, –0.176, –0.3048, 7.2955, 0.352, 0., 7.2955, 0.0191
```

It is important to notice here that this standard section starts with the wire at tag 104, segment 1 and it includes five more wires, each with tag 104 and each with one segment. The entire section carries the tag 104 and there are a total of six segments in the standard section. Therefore, the standard section starts with wire tag 104, segment 1, and it ends with wire tag 104, segment 6. Please review the Segmentation Data in a NEC-2 output file with special attention being paid to the Segment Number and the associated Tag number to see how they relate.

Also, please read the description of the GM command in Appendix A before continuing.

Because the tower sections will only be stacked vertically, the GM card is written with no rotation and no movement in the X-Y directions. The standard section is repeated fourteen times with only an upward movement of 3.048 meters each time. Also note that the wire tag will not be incremented. Thus, the GM command is:

```
GM, 0, 14, 0., 0., 0., 0., 0., 3.048, 104., 1., 104., 6.
```

A bit of reassurance is in order at this time. We have just used 28 lines to describe one tower and these lines have required considerable effort to generate. It would then appear that an eight-tower array will require 224 hard-earned lines to describe the entire array. But such is not the case.

If all towers in the array are identical, then the GM command can be used to duplicate the entire tower with a single line. Thus, an eight-tower array will require only 7 more lines, all of which can be generated with relative ease.

As an example, we can duplicate the entire tower above (which is located at the origin) at a new location 50 meters north with this single command:

```
GM, 100, 1, 0., 0., 0., 50.0, 0., 0., 101., 1., 104., 90.
```

Proceeding along this GM command, the number 100 increments the existing tag numbers to put the tags in the 200 series on this tower 2. The numeral 1 indicates that one additional tower will be generated and the next three zeros show that the tower is not rotated in the move. The following three numbers are the coordinates of the new location; that is, X = 50 meters, Y = 0 meters, and Z = 0 meters. The next two numbers indicate the first segment in the move, tag 101, segment 1. The last two numbers indicate the last tag and segment of the tower and require a bit of explanation.

It is clear that tag 104 is indeed the last tag number. But tag 104 contains multiple segments so it is necessary to determine the number of the last segment of tag 104. This can be reasoned as follows. Tag 104 was first used on the starter section's six wires with one segment on each wire. Tag 104 was used again to vertically stack fourteen copies of the starter section, so it used $6 \times 14 = 84$ segments in the stacking process. Therefore, the last segment of tag 104 is $6 + 84 = 90$.

Thus, the total tower structure starts at tag 101, segment 1, and ends at tag 104, segment 90.

Again, you are encouraged to review the GM command in the appendix to understand its coding better.

Simplified Lattice Model

The tower model shown in Figure 3-1(e) is essentially the same as that shown in Figure 3-1(d) with the tower base and insulator replaced by a single drive wire (refer to page 30). Notice that the single drive wire includes the spider and ring girth used to connect to the triangular tower.

In one method of generating this tower configuration, the overall tower height is first defined. Then the center height of the insulator is taken as the center point of the drive wire. This defines the segment length as being twice the center height of the insulator. That same segment length is then used for the entire tower, so the number of segments is determined by dividing the tower height by the segment length.

For example, consider a 100-meter tower with the insulator center point located 2.5 meters above ground. The segment length will be $2 \times 2.5 = 5$ meters. The total number of segments is $100/5 = 20$ segments. The drive wire uses one 5-meter segment, the standard section uses another, and then the GM command is used to stack eighteen more 5-meter segments to complete the total of twenty 5-meter segments making up the full tower height.

This model appears to work quite well and is the lattice model choice of this writer. When this configuration is used to model a 90° tower, the calculated self-impedance compares favorably with the published measured value, with the resistive component being reasonably close but with the reactive component being somewhat small.

3.4 Viewing Tower Configuration

The code for tower configurations as complex as the lattice are almost impossible to verify as error free without some computer help. Many of the commercial NEC-2 programs include a viewing capability that draws a 3-D view of the structure and thus reveals any errors in the coding. The public domain NEC-2 does not have that capability. Fortunately, however, there are several other public domain programs intended to work with NEC-2 to display the antenna geometry. Most, however, are tailored to work with the conventional NEC-2 coordinate system and incorrectly display files that use the broadcast coordinate system, which is described in Chapter 4.

Glenn Stumpff (*gstumpff@yahoo.com*) has modified a viewing program called NV.EXE such that it accommodates both the use of the GM command and the modified coordinate system. Stumpff has called the modified program NVCOMP.EXE and has placed it on the Internet as a public domain program. At the time of this writing, the file nvnew.zip, which contains NVCOMP.EXE and other programs, can be downloaded from *http://www.si-list.net/swindex.html* or *http://www.home.earth-link.net/~gstumpff/nvnew.zip*.

A copy of NVCOMP.EXE is available on the CD that is included with this book.

NVCOMP.EXE reads the NEC-2 input file and draws a 3-D view of the antenna structure on the screen. If a multitower array is included in the NEC-2 file, all towers of the array are displayed in their proper positions. The display can be zoomed, moved, and rotated about all three axes and the image can be stored. On demand, NVCOMP.EXE can highlight each wire on the display, display the coordinates of each wire end, and show each wire radius. Instructions for using NVCOMP.EXE are given in Appendix C.

3.5 Exercises

3-1. Write the input file code to model a four-sided tower of the same configuration as shown in Figure 3-1(e). Make each face 48 inches and the total tower height 152.4 meters. Use a 10-foot standard section for stacking.

3-2. Verify the correctness of the model by viewing it using NVCOMP.EXE.

3-3. Use the GM command to add a second tower, identical to that in exercise 3-1, at a location 141.4214 meters northeast of the existing tower.

3-4. Verify the correctness of both towers by viewing the pair using NVCOMP.EXE.

3-5. Save the NVCOMP.EXE image of both towers as a .BMP file.

Array Geometry

4

4.1 The Coordinate System

An antenna array is described to NEC-2 as a series of straight wires whose locations are specified in terms of their end coordinates. To specify the end coordinates, NEC-2 uses the conventional spherical coordinate system commonly used in mathematics, as sketched in Figure 4-1.

Azimuth displacement (Φ) in the X-Y plane is measured from the +X-axis and increases in the counterclockwise direction. The elevation angle (Θ) is measured from the +Z-axis with the zenith being 0°.

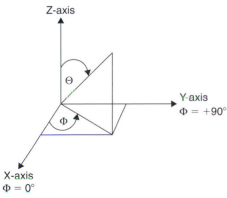

FIGURE 4-1

Conventional spherical coordinate system.

The broadcaster, on the other hand, identifies points in the geographical coordinate system by employing the compass heading and the distance from a given reference point. The compass heading, designated phi (Φ), is measured from true north and increases in the clockwise direction. The broadcaster measures the elevation angle, theta (Θ), referenced to the horizon with the zenith being taken as 90°.

It is plain that the two coordinate systems differ, so those of us who use NEC-2 for broadcast work have to reconcile these differences by defining a coordinate system that is convenient for the broadcaster to use and is also acceptable to NEC-2. Fortunately, that is not a difficult task.

NEC-2 expects to receive XYZ coordinates. The X coordinate and the Z coordinate are specified the same by both NEC-2 and the broadcaster, so no change is required in specifying those two coordinates.

The elevation angles differ only in definition. NEC-2 defines the zenith as 0° and the broadcaster's convention is to define the horizon as 0°. The simplest reconciliation here is for the broadcaster to accept the NEC-2 definition. If a horizontal pattern is desired, just make the NEC-2 calculation at 90° instead of 0°, and so on. That is not difficult and is the convention followed in the remainder of this book.

This leaves only the Y coordinate and the direction of rotation of the angle Φ, to be resolved.

Figure 4-2(a) shows a projection of the X-Y plane used in the NEC-2 coordinate system with the axis rotated to point the +X-axis ($\Phi = 0°$), upward to correspond to the usual north on the compass rose. When this is done, notice that the $-$Y-axis corresponds to the east direction which, in this coordinate system, corresponds to $\Phi = 270°$, as opposed to the 90° normally shown on the compass rose. This can be corrected simply by reversing the direction of rotation of the angle Φ by reversing the direction of the Y-axis, as shown in Figure 4-2(b).

These changes result in the coordinate system shown in Figure 4-3. It allows the broadcaster to use the familiar spacing/bearing description and at the same time, it provides NEC-2 with an acceptable XYZ Cartesian coordinate system. A tower location having a particular bearing and spacing can be laid out in the coordinate system of Figure 4-3 and the corresponding X-Y coordinates will be compatible with the requirements of NEC-2. The Z coordinates are the same in either system.

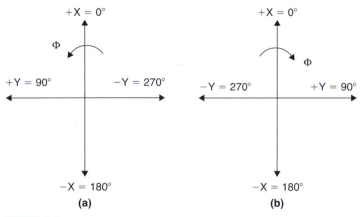

FIGURE 4-2

(a) X-Y projection of spherical coordinates; (b) X-Y projection with Y-axis reversed.

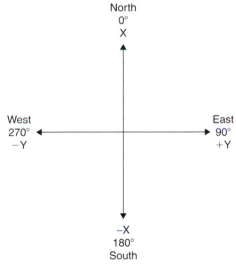

FIGURE 4-3

Coordinate system as used for broadcast applications.

The points to remember about NEC-2's broadcast coordinate system are summarized as follows:

1. The horizon is an elevation angle of $\theta = 90°$; the zenith is $0°$.

2. North corresponds to $+X$; south corresponds to $-X$.

3. East corresponds to $+Y$; west corresponds to $-Y$.

4. Height corresponds to $+Z$; there is no $-Z$.

Also, keep in mind that the units of length measurement must be meters, not feet and not degrees.

4.2 Array Geometry: An Example

Consider a tower arrangement designed to operate at 1500 kHz and described in Table 4-1. In this example, the spacing and height are given in electrical degrees at the operating frequency and orientation is expressed in degrees of azimuth. Because NEC-2 expects units of length to be expressed in meters, it is necessary to convert the spacing from degrees to meters as follows.

$$\lambda = c/f = 299.8/1.5 = 199.87 \text{ meters}$$

$$\#2 \text{ Spacing(meters)} = \#2 \text{ Spacing(degrees)} \times \lambda/360$$

$$= 270 \times 199.87/360$$

$$= 149.9025 \text{ meters}$$

Similarly, #3 spacing is also 149.9025 meters. Also tower 1 height above ground is 49.9675 meters and the height of towers 2 and 3 is 124.9188 meters.

It is now necessary to express each tower location in the X-Y coordinates of Figure 4-3. Notice that Tower 1 has zero spacing at zero angle so it is located at the origin of the coordinate system. The other towers have non-zero coordinates where:

$$X = \text{Spacing(meters)} \times \cos(\text{bearing}°)$$

and

$$Y = \text{Spacing(meters)} \times \sin(\text{bearing}°)$$

so

$$X_2 = 149.9025 \times \cos(45°) = 105.9971 \text{ meters}$$

$$Y_2 = 149.9025 \times \sin(45°) = 105.9971 \text{ meters}$$

Table 4-1 Three Tower Array Parameters

Tower	Spacing	Bearing	Height
1	0.0°	0.0°	90°
2	270°	45°	225°
3	270°	−45°	225°

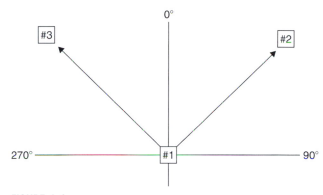

FIGURE 4-4

CALL.NEC tower locations in X-Y plane.

In a like manner, the X-Y coordinates for tower 3 is:

$$X_3 = 149.9025 \times \cos(-45°) = 105.9971 \text{ meters}$$

$$Y_3 = 149.9025 \times \sin(-45°) = -105.9971 \text{ meters}$$

The towers are now located on the ground (in the X-Y plane). They are plotted in the X-Y plane, as shown in Figure 4-4.

The ends of each tower can be expressed in terms of these X and Y coordinates plus the Z coordinate. The bottom ends of the towers are on the ground where Z = 0 meters. The top of tower 1 is (by definition) located at height Z = 49.9675 meters. Therefore, tower 1 is uniquely defined as:

$$\text{End 1 } (X_{11}, Y_{11}, Z_{11}) = (0., 0., 0.)$$

$$\text{End 2 } (X_{21}, Y_{21}, Z_{21}) = (0., 0., 49.9675)$$

Assuming that this tower has been assigned tag 101, that the tower will be divided into 20 segments, and that it has a radius of 0.1456 meters, this information is entered in the GW command as follows:

GW, 101, 20, 0., 0., 0., 0., 0., 49.9675, 0.1456

There are 20 segments on the wire and segment 1 is at end 1, segment 20 is at end 2. The tops of towers 2 and 3 are both at 124.9188 meters, so for tower 2,

$$\text{End 1 } (X_{12}, Y_{12}, Z_{12}) = (105.9971, 105.9971, 0.)$$

$$\text{End 2 } (X_{22}, Y_{22}, Z_{22}) = (105.9971, 105.9971, 124.9188)$$

The resulting GW command is

GW, 201, 20, 105.9971, 105.9971, 0., 105.9971, 105.9971, 124.9188, 0.1456

In a like manner, GW commands for tower 3 are written. The complete set of GW commands to describe this array using a one-wire tower model is:

GW, 101, 20, 0., 0., 0., 0., 0., 49.9675, 0.1456
GW, 201, 20, 105.9971, 105.9971, 0., 105.9971, 105.9971, 124.9188, 0.1456
GW, 301, 20, 105.9971, -105.9971, 0., 105.9971, -105.9971, 124.9188, 0.1456

4.3 The Array Input File

It is sometimes easier to modify an existing file than it is to generate a new one because the existing file can be used as a template to remind the user of the need for, and the format of, the various lines of code. The input file shown as Listing 2-1 in Chapter 2 can be used for that purpose in this instance to create an input file for this three-tower array. The input file of Chapter 2 is repeated here as Listing 4.1 for convenience.

To get started, we should first change the comment commands to establish a record of the file.

CM This is a simplified 3-tower array
CE created for illustration only.

Listing 4-1

```
CM This is a comment line – usually shows the file name, CALL.NEC
CM The comment lines will be printed in the Output file.
CE The last comment line must use the CE designation.
GW, 101, 20, 0., 0., 0., 0., 0., 115, 0.5
GE, 1
GN, 1
FR, 0, 1, 0, 0, 1.5, 0.
EX, 0, 101, 1, 00, 1266.084, 0.
RP, 0, 1, 9, 1001, 90., 0., 0., 45., 1609., 0.
EN
```

Next, the existing single GW command is replaced with the three GW commands that describe the towers used in the simplified array.

```
GW, 101, 20, 0., 0., 0., 0., 0., 49.9675, 0.1456
GW, 201, 20, 105.9971, 105.9971, 0., 105.9971, 105.9971, 124.9188, 0.1456
GW, 301, 20, 105.9971, -105.9971, 0., 105.9971, -105.9971, 124.9188, 0.1456
```

Finally, replace the voltage drive to the single tower with drive voltages to each of the three towers in the array so as to generate the desired pattern. How these voltages are determined is described in Chapter 6.

```
EX, 0, 101, 1, 00, 626.43, 432.98
EX, 0, 201, 1, 00, -216.62, 140.12
EX, 0, 301, 1, 00, -216.62, 140.12
```

There is a drive voltage for each tower. The tag number identifies both the tower and the wire on that tower that receives the drive voltage. Thus tag 101 shows that tower 1 is driven on wire 1 of tower 1. Tag 201 shows that tower 2 is driven on wire 1 of tower 2, and so on.

The digit 1 following the tag indicates the wire segment that receives the drive voltage. Referring back to the GW command, notice that each tower is divided into 20 segments. Thus, the drive voltage is applied to the first of those 20 segments. Remember that segment 1 is next to end 1, which is at ground level as defined by the GW command. This puts the drive voltage at the base of the tower, as is appropriate.

Also, notice that the drive voltage to the tower is a complex number having a magnitude and phase relative to the reference tower.

NEC-2 accepts this complex number expressed in terms of its real and imaginary parts, the first entry being the real part and the second being the imaginary part.

Putting these changes together with the unchanged parts of the original input file gives Listing 4-2.

The RP command has been changed to cause a calculation of the far field at every 1° of azimuth (in lieu of 45°) to produce a smoother plot of the horizontal radiation pattern.

The single tower input file of Chapter 2 was modified to create the three-tower input file of Listing 4-2 to emphasize the utility of using a template file. A template file is a pro forma file that can be modified for a particular use. It provides a guide to the types of commands that must be included in the file and it illustrates the format of those commands. Such use saves time by reducing the need to refer to the command descriptions. Therefore, to complete a usable template file from Listing 4-2, we can add some load (LD) commands and we will do this by including loss in the tower model.

The FCC requires that the tower model include a loss of at least 1 ohm at the height of maximum current. We will add 1.5 ohm for good measure. Since the height of tower 1 in the three-tower input file is 90°, maximum current occurs at the base. Therefore, the following command will place 1.5-ohm series resistance in the first segment of tower 1.

```
LD, 0, 101, 1, 1, 1.5, 0., 0.
```

Towers 2 and 3 are both taller than 90° so the current maximum occurs above the base. The method used to locate the segment at which the current maximum occurs is explained in Chapter 7. For now it is sufficient to say that the 1.5-ohm resistance will be placed in segment 4 on both towers 2 and 3. The commands placing these loads are:

```
LD, 0, 201, 4, 4, 1.5, 0., 0.
LD, 0, 301, 4, 4, 1.5, 0., 0.
```

Please review the description of the LD command as it appears in Appendix. The complete file is shown in Listing 4-3.

Listing 4-2

```
CM This is a simplified 3-tower array
CE created for illustration only.
GW, 101, 20, 0., 0., 0., 0., 0., 49.9675, 0.1456
GW, 201, 20, 105.9971, 105.997, 0., 105.997, 105.997, 124.9188, 0.1456
GW, 301, 20, 105.997, –105.997, 0., 105.997, –105.997, 124.9188, 0.1456
GE, 1
GN, 1
FR, 0, 1, 0, 0, 1.5, 0
EX, 0, 101, 1, 00, 626.43, 432.98
EX, 0, 201, 1, 00, –216.62, 140.12
EX, 0, 301, 1, 00, –216.62, 140.12
RP, 0, 1, 361, 1001, 90., 0., 1., 1., 1000., 0.
EN
```

Listing 4-3

```
CM TEMP.NEC
CM This is a 3-tower array containing
CM 1.5 ohm loss resistance and created for use
CE as an input file template.
GW, 101, 20, 0., 0., 0., 0., 0., 49.9675, 0.1456
GW, 201, 20, 105.9971,105.997, 0., 105.997, 105.997, 124.9188, 0.1456
GW, 301, 20, 105.997, –105.997, 0., 105.997, –105.997, 124.9188, 0.1456
GE,1
GN,1
FR, 0, 1, 0, 0, 1.5, 0
LD, 0, 101, 1, 1, 1.5, 0., 0.
LD, 0, 201, 4, 4, 1.5, 0., 0.
LD, 0, 301, 4, 4, 1.5, 0., 0.
EX, 0, 101, 1, 00, 626.43, 432.98
EX, 0, 201, 1, 00, –216.62, 140.12
EX, 0, 301, 1, 00, –216.62, 140.12
RP, 0, 1, 361, 1001, 90., 0., 1., 1., 1000., 0.
EN
```

Notice that the comment commands have been changed to properly describe the file and the XQ command has been omitted because the RP command serves to execute the program.

It would be useful to enter the above commands into a file named TEMP.NEC and use it as a template file. Remember that the commands in an input file must begin in column 1 of line 1. Each successive command must also begin in column 1. Do not indent the commands or use spaces at the beginning of the commands and do not use blank lines. Be sure to save the file as a text file.

Table 4-2 Four Tower Array Parameters

Tower	Spacing	Bearing	Drive Voltage
1	0.0°	0.0°	130.76 – j334.9
2	87.6°	348°	421.17 – j383.72
3	170.0°	334°	249.86 – j720.98
4	255.9°	338°	572.72 – j187.49

4.4 Exercises

Conduct a NEC-2 calculation on the four-tower array described in Table 4-2. Make the tower configurations as shown in Chapter 3, Figure 3-1(c), with all tower heights being 121.8786 meters. Drive the first segment of each tower using the drive voltages shown in Table 4-2.

Use 20 segments per tower. The radius of all feed segments is 0.03 meter and the radius of all towers is 0.5 meter. The operating frequency is 550 kHz.

4-1. What is the total power to the array? What is the power assignment to each tower?

4-2. If the antenna monitor sample is taken using a current transformer at the drive point, what will be the antenna monitor indications?

4-3. How many lobes does the horizontal far-field radiation pattern contain?

Loads, Networks, and Transmission Lines

5.1 Modeling Impedance Loads

Modeling lumped R-L-C impedance loads on one or more segments of a wire is accomplished using the LD command. Series and parallel circuits can be generated in addition to a finite wire conductivity. To review the syntax of the LD command, see the description in Appendix A.

LD,	I1,	I2,	I3,	I4,	F1,	F2,	F3
	LDTYP	LDTAG	LDTAGF	LDTAGT	ZLR	ZLI	ZLC

Here is a typical broadcast application:

LD, 0, 101, 1, 1, 0., 2.5E-06, 0.

More often than not, the LD command is used by setting I1 = 0 to add a series impedance to a wire such as might be found in the inductance of a lead or the loss resistance of a wire. It is also commonly used to create an open circuit that is shunted by a capacitor such as might exist at the base insulator of the tower. The finite Q of an inductance can be represented by the LD command with I1 = 0 by showing both R and L in series.

The setting I1 = 1 places a parallel R-L-C circuit in series with a wire. This might be used to represent the shunting effect of the lighting choke in parallel with the base insulator capacity, or perhaps a parallel resonant L-C trap in a wire.

Setting I1 equal to other values is less common in broadcast applications, although it is conceivable that one might want to represent tower loss by modeling the tower appropriately and setting I1 = 5 to specify the conductivity of the tower steel. See Appendix A for full details on using the LD command.

The setting I2 identifies the tag number of the wire containing the load. Settings I3 and I4 indicate the segments of that tag receiving the load. If I4 is equal to I3, then the load is placed only in the segment identified by I3. I4 can be greater (but not less) than I3, in which case the LD command will place the specified load in every segment between I3 and I4 inclusive. This feature can be used to model guy wires in which the break-up insulators are represented by a small capacitor that is placed in segments of the guy wire that are of a length equal to the insulator spacing.

The floating-point numbers in the LD command define the value of the R-L-C components in that order. A zero in any R-L-C field indicates that no component is present as opposed to a zero value for that component. For example, in a series R-L-C circuit (LD 0 …), a zero value is the same as a short circuit; in a parallel R-L-C circuit (LD 1 …), a zero value is the same as an open circuit. If a zero value for the component is desired, then a very small number must be entered, such as 1.0E-10.

When an inductance or capacity is entered on an LD command, the resulting reactance is automatically scaled as frequency changes. When reactance is entered on the LD command (I1 = 4), the reactance is not automatically scaled with frequency.

Load commands are normally input in groups to achieve a desired structure loading. If a segment is loaded more than once by a group of loading commands, the loads are assumed to be in series.

When a load is placed in a segment that also carries a voltage source, the load appears on the segment in series with the voltage source. If it is desired to have the load appear on the segment in parallel with the voltage source, as might be the case when applying the voltage across the capacity of a base insulator, then the LD command cannot be used. In that case, the NT network command is used.

5.2 **Modeling Nonradiating Networks**

The NT command generates a two-port nonradiating network connected between specified segments of the structure. Since the network is nonradiating, the physical location of the segments to which the network connects is irrelevant in terms of how the network operates.

The network can be made up of R-L-C components with the network characteristics being specified by its short-circuit admittance matrix parameters. Typical network uses include impedance matching and phasing networks, but more useful applications in a NEC-2 analysis include special kinds of shunt impedance loads and methods for generating tower feeds. The reader is encouraged to review the syntax of the NT card in Appendix A.

NT,	I1,	I2,	I3,	I4,	F1,	F2,	F3,	F4,	F5,	F6
	TAG1	SEG1	TAG2	SEG2	Y11R	Y11I	Y12R	Y12I	Y22R	Y22I

Here is a typical broadcast application:

NT, 100, 1, 101, 1, 0.01, −0.01, 1.0E−10, 0., 1.0E+10, 0.

The entries I1 and I2 identify the wire tag and segment number to which port 1 of the network is connected. Entries I3 and I4 identify the wire tag and segment number to which port 2 of the network is connected. The network is described in terms of its complex short-circuit admittance parameters, Y11, Y12, and Y22. The entries Y11R and Y11I in the NT command are the real and imaginary parts of Y11. Y12R and Y12I are the real and imaginary parts of Y12. And Y22R and Y22I are the real and imaginary parts of Y22.

Figure 5-1 shows a two-port network. The Y-parameters are calculated in the usual way.

$$Y11 = I_1/E_1 \quad \text{with} \quad E_2 = 0$$

$$Y12 = -I_1/E_2 \quad \text{with} \quad E_1 = 0$$

$$Y22 = I_2/E_2 \quad \text{with} \quad E_1 = 0$$

FIGURE 5-1

General two-port network.

It is important to recognize that the Y-parameters do not scale with frequency, and they must be recalculated and repeated for each frequency.

5.2.1 Typical Networks

Figure 5-2 shows the network configuration of some networks commonly used in broadcasting. The following are Y-parameters for the networks in Figure 5-2:

(a) $Y11 = 1.0E+10 + j0$

    $Y12 = -1.0E+10 + j0$

    $Y22 = 1.0E+10 + j0$

(b) $Y11 = 1/Z_1$

    $Y12 = -1/Z_1$

    $Y22 = 1/Z_1$

(c) $Y11 = 1.0E+0 + j0$

    $Y12 = 0 + j0$

    $Y22 = 1/Z_1$

(d) $Y11 = 1/Z_1$

    $Y12 = -1/Z_1$

    $Y22 = (Z_1 + Z_2)/Z_1 Z_2$

(e) $Y11 = (Z_2 + Z_3)/(Z_1(Z_2 + Z_3) + Z_2 Z_3)$

    $Y12 = -Z_3/(Z_2(Z_1 + Z_3) + Z_1 Z_3)$

    $Y22 = (Z_1 + Z_3)/(Z_2(Z_1 + Z_3) + Z_1 Z_3)$

(f) $Y11 = (Z_1 + Z_2)/Z_1 Z_2$

    $Y12 = -1/Z_2$

    $Y22 = (Z_2 + Z_3)/Z_2 Z_3$

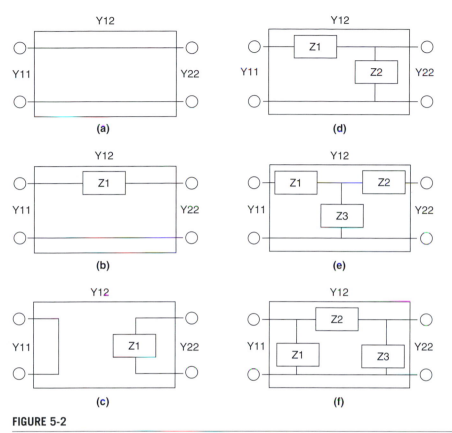

FIGURE 5-2

Common network configurations.

5.2.2 Typical Network Applications

The networks shown in Figure 5-2 are often used as follows:

Network (a) is a pass-through network generally for combining or for use during an analytical in/out comparison of another network.

Network (b) is useful to place an impedance in series with the drive signal, such as to simulate the effect of the small resistance of the spring clips or to include the inductance of the tower lead-in.

Network (c) is used to place an impedance in parallel with a source voltage. Recall that when the LD command is used to place a load in a segment that also carries a voltage source, that load appears on the segment in series with the voltage source. However, when a NT command is used to place a network in a segment that also carries a voltage source, that network appears on the segment in parallel with the voltage source.

For this application, a dummy segment may be defined to accept port 1 of the network. Port 2 will connect to the segment that carries the voltage source. The dummy segment is made to be nonradiating by making it very small and placing it in a far-off location.

An input file that places a drive voltage across a base insulator having 100 pf shunt capacity would contain all the normal commands plus the following:

```
GW, 100, 1, 999., 999., 999., 999., 999., 999.01, 0.001
GW, 101, 20, 0., 0., 0., 0., 0., 50., 0.25
NT, 100, 1, 101, 1, 1.0E+10, 0., 0., 0., 0., 6.28E-4
EX, 0, 101, 1, 00, 325.0, 0
```

The first GW command creates the dummy segment as segment 1 of the wire having tag 100. The wire is located far away (999.,999.,999.); it is vertical and very small (0.01 meter high with 0.001 meter radius). The second GW command creates the driven tower radiator having the wire tag 101 and 20 segments. The NT command connects the network between wire tag 100, segment 1 and wire tag 101, segment 1. The Y-parameters of the network are:

$$Y11 = 1.0E+10 + j0$$

$$Y12 = 0 + j0$$

$$Y22 = 0 + j6.28E-4$$

The EX command places the drive voltage in parallel with the network on wire tag 100, segment 1.

Network (d) is used to include both a series impedance and a shunt impedance in the drive path. This might represent the series inductance of a tower feed and the shunt capacity of the insulator.

Network (e) is the common T-network used for matching and phasing.

Network (f) is a Pi-network that might represent the case where there is a shunt impedance at the feed point plus a lead with series inductance feeding the shunt capacity of the base insulator.

Other network configurations may be used in which case the Y-parameters would be calculated as described in Section 5.2 for those particular networks.

5.2.3 General Guidelines for Networks

Network commands may be used in groups to specify several networks on a structure. All network commands for a network configuration must occur together with no other commands (except TL commands) separating them. When the first NT command is read following a command other than a NT or TL command, all previous network and transmission line data are destroyed. Hence, if a set of network data is to be modified, all network data must be input again in the modified form.

One or more network ports can be connected to any given segment. Multiple network ports connected to one segment are connected in parallel.

If a network is connected to a segment that has been impedance loaded (i.e., through the use of the LD command), the load acts in series with the network port on the segment. Figure 5-3 shows a series load and a shunt voltage source.

5.3 Modeling Transmission Lines

The TL command is a special version of the NT command and is used to generate a transmission line between any two segments on the structure. Characteristic impedance, length, and shunt admittance are the defining parameters.

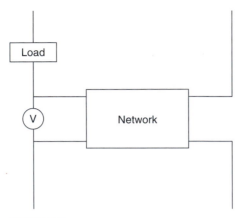

FIGURE 5-3

Relation of load, network, and voltage source.

TL, I1, I2, I3, I4, F1, F2, F3, F4, F5, F6

Here is a typical broadcast application:

TL, 102, 1, 101, 1, 50., 62.0

Entries I1 and I2 define the tag and segment number to which end 1 of the transmission line is connected. Entries I3 and I4 define the tag and segment number to which end 2 is connected.

Entry F1 specifies the characteristic impedance of the transmission line in ohms. A negative sign in front of the characteristic imped-ance acts as a flag for generating the transmission line with a 180-degree phase reversal (crossed line) if this is desired.

Entry F2 specifies the length of transmission line in meters. If this field is left blank, the program will use the straight line distance between the specified connection segments. If the length of the transmission line is originally specified in degrees, then it must be converted to meters with the expression

$$F2(meters) = length(degrees) \times wavelength(meters) \div 360°.$$

The remaining four floating-point fields are used to specify the real and imaginary parts of the shunt admittances at end 1 and end 2, respectively.

The rules for transmission line commands are the same as for network commands. All transmission line commands for a particular configuration must occur together with no other commands (except NT commands) separating them.

When the first TL or NT command is read following a command other than a TL or NT command, all previous network or transmission line data are destroyed. Hence, if a set of TL commands is to be modified, all transmission line and network data must be input again in the modified form.

One or more transmission lines may be connected to any given segment. Multiple transmission lines connected to one segment are connected in parallel.

If a transmission line is connected to a segment that has been impedance loaded (i.e., through the use of an LD command), the load is placed on the segment in series with the transmission line input, similar to a network, as shown in Figure 5-3.

5.4 Network Output File Listing

If a NEC-2 run uses networks, data pertaining to those networks are listed under three categories in the output file. An excerpt from such an output file is explained as follows.

5.4.1 Network Descriptions

The network description provided by the NT commands of the NEC-2 input file is listed for confirmation under the heading - - - NETWORK DATA - - -.

Output 5-1 shows a three-tower array being driven through the antenna tuning networks. It shows the From–To listing (input/output) of the networks and the Y11, Y12, and Y22 parameters that describe the networks.

Output 5-1

- - - NETWORK DATA - - -
- - ADMITTANCE MATRIX ELEMENTS (MHOS) - -

-FROM-		-TO-		(ONE,ONE)		(ONE,TWO)		(TWO,TWO)	
TAG NO.	SEG. NO.	TAG NO.	SEG. NO.	REAL	IMAG.	REAL	IMAG.	REAL	IMAG.
100	1	101	2	0.0000E+00	−1.8908E−02	0.0000E+00	2.2193E−02	0.0000E+00	−1.7706E−03
200	186	201	187	0.0000E+00	−4.9734E−01	0.0000E+00	−5.5729E−01	0.0000E+00	−6.8056E−01
300	371	301	372	0.0000E+00	−9.6590E−04	0.0000E+00	2.5770E−02	0.0000E+00	−1.0415E−02

Output 5-2

- - - STRUCTURE EXCITATION DATA AT NETWORK CONNECTION POINTS - - -

TAG NO.	SEG. NO.	VOLTAGE (VOLTS)		CURRENT (AMPS)		IMPEDANCE (OHMS)		ADMITTANCE (MHOS)		POWER
		REAL	IMAG.	REAL	IMAG.	REAL	IMAG.	REAL	IMAG.	WATTS
101	2	−3.067E+1	−6.707E+2	−7.452E+0	−8.399E+0	4.649E+1	3.759E+1	1.301E−2	−1.052E−2	2.931E+3
201	187	9.052E+1	−2.005E+2	1.373E+1	1.402E−1	6.445E+0	−1.468E+1	2.508E−2	5.712E−2	6.071E+2
301	372	2.219E+2	−2.005E+2	9.072E+0	−4.649E+0	2.834E+1	−7.581E+0	3.293E−2	8.808E−3	1.472E+3
100	1	3.760E+2	−3.893E+2	1.214E−6	1.173E−6	−8.193E+2	−3.206E+8	−7.969E−15	3.119E−9	−1.17E−9
200	186	−1.103E+2	2.203E+2	−6.870E−7	−3.439E−7	1.200E+2	−3.206E+8	1.167E−15	3.119E−9	3.54E−11
300	371	2.701E+2	2.710E+2	−8.451E−7	8.423E−7	−7.450E+2	−3.206E+8	−7.247E−15	3.119E−9	−5.3E−10

5.4.2 Source and Load Impedance to the Networks

The - - - STRUCTURE EXCITATION DATA AT NETWORK CONNECTION POINTS - - - heading in Output 5-2 lists what amounts to the source and load impedances presented to each network; that is, it shows what the network sees when looking back into the structure feeding the network, and what the network sees when looking forward into the structure the network is feeding.

In the case of ATU 1, its load is the drive point of tower 1 (wire tag 101, segment 2), listed under "IMPEDANCE(OHMS)" as 46.49 + j37.59. Its source in this case is the very short dummy wire provided as the means to feed the network (wire tag 100, segment 1). So, looking back into the structure, the network sees −8.19 − j3.2E + 08, which is the primarily capacitive reactance of the very short wire.

ATU 2 and ATU 3 are shown in a like manner.

Output 5-3

		- - - ANTENNA INPUT PARAMETERS - - -								
TAG	SEG.	VOLTAGE (VOLTS)		CURRENT (AMPS)		IMPEDANCE (OHMS)		ADMITTANCE		POWER
NO.	NO.	REAL	IMAG.	REAL	IMAG.	REAL	IMAG.	REAL	IMAG.	WATTS
100	1	3.760E+2	–3.893E+2	7.523E+0	–7.790E+0	4.998E+1	6.013E–3	2.001E–2	–2.407E–6	2.931E+3
200	186	–1.103E+2	2.203E+2	–2.212E+0	4.405E+0	4.998E+1	–5.667E–2	2.001E–2	2.269E–5	6.071E+2
300	371	2.700E+2	2.710E+2	5.429E+0	5.456E+0	4.970E+1	3.998E–2	2.012E–2	1.618E–5	1.472E+3

5.4.3 Network Input Parameters

The impedance seen looking into the input terminals of the network is listed in Output 5-3 under the - - - ANTENNA INPUT PARAMETERS - - - heading along with the voltage appearing across the input terminals, the current into the network, and the power taken by the network.

In the case of tower 1, the input impedance presented by the ATU is $49.98 + j0.006$. The input current is $7.52 - j7.79$ amps peak and the network is taking 2931 watts. Towers 2 and 3 are listed in a like manner.

5.5 Exercises

5-1. Use Listing 2-1 given in Chapter 2, Section 2.3.4 as the input file for a bnec.exe run and record the drive point impedance. Modify Listing 2-1 to add 150 pf capacity in parallel with the drive voltage and do a bnec.exe run using the modified code as the input file. Compare the resulting drive point impedance with the original.

5-2. Repeat the steps in exercise 5-1 but add 300 pf capacity instead of 150 pf.

5-3. Modify the input file created in exercise 5-2 to add a network that matches the drive point impedance to 50 ohms using a 90° T-network.

Calculating Base Drive Voltages

6

6.1 Base Drive Voltages

NEC-2 requires the broadcaster to change his starting parameters from field ratios to the voltages present at the drive point of the towers. Although there are several ways to accomplish that, this section describes a modified version of the method given by Trueman in *IEEE Transactions on Broadcasting*, March 1988. The process, as applied to broadcasting, is explained in the sections that follow.

First, however, a word of encouragement is in order at this point. The sections that follow present some rather laborious and boring mathematics. They develop the procedure for calculating the drive point voltages that create the target field ratios and it is important to thoroughly understand the process involved. However, software has been provided on the CD included with this book to read the NEC-2 output files and to make the necessary calculations with a minimum of human effort. Thus, you may use the software in lieu of making the detailed calculations. However, it is still worthwhile to wade through the mathematics to understand the process.

6.2 Direct and Induced Currents

Recognize that the drive voltage at the base of a tower causes a current to flow in that tower. If there are other towers nearby, then the current flowing in the driven tower will induce a current flow in those nearby towers even though the nearby towers have no drive voltage of their own. Consequently, when all towers are driven, the current flowing in a given tower is the result not only of the drive voltage at its base, but also of the current flowing in the neighboring towers. In the case of three towers,

$$I_1 = I_{11} + I_{12} + I_{13}, \tag{1}$$

where I_1 is the total current flow in tower 1, I_{11} is the current flow in tower 1 due exclusively to its own excitation, I_{12} is the induced current flow in tower 1 due to the excitation of tower 2, and I_{13} is the induced current flow in tower 1 due to the excitation of tower 3. Similar equations can be written for towers 2, 3, and so on.

NEC-2 makes it easy to view these current components. For example, a NEC-2 simulation of such a three-tower array, with each tower having been divided into twenty segments, will have a total of sixty segments displayed in the NEC-2 output file—twenty segments on tower 1, twenty additional segments on tower 2, and another twenty segments on tower 3.

If tower 1 is driven and there is no drive on towers 2 and 3, the NEC-2 output file will show I_{11}, (which is the current distribution of tower 1) on segments 1 through 20. It will also show I_{21}, (the induced current distribution of tower 2), on segments 21 through 40. Finally, it will show I_{31}, (the induced current distribution of tower 3), on segments 41 through 60. Therefore, the NEC-2 output file will have a listing of the current distribution on all three towers, although only tower 1 is driven. For example,

- I_{11} is the current on tower 1 due to the drive on tower 1, and the distribution appears on segments 1 through 20.

- I_{21} is the current on tower 2 due to the drive on tower 1, and the distribution appears on segments 21 through 40.

- I_{31} is the current on tower 3 due to the drive on tower 1, and the distribution appears on segments 41 through 60.

In a like manner, if in the NEC-2 simulation, only tower 2 is driven and there is no drive on towers 1 and 3, then in the NEC-2 output file,

- I_{12} is the current on tower 1 due to the drive on tower 2, and the distribution appears on segments 1 through 20.

- I_{22} is the current on tower 2 due to the drive on tower 2, and the distribution appears on segments 21 through 40.

- I_{32} is the current on tower 3 due to the drive on tower 2, and the distribution appears on segments 41 through 60.

Finally, if the simulation drives only tower 3 while towers 1 and 2 are not driven, then in the NEC-2 output file,

- I_{13} is the current on tower 1 due to the drive on tower 3, and the distribution appears on segments 1 through 20.

- I_{23} is the current on tower 2 due to the drive on tower 3, and the distribution appears on segments 21 through 40.

- I_{33} is the current on tower 3 due to the drive on tower 3, and the distribution appears on segments 41 through 60.

Now if this three-tower simulation is written so that all three towers are driven simultaneously, then each tower will have three current components flowing—the current due to its own excitation plus the current component induced from the excitation of each of the other two towers. In that case, the NEC-2 simulation output file will list the following currents by segment:

- I_1, which is composed of $I_{11} + I_{12} + I_{13}$, and the distribution appears on segments 1 through 20.

- I_2, which is composed of $I_{21} + I_{22} + I_{23}$, and the distribution appears on segments 21 through 40.

- I_3, which is composed of $I_{31} + I_{32} + I_{33}$, and the distribution appears on segments 41 through 60.

Notice that these currents are of the form described in equation (1).

6.3 Current Moments

The field radiated by a tower is proportional to the total current flowing in that tower. At the horizon

$$E(\Phi) = \left(1/\sqrt{2}\right)\left(j\eta\beta e^{-j\beta r}/2\pi r\right)\left[\int_0^h I_i(z)dz\right], \tag{2}$$

where $I_i(z)$ is the total current flowing in tower i as a function of height and is defined by

$$I_i = I_{i1} + I_{i2} + I_{i3} + \cdots$$

The current on tower i is the current caused by exciting tower i plus those currents induced on tower i as a result of the drive on the companion towers.

Because the current distribution on a tower is not uniform, nor is it commonly defined, the integral within the brackets of equation (2) is not easily evaluated. To overcome this difficulty, in some calculation methods, the current distribution has been assumed to be sinusoidal, thus making the integral easily evaluated. This assumption is satisfactory for many situations but it leads to error when working with tall towers and other complex configurations.

Therefore, in the NEC-2 analysis and for purposes of the explanations in this section, rather than make this sinusoidal distribution assumption, the current distribution is approximated by dividing the tower into a number of short segments, each of which carries a current of constant amplitude whose value is defined as the current that exists at the center of that particular segment. Then with the current distribution on the tower approximated by a number of segments, each of which has a particular length and each of which carries a particular current of constant amplitude over the entire length of that segment, the integral can be approximated with satisfactory accuracy by a summation of the product of current and segment length, thus

$$\int_0^h I_i(z)dz \approx \sum_{j=1}^N \Delta_j I_j, \tag{3}$$

where I_j is the current in segment j and Δ_j is the length of segment j and the product is summed over N, the total number of segments. Values for both $I_j(z)$ and Δ_j can be obtained from the NEC-2 output file under the heading CURRENTS AND LOCATION.

Recall that the current moment is defined as the product of the current flowing in a particular segment multiplied by the length of that segment and because the current has a phase relative to some reference, the current moment is a complex number.

The term on the right side of equation (3) is seen to be the current moment of the tower furnishing the data and its value is easily obtainable from the NEC-2 output file. Stating this in general terms gives

$$C_i = \sum_{j=1}^{N_i} \Delta_{ij} I_{ij}, \qquad (4)$$

where C_i is the total current moment of tower i, N_i is the number of segments on tower i, Δ_{ij} is the length of segment j on tower i, and I_{ij} is the current on segment j of tower i.

To accommodate the case where Δ_{ij} is not vertical, then the factor $\sin \alpha_{ij}$ is added within the summation where α_{ij} is alpha, the vertical angle of Δ_{ij}, as read from the NEC-2 output file. Equation 4 then becomes

$$C_i = \sum_{j=1}^{N_i} \Delta_{ij} I_{ij} \sin \alpha_{ij}, \qquad (5)$$

6.4 Development Concept

The task now is to describe a method that can be implemented in a postprocessing computer program to convert the desired field ratios to a set of base drive voltages that will generate those field ratios.

From Section 6.2, we see that we can determine the current distribution of the various components of current flowing in each tower by individually driving each tower while the companion towers are left with no drive. Then Section 6.3 shows how the current moments are calculated from those current distributions. This section uses a three-tower array to explain a special utilization of those procedures to determine the desired base drive voltages.

To generate the data for this analysis, it is necessary to make three NEC-2 runs with an input file and an output file for each run. The first NEC-2 run calls for driving each tower individually with $1 + j0$ volt while the companion tower bases are shorted to ground to ensure zero volts at each base. Next, we make a second NEC-2 run using a set of normalized drive voltages that have been determined from the results of the first run. The normalized drive voltages generate the correct pattern shape but not the correct pattern size. Finally, to create the correct pattern size, a third NEC-2 run is made using final drive voltages, which are obtained by scaling the normalized voltages to the full power level.

To keep track of the several files, it is helpful to be consistent in naming them. In this work, the files associated with the unity excitation have been named CALL_1.NEC and CALL_1.OUT to identify the NEC-2 input file and the corresponding output file. The NEC-2 runs using the normalized drive voltages are named CALL_N.NEC and CALL_N.OUT and the files for the final run are named simply CALL.NEC and CALL.OUT.

6.4.1 Unity Drive

The first step is to characterize the array. This is done by individually driving each tower of the array with $1.0 + j0.0$ volt while the companion towers are grounded. The tower currents as described in Section 6.2 will be obtained as a result of this unity drive and the related current moments can then be determined as described in Section 6.3.

Excitation to the driven tower is placed on the base insulator segment and the other towers are grounded by giving them no excitation.

It is not necessary to run NEC-2 three times to create the three current files necessary to calculate the unity drive current moments. This can be done in a single NEC-2 run by repeating the drive commands. For example, including these NEC-2 commands

```
EX, 0, 101, 1, 00, 1.0, 0.
XQ,
EX, 0, 201, 1, 00, 1.0, 0.
XQ,
EX, 0, 301, 1, 00, 1.0, 0.
XQ,
```

in the CALL_1.NEC file will place the 1.0 + j0 volt drive on tower 1 with the companion towers grounded, then execute a NEC-2 analysis. Following that, it will place the 1.0 + j0 drive on tower 2 with the companion towers grounded, then execute another NEC-2 analysis. Finally, the commands will place the 1.0 + j0 drive on tower 3 with the companion towers grounded and execute yet another NEC-2 analysis. Each NEC-2 execution will generate the corresponding current listings in the output file for each excitation command.

6.4.2 Normalized Drive

Since the towers of the three-tower array were driven with 1.0 + j0 volt, the current moments calculated from the resulting current sets will be the current moment *per volt* with units of ampere-meter per volt (A-M/V). Thus, to obtain the current moment for any other drive voltage on the tower, the current moment per volt can be multiplied by the applied volts, which may be, and in this case is, a complex number. For example, with a drive voltage of V_1 on tower 1,

$$C_1 = C_{11} V_1, \qquad C_2 = C_{21} V_1, \qquad \text{and} \qquad C_3 = C_{31} V_1.$$

In a like manner, if tower 2 is driven with V_2 volts and towers 1 and 3 shorted, the resulting current moments will be

$$C_1 = C_{12} V_2, \qquad C_2 = C_{22} V_2, \qquad \text{and} \qquad C_3 = C_{32} V_2.$$

Also, driving tower 3 with V_3 and towers 1 and 2 shorted gives

$$C_1 = C_{13} V_3, \qquad C_2 = C_{23} V_3, \qquad \text{and} \qquad C_3 = C_{33} V_3.$$

Finally, if all three towers are driven simultaneously with V_1, V_2, and V_3, then each induces a current in the others with the resulting total current moments being

$$C_1 = C_{11} V_1 + C_{12} V_2 + C_{13} V_3 \tag{5}$$

$$C_2 = C_{21} V_1 + C_{22} V_2 + C_{23} V_3 \tag{6}$$

$$C_3 = C_{31} V_1 + C_{32} V_2 + C_{33} V_3 \tag{7}$$

Stated in general terms,

$$C_i = \sum_{j=1}^{N} C_{ij} V_i.$$

Since the field is directly proportional to the current moment, then the field ratio is

$$F_j = C_j/C_k$$

where C_k is the current moment of the reference tower. If we select tower 1 to be the reference tower, then

$$C_k = C_l.$$

At this point, this development deviates from that of Trueman to take a less rigorous but somewhat more convenient path.

Dividing equations (5), (6), and (7) by the current moment of the reference tower, C_k, and recognizing that $C_i/C_k = F_i$ results in

$$F_1 = C_{11}\, V_1' + C_{12}\, V_2' + C_{13}\, V_3', \text{and} \tag{8}$$

$$F_2 = C_{21}\, V_1' + C_{22}\, V_2' + C_{23}\, V_3', \text{and} \tag{9}$$

$$F_3 = C_{31}\, V_1' + C_{32}\, V_2' + C_{33}\, V_3', \tag{10}$$

where the left side of the equations can be the desired field ratios, in which case the primed V's represent the base drive voltages normalized to the current moment of the reference tower. The normalized drive voltages have the units of volts per ampere-meter.

We now reason that there exists a set of complex voltages for V_1', V_2', and V_3' that will operate on the set of current moments to yield the desired field ratios. We have values for all the variables except the three normalized drive voltages, therefore we have a set of simultaneous equations consisting of three equations with three unknowns. We can now solve for those unknown normalized drive voltages, taking due notice that all variables are complex.

The result thus obtained is not the final answer, however. Because the drive voltages have been normalized to the reference current moment, they will create the desired pattern shape but they will not create the correct pattern size.

6.4.3 Full Power Drive

To get the correct pattern size, we must do a NEC-2 run using the normalized drive voltages. It is suggested that these input and output files be named CALL_N.NEC and CALL_N.OUT, respectively. Review the output file thus obtained (CALL_N.OUT) and take note of the total input power listed under the heading - POWER BUDGET-. Call this value P_n and call the desired full power P_f. Then, to obtain the full power drive voltages, we must scale the normalized drive voltages by the factor

$$K = \sqrt{P_f/P_n}. \tag{11}$$

Finally, a third NEC-2 run can be made (naming input and output files CALL.NEC and CALL.OUT) using the scaled full power drive voltages to obtain the correct pattern size and power level.

6.4.4 Shunt Reactance and Networks

It is important to know that if the tower model includes a reactance in parallel with the exciting voltage, such as might be implemented using the network configuration described in Figure 5-2(c), then that reactance may be in place on the excited tower when the individual towers are excited with $1.0 + j0.0$ volts, as described in Section 6.4.1. However, be aware that while an individual tower is being excited, the remaining towers of the array must be grounded. Therefore, any reactance that appears in series with the tower must not be in place on towers that are to be grounded. In short, the NT command should be paired with the corresponding EX command in defining the excitation, as opposed to leaving all NT commands in place during the individual excitations.

Of course, the shunting reactance should be in its proper place throughout the remaining steps of the excitation voltage calculation.

Moreover, if the tower model includes both a shunt reactance and a series reactance, be careful about using the network described in

Figure 5-2(d). The transfer function of that network varies with the terminating impedance; thus, it is not possible to accurately transfer the base drive voltage from the tower base to the input of the network. The work-around for this is to use the network configuration in Figure 5-2(c) to simulate the shunt reactance while calculating the base drive voltages. Once the drive point impedances have been determined, simply mentally add the series reactance to the calculated drive point impedance.

6.5 Example: A Three-Tower Array

The procedure for calculating the driving point voltage will be summarized with a simple three-tower example using a transmitter operating on 1500 kHz with 5000 watts and seeking the array parameters shown in Table 6-1.

This example was chosen to demonstrate that the procedure can accommodate various conditions including tall towers and towers of different heights as well as widely differing field ratios.

6.5.1 Create a Unity Drive File

The first task in determining base drive voltages is to generate a NEC-2 input file that will drive each of the towers individually and sequentially with 1.0 + j0.0 while the companion towers are grounded. Listing 6-1 defines the geometry of the array, installs the operating parameters, and drives each tower in sequence. Notice particularly how the EX commands are listed and executed individually.

Table 6-1 Three-Tower Array

Tower	Ratio	Phase	Spacing	Bearing	Height
1	1.0	0°	0°	0°	90°
2	0.05	0°	270°	45°	225°
3	0.05	0°	270°	−45°	225°

Listing 6-1

```
CM SQR_1.NEC
CM 3-tower pattern
CE
GW, 101, 20, 0., 0., 0., 0., 0., 49.9675, 0.1456
GW, 201, 20, 105.997, 105.997, 0., 105.997, 105.997, 124.9188, 0.1456
GW, 301, 20, 105.997, -105.997, 0., 105.997, -105.997, 124.9188, 0.1456
GE, 1
GN, 1
FR, 0, 1, 0, 0, 1.5, 0.
EX, 0, 101, 1, 00, 1.0, 0.
XQ
EX, 0, 201, 1, 00, 1.0, 0.
XQ
EX, 0, 301, 1, 00, 1.0, 0.
XQ
EN
```

You are encouraged to run this input file and create an output file named SQR_1.OUT. Refer to your output file for the following discussion.

6.5.2 Calculate Unity Drive Current Moments

The unity drive current moments are used in conjunction with equations (8), (9), and (10) to calculate the normalized drive voltage. For this three-tower array, three current moments are calculated for each of the three towers.

Tower 1 Moments

The SQR_1.OUT output file will contain three sets of current listings. The first listing will be under the heading - CURRENTS AND LOCATIONS - and will follow the listing of the first EX card, which shows that tower 1 is the driven tower. That current listing contains the current distribution on each of the three towers as a result of driving tower 1.

Segments 1 through 20 show I_{11}, which is the current on tower 1 due to its own drive. Segments 21 through 40 show I_{21}, which is the current on tower 2 due to the drive on tower 1, and segments 41 through 60 show I_{31}, which is the current on tower 3 due to the drive on tower 1.

The current moment components C_{11}, C_{21}, and C_{31} of equations (5), (6), and (7) can be computed from these current distributions by noting that the - CURRENTS AND LOCATIONS - listing shows the length of each segment in addition to the current on each segment. These can be applied to equation (4) to determine the current moment; for example,

$$C_{11} = \Delta_{1j} \sum_{j=1}^{20} I_{1j} \tag{11}$$

where j represents the segment number, in this instance running from 1 to 20 on tower 1.

In this example, notice that the segment length is constant on each tower, so it was factored out of the summation as a multiplier. Also notice that all segments are vertical, so the factor sin α is not required. Do not overlook the fact that in the output file, the segment length is given in units of wavelength. This must be converted to meters by multiplying the listing by the wavelength. In the instance of tower 1, the segment length is 0.0125 $\times$ 199.87 meters = 2.498 meters. Thus, equation (11) becomes

$$C_{11} = 2.498[(1.68 \times 10^{-2} - j1.02 \times 10^{-2})$$
$$+ (1.671 \times 10^{-2} - j1.051 \times 10^{-2}) \tag{12}$$
$$+ (1.652 \times 10^{-2} - j1.069 \times 10^{-2}) + \cdots],$$

with the result that $C_{11} = (0.55278 - j0.38736)$

The current is taken in the real/imaginary form rather than the polar form to facilitate the addition.

In a like manner, C_{21} and C_{31} can be determined from the remainder of the current listing using

$$C_{21} = \Delta_{2j} \sum_{j=21}^{40} I_{2j} \tag{13}$$

where the segments on tower 2 run from 21 through 40 with the segment length = 0.03125 λ, or 6.246 meters, resulting in

$$C_{21} = (-0.0356 - j0.05832).$$

And finally,

$$C_{31} = \Delta_{3j} \sum_{j=41}^{60} I_{3j} \tag{14}$$

where the segments on tower 3 run from 41 through 60 with segment length $= 0.03125\lambda$, or 6.246 meters, so

$$C_{31} = (-0.0356 - 0.05832).$$

Tower 2 Moments

Next, following the listing of the EX command, driving tower 2 will be the set of current listings resulting from the drive on tower 2. It, too, will be under a heading - CURRENTS AND LOCATIONS -. Again, segments 1 through 20 show the current distribution on tower 1 due to the drive on tower 2, segments 21 through 40 show the current on tower 2 due to its own drive, and segments 41 through 60 show the current on tower 3 due to the drive on tower 2.

The current moment components C_{12}, C_{22}, and C_{32} of equations (5), (6), and (7) can be computed from these current distributions by following the same procedure described previously and again noting that in the instance of towers 2 and 3, the segment length is 0.03125×199.87 meters $= 6.246$ meters.

$$C_{12} = \sum_{j=1}^{20} \Delta_{1j} I_{1j} \tag{15}$$

so

$$C_{12} = (-0.02956 - j0.01297).$$

Also

$$C_{22} = \sum_{j=21}^{40} \Delta_{2j} I_{2j} \tag{16}$$

then

$$C_{22} = (0.02983 - j0.22645).$$

Finally,

$$C_{32} = \sum_{j=41}^{60} \Delta_{3j} I_{3j} \tag{17}$$

and

$$C_{32} = (0.00474 + j0.01324).$$

Tower 3 Moments

Following the listing of the EX command driving tower 3 will be the third set of current listings. It too will be under the heading - CURRENTS AND LOCATIONS -. Segments 1 through 20 show the current distribution on tower 1 due to the drive on tower 3, segments 21 through 40 show the current on tower 2 due to the drive on tower 3, and segments 41 through 60 show the current on tower 3 due to its own drive.

In a manner similar to that above, the current moment components C_{13}, C_{23}, and C_{33} of equations (5), (6), and (7) can be computed from these current distributions by following the same procedure described previously.

$$C_{13} = \sum_{j=1}^{20} \Delta_{1j} I_{1j} \tag{18}$$

results in

$$C_{13} = (-0.02956 - j0.01297).$$

Also

$$C_{23} = \sum_{j=21}^{40} \Delta_{2j} I_{2j} \tag{19}$$

so

$$C_{23} = (0.00474 + j0.01324).$$

Finally,

$$C_{33} = \sum_{j=41}^{60} \Delta_{3j} I_{3j} \tag{20}$$

and

$$C_{33} = (0.02983 - j0.22645).$$

6.5.3 Solve for the Normalized Drive Voltages

The current moments just calculated can be placed in equations (8), (9), and (10). Then both sides of the equations are divided by the current moment of the reference tower (C_1). Since $C_i/C_1 = F_i$, we can replace the left side of equations (8), (9), and (10) with the desired field ratios. The results are:

$$1.0 = (0.55278 - j0.38736)V_1' + (-0.02956 - j0.01297)V_2' + (-0.02956 - j0.01297)\ V_3'$$

$$0.05 = (-0.0356 - j0.05832)V_1' + (0.02983 - j0.22645)V_2' + (0.00474 + j0.01324)\ V_3'$$

$$0.05 = (-0.0356 - j0.05832)V_1' + (0.00474 + j0.01324)V_2' + (0.02983 - j0.22645)V_3',$$

where the V' values are the drive voltages normalized to the reference current moment.

These three equations leave only the values for the three normalized drive voltages as unknowns, so they can be solved as a set of simultaneous equations.

A small postprocessing computer program has been written to read the SQR_1.OUT file and calculate the current moments thus generated. Thereafter, it solves the N equations in N unknowns to obtain the normalized drive voltages. The program NECDRV2.EXE performs that function and is included on the CD included with this book.

In this instance, using the parameters given earlier and running NECDRV2.EXE yields the following results for the normalized drive voltages:

$$V_1' = 1.1706 + j0.8297$$

$$V_2' = -0.4149 + j0.2703$$

$$V_3' = -0.4149 + j0.2703$$

These normalized drive voltages are now used to drive the three towers simultaneously by placing these drive voltages in a SQR_N.NEC

Listing 6-1(a)

```
EX, 0, 101, 1, 00, 1.1706, 0.8297
EX, 0, 201, 1, 00, -0.4149, 0.2703
EX, 0, 301, 1, 00, -0.4149, 0.2703
```

Listing 6-1(b)

```
EX, 0, 101, 1, 00, 616.21, 436.76
EX, 0, 201, 1, 00, -218.4, 142.29
EX, 0, 301, 1, 00, -218.4, 142.29
```

file. This is most conveniently done by copying the SQR_1.NEC file to SQR_N.NEC and modifying the EX commands to read as shown in Listing 6-1(a).

Once created, the SQR_N.NEC file is run using bnec.exe to generate the SQR_N.OUT file.

6.5.4 Determine the Full Power Drive Voltage

The SQR_N.OUT file shows the correct drive point impedances and other parameters but it does not create the correct power level, nor would it create the correct pattern size. This is corrected by scaling the normalized drive voltages by the square root of the ratio of desired power to the normalized power.

Under the heading - POWER BUDGET -, the SQR_N.OUT file shows a total normalized power of 1.8044E-02 watts. The scale factor to get this up to 5000 watts is

$$K = \sqrt{5000/1.8044 \times 10^{-2}} = 526.40.$$

The full power drive voltages are obtained by multiplying the normalized drive voltages by the factor 526.40. Thus,

$$V_1 = 616.21 + j436.76$$

$$V_2 = -218.4 + j142.29$$

$$V_3 = -218.4 + j142.29$$

The SQR_N.NEC normalized input file is copied to SQR.NEC, and SQR.NEC is edited to replace the normalized voltages on the EX commands with the full power drive voltages, as shown in Listing 6-1(b).

Running SQR.NEC generates SQR.OUT, which is the full power output file that is usually created in a normal NEC-2 design analysis. SQR. OUT contains all the information necessary for the usual array design and is where the design effort would normally stop.

6.6 Exercises

Consider a two-tower array having the parameters shown in Table 6-2. The transmitter operates on 870 kHz with a power of 50,000 watts. The towers are identical. Use the tower model shown in Figure 3-1(c) with twenty segments. The drive wire is the length of one segment with a radius equal to 6 inches. The remainder of the radiator is a triangular tower having a face width of 48 inches.

Table 6-2 Two-Tower Array

Tower	Ratio	Phase	Spacing	Bearing	Height
1	1.00	0°	0°	0°	182.1°
2	1.25	67°	138°	180°	182.1°

6-1. Give NEC-2 calculated values for the following:
   (a) Drive point impedance of each tower
   (b) Power to be delivered to each tower.
   (c) Expected antenna monitor reading if tower currents are sampled with current transformers located at the output of the antenna-tuning network
   (d) At what height on the towers should a sampling loop be mounted so that the antenna monitor readings will closely approximate the far-field ratios?

6-2. Repeat exercise 6-1 with 250 pf shunting the drive voltages.
   (a) What effect does the shunting capacity have on the drive point impedance? Why?
   (b) What effect does the shunting capacity have on the power required by each tower. Why?

(c) Does the shunting capacity affect the antenna monitor readings?

(d) What characteristic of this array suggests that it is sensitive to the capacity shunting the drive voltage?

(e) What is a likely source of this shunting capacity?

Using Data from the Output File

7.1 Overview

NEC-2 output reports are quite voluminous and have long lines that make them difficult to read and difficult to print. A convenient way to view them is to open the file in WordPad using the command "Wordpad CALL.OUT". To conveniently print a hard copy of the file, select the entire file and reduce the font to size 6 so the long lines will fit on $8\frac{1}{2} \times 11$ paper in the portrait orientation. A larger font can be used to print it in the landscape orientation.

Not all of the output report is necessary for the usual broadcast work. For example, the segmentation data adds considerably to the volume of the report and contributes very little in usual broadcast work. Also, the far-field pattern listing adds more that 361 lines to the report but they are used only to plot the pattern. Therefore, one might want to create a condensed output file by copying the CALL.OUT file to CALL_C.OUT and from the latter, delete unwanted portions to generate a smaller working file. In any event, the original CALL.OUT file should be retained so the entire file is available for future reference.

For an even more concise output report, a simple computer program can be written to read the CALL.OUT file and print pertinent information such as drive point impedance, power budget, and base currents.

The NEC-2 output file is a source of much information that is not listed directly in the file. With a little manipulation of the output file content, the additional information can be retrieved to yield a deeper insight. Simple computer programs may be written to read the NEC-2 output file directly and then process the data as desired. It is beyond the scope of this book to cover programming methods to accomplish this, but the necessary methods are well known to those who are knowledgeable in computer programming. The sections that follow describe the concepts embodied in those computer programs and provide some examples.

7.2 Verify the Field Ratios

Once the base drive voltages have been computed and used to render a NEC-2 output file, it is very reassuring to know that the voltages as calculated do, in fact, create the desired field ratios.

The NEC-2 output file contains the current distribution listing that resulted from the actual drive voltages used to create that file. As explained earlier, the current moments can be calculated from these current distributions and the field ratios can then be determined from those current moments. In the case of the example file SQR_N.OUT created in Chapter 6, the current moments are

$$C_1 = 199.8717 @ -1.237\text{E-}3°,$$

$$C_2 = 9.9937 @ -9.592\text{E-}3°,$$

$$C_3 = 9.9937 @ -9.592\text{E-}3°.$$

Recalling that Fi = Ci/Ck, we can write

$$F_1 = C_1/C_1 = (199.8717 @ -1.237\text{E-}3°)/(199.8717 @ -1.237\text{E-}3°)$$
$$= 1.00 @ 0.0°,$$

$$F_2 = C_2/C_1 = (9.9937 @ -9.592\text{E-}3°)/(199.8717 @ -1.237\text{E-}3°)$$
$$= 0.05 @ 0.0°,$$

$$F_3 = C_3/C_1 = (9.9937 @ -9.592\text{E-}3°)/(199.8717 @ -1.237\text{E-}3°)$$
$$= 0.05 @ 0.0°,$$

which agree perfectly with the desired field ratios listed in the example.

7.3 **Plot Far-Field Radiation Pattern**

The RP command creates a listing of the radiation pattern in the output file. Once this listing is made, a postprocessing program can be written to read the output file and plot the resulting pattern. If the vertical angle (θ) is held constant while the azimuth angle (Φ) is varied, the horizontal pattern is generated. An example of such a plot is shown in Figure 7-1 where the data is taken from the file SQR.OUT as created in Chapter 6.

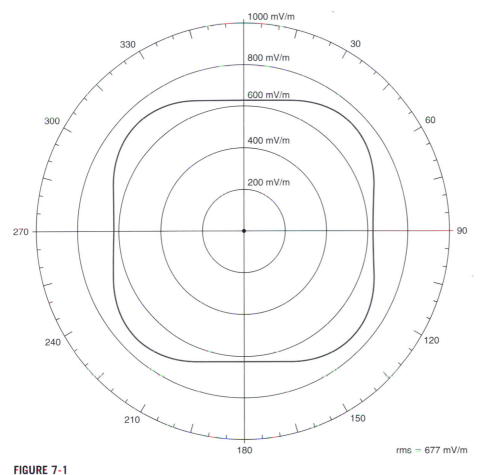

FIGURE 7-1

Radiation pattern of SQR.OUT.

If Φ is held constant while θ is varied, then the vertical pattern is generated.

As an alternative, the PL command may be used to generate a separate data file to hold only the radiation pattern data. A typical PL command is

PL,3,1,1,3

The command will generate a table of values that can be adapted to any available plotting routine. Refer to the PL command in Appendix A for additional details.

7.4 Detuning Unused Towers

When it is desirable to create a circular radiation pattern by restricting all radiation to a single tower of a multiple tower array, two approaches are possible and both can be simulated by a NEC-2 analysis. The first approach is to handle the generation of the circular pattern as one might handle any other pattern; that is, calculate the drive voltages that yield a field ratio of 1 @ 0° for the driven tower and 0 @ 0° for all unused towers. This creates a perfectly circular pattern and is an excellent analysis tool. Unfortunately, the method suffers the disadvantage of requiring the expense of a complete power dividing and phasing capability to physically implement such arrangement.

The second approach is much less expensive and therefore is the most often used. Recall that the driven tower induces a current flow in the unused towers of an array and that the induced current flow radiates a field that causes the distortion of the desired nondirectional pattern. The radiated field caused by the induced current is expressed mathematically as

$$E_i = (1/\sqrt{2})(j\beta\eta e^{-j\beta r}/2\pi r)\int_0^h I(z)dz,$$

where $I(z)$ is the induced current as a function of height and the integral in the expression is the current moment of the unused tower. It is clear, then, that if the current moment can be made to be 0 (or near 0), then the radiated field from the unused tower is also made to be 0 (or near 0). That is the principle upon which the concept of detuning an unused tower is based.

There are several options available to accomplish the task. The first option, and perhaps the least expensive, is to simply open the base of the unused towers, thus reducing the current moment by reducing the current flow. This is usually satisfactory for short towers but the taller towers require a bit more attention to nullify the effect of the current that continues to flow even when the tower base is opened. In that case, base loading may be used to reduce the current moment created by the induced current.

7.4.1 Detuning by Base Loading

The process of base loading an unused tower to reduce its parasitic radiation includes grounding the tower base through an inductance whose value has been selected so as to create a current distribution on the tower that minimizes the current moment. A good starting value for the base load inductance can be obtained by making a NEC-2 analysis in which all towers are driven to create a field ratio of 1.0 @ 0° for the nondirectional tower and 0.0 @ 0° for each unused tower.

From the output file generated by that analysis, the drive point impedance of each unused tower is examined and the conjugate of the reactive component is taken as a good estimate of the base loading reactance necessary to detune that unused tower. The conjugate reactance is called a good estimate because some adjustment to that value may be necessary if the resistive component of the unused tower's drive point impedance is large. Therefore, the value of the base loading reactance should be verified by iterating larger and smaller values. If more than one unused tower is involved, then using the average value of inductance in all unused towers will usually be effective if the towers are identical.

The appropriate value of inductance can also be determined entirely by an iteration process, that is, by arbitrarily selecting a starting value for the base load inductance (perhaps 10 to 50 μH) then running a NEC-2 simulation to calculate the resulting current moments for the towers of interest. That process is then repeated with changing inductance values until the value of inductance is found that reduces the current moments sufficiently to produce a satisfactory circular radiation pattern from the driven tower.

Example: Detuning by Base Loading

This example describes the detuning of seven of the eight towers in an array configured in two rows of four towers each. Each tower is 203° in height and the spacing between towers is in the order of 100°. Tower 7 is fed with 1000 watts while the other towers are detuned in an effort to create a circular pattern.

Taller towers exhibit a different behavior than do shorter towers. Shorter towers cause the most severe pattern distortion when the unused towers are connected to ground. In this example using taller towers, the most severe pattern distortion occurs when the unused towers are left open.

See Figure 7-2 for the pattern obtained when the bases are left open and Figure 7-3 for the pattern obtained when the bases are shorted directly to ground.

Both patterns fail to meet the requirement for a circular pattern, so it is mandatory that some means be used to improve the circularity. To determine the base loading inductance, a NEC-2 analysis was run to determine the drive voltages necessary to create a field ratio of 1 @ 0° for tower 7 and 0 @ 0° for the companion towers. The output file for this analysis was studied to confirm the circularity of the pattern and also to determine the drive point impedance of each companion tower. From the drive point impedances, the conjugate of the reactive part was taken as the reactance for base loading. For the eight-tower array being considered, the conjugate reactances ranged from + j118 to + j136, corresponding to inductances within the range 13.62 μH to 15.54 μH. A base loading inductance of 15 μH was selected for each of the companion towers.

A NEC-2 simulation was run with the base of the unused towers connected to ground through the 15 μH inductor. The resulting NEC-2 output file was processed to calculate the field ratios that resulted from the induced current in each tower, and those field ratios were summed as a figure of merit. The value of inductance was iterated and the field

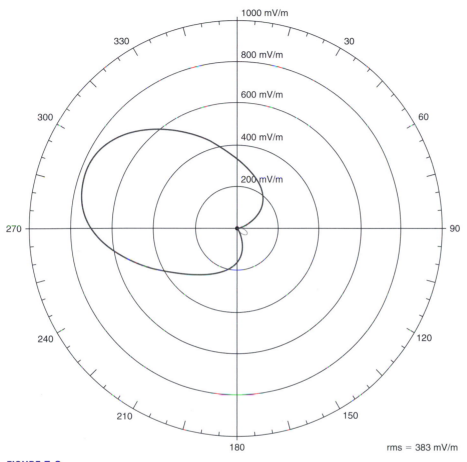

FIGURE 7-2

Nondirectional pattern of an eight-tower array with the unused towers open.

ratios were calculated and their magnitude summed for each value of inductance. The 15 µH inductor was verified as that value that produced the smallest field ratio sum. The calculated field ratios were:

$$F(1) = 0.035 \qquad F(5) = 0.037$$

$$F(2) = 0.054 \qquad F(6) = 0.049$$

$$F(3) = 0.065 \qquad F(7) = 1.000$$

$$F(4) = 0.045 \qquad F(8) = 0.055$$

The minimum field ratio sum was 0.3389.

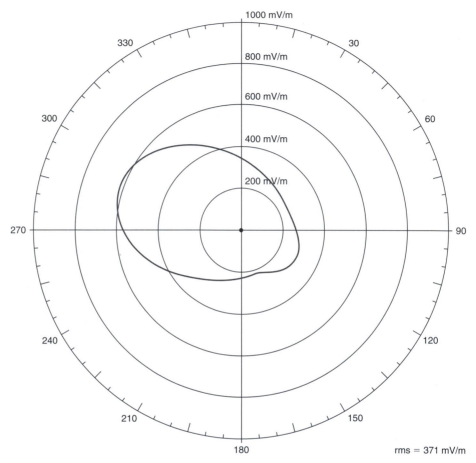

FIGURE 7-3

Nondirectional pattern of an eight-tower array with the unused towers grounded.

The resulting radiation pattern is shown in Figure 7-4. While the result is less than ideal, it is indeed an improvement over that obtained by simply grounding the bases or leaving them open. An attempt was made to further reduce the field ratios by using the base loading inductance individually calculated for each unused tower, but the reduction was not significant.

Base Loading Input File Listing

The following NEC-2 input file (Listing 7.1 on page 90) generates the radiation pattern shown in Figure 7-4. The LD commands provide the base loading.

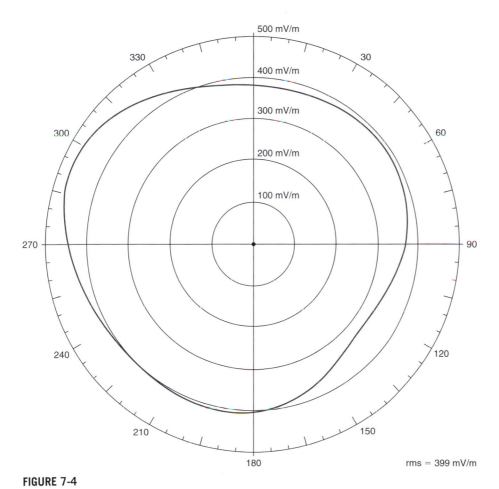

500 mV/m
400 mV/m
300 mV/m
200 mV/m
100 mV/m

rms = 399 mV/m

FIGURE 7-4

Nondirectional pattern of an eight-tower array using base loading.

7.4.2 **Detuning by Skirting**

The previous example demonstrates that tall towers do not respond well to detuning by base loading. Somewhat better results can be obtained by using a 90° skirt at the top of the tower to create the effect of a shorter tower. The example that follows demonstrates that concept.

Example: Detuning by Skirting

The array used in the previous example will be used in this example to demonstrate the increased effectiveness of detuning by using a skirt

Listing 7-1

```
CM   ND.NEC - nondirectional operation of 8-tower array
CM      Single Wire Tower, 4' face, 405' AGL, 20 segments
CM      Perfectly conducting ground
CE      Exciting tower 7 with others grounded thru 15uH
GW, 101, 20, 0., 0., 0., 0., 0., 123.44, 0.582
GW, 201, 20, 61. 043, 24.663, 0., 61.043, 24.663, 123.44, 0.582
GW, 301, 20, 122.086, 49.326, 0., 122.086, 49.326, 123.44, 0.582
GW, 401, 20, 183.129, 73.989, 0., 183.129, 73.989, 123.44, 0.582
GW, 501, 20, –3.135, –59.811, 0., –3.135, –59.811, 123.44, 0.582
GW, 601, 20, 57.867, –35.073, 0., 57.867, –35.073, 123.44, 0.582
GW, 701, 20, 119.024, –10.455, 0., 119.024, –10.455, 123.44, 0.582
GW, 801, 20, 179.881, 14.22, 0., 179.881, 14.22, 123.44, 0.582
GE, 1
GN, 1
FR, 0, 1, 0, 0, 1.39, 0.
LD, 0, 101, 1, 1, 0., 15.E–6, 0.
LD, 0, 201, 1, 1, 0., 15.E–6, 0.
LD, 0, 301, 1, 1, 0., 15.E–6, 0.
LD, 0, 401, 1, 1, 0., 15.E–6, 0.
LD, 0, 501, 1, 1, 0., 15.E–6, 0.
LD, 0, 601, 1, 1, 0., 15.E–6, 0.
LD, 0, 801, 1, 1, 0., 15.E–6, 0.
EX, 0, 701, 1, 00, 1279.46, 0.
RP, 0, 1, 361, 1001, 90., 0., 1., 1., 1000., 0.
EN
```

on a tall tower. For convenience, a four-wire skirt is used with the top end connected to the top of the tower. The skirt extends 90° from the top of the tower and its lower end effectively terminates the tower in a high impedance at the lower end of the skirt. The 203° skirted tower now behaves as though it were a simple 113° tower, and thus it can be detuned effectively by simply leaving its base open.

The details of creating the skirt are described in Chapter 9, Top Loaded and Skirted Towers. For now it is sufficient to explain that the tower with skirt wires was modeled as tower 1. then the GM command was used to copy the entire skirted tower to the locations of towers 2 through 6 and again at the location of tower 8. Tower 7 was not skirted because it is the driven tower in the nondirectional mode. The viewing program, NVCOMP.EXE, was used to verify the correctness of the total array. Figure 7-5 shows the NVCOMP.EXE display of the array. Tower 1 is the rightmost tower on the back row with tower 5 being in front of tower 1.

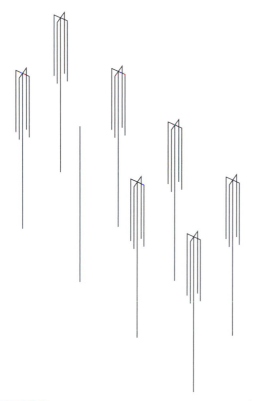

FIGURE 7-5

NVCOMP.EXE display of eight-tower array detuned with top skirts.

It is worthwhile to note here that from a practical standpoint, a system such as this can be implemented by using a contactor to connect the lower end of the skirt to the tower when the array is in the directional mode. The contactors will be open in the nondirectional mode.

With the skirts in place and the tower bases open, the calculated field ratios are:

$$F(1) = 0.027 \qquad F(5) = 0.025$$

$$F(2) = 0.034 \qquad F(6) = 0.033$$

$$F(3) = 0.033 \qquad F(7) = 1.000$$

$$F(4) = 0.030 \qquad F(8) = 0.032$$

The minimum field ratio sum is 0.2140.

These values are somewhat smaller than those given in the Example: Detuning by Base Loading section when base loading was used. The resulting radiation pattern is shown in Figure 7-6 and is indeed an improvement over that shown in Figure 7-4.

In an attempt to improve the circularity even more by combining the skirted method with base loading, the tower bases were connected to ground through selected values of inductance. The smallest field ratio sum was obtained with an inductance of 47 μH in each base and the field ratio sum decreased significantly to 0.0220. Surprisingly, however, the circularity of the radiation pattern showed no practical

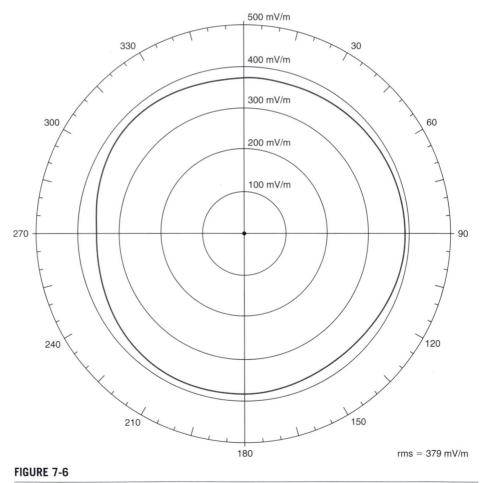

FIGURE 7-6

Nondirectional pattern of eight-tower array using skirt detuning.

improvement. Where the pattern in Figure 7-6 shows a compression at 270°, the revised pattern showed an equivalent bulge at 110°. The improvement did not appear to warrant the change.

Input File Listing: Detune by Skirting

Listing 7-2 is the NEC-2 input file that yields the pattern of Figure 7-6.

The LD commands in Listing 7-2 insert a 1 pF capacitor in the bottom segment of the unused towers to create the open base. The GW, 100 series commands create tower 1 and its skirt. The GM commands

Listing 7-2

```
CM   SK2.NEC - nondirectional operation of 8-tower array
CM       Single Wire Tower, 4' face, 405' AGL, 20 segments
CM       Perfectly conducting ground
CM       Exciting tower 7 for 1000 watts
CE       Using a 4-wire 90° skirt on unused towers
GW, 101, 20,  0., 0., 0., 0., 0., 123.444, 0.582
GW, 102, 1,0., 0., 123.444, 5.6, 0., 123.444, 0.0254
GW, 103, 8, 5.6, 0., 123.444, 5.6, 0., 74.0664, 0.0254
GW, 104, 1, 0., 0., 123.444, 0., 5.6, 123.444, 0.0254
GW, 105, 8, 0., 5.6, 123.444, 0., 5.6, 74.0664, 0.0254
GW, 106, 1, 0., 0., 123.444, –5.6, 0., 123.444, 0.0254
GW, 107, 8, –5.6, 0., 123.444, –5.6, 0., 74.0664, 0.0254
GW, 108, 1, 0., 0., 123.444, 0., –5.6, 123.444, 0.0254
GW, 109, 8, 0., –5.6, 123.444, 0., –5.6, 74.0664, 0.0254
GM, 100, 1, 0., 0., 0., 61.043, 24.663, 0., 101., 1., 109., 8.
GM, 200, 1, 0., 0., 0., 122.086, 49.326, 0., 101., 1., 109., 8.
GM, 300, 1, 0., 0., 0., 183.129, 73.989, 0., 101., 1., 109., 8.
GM, 400, 1, 0., 0., 0., –3.135, –59.811, 0., 101., 1., 109., 8.
GM, 500, 1, 0., 0., 0., 57.867, –35.073, 0., 101., 1., 109., 8.
GM, 700, 1, 0., 0., 0., 179.881, 14.22, 0., 101., 1., 109., 8.
GW, 701, 20, 119.024, –10.455, 0., 119.024, –10.455, 123.444, 0.582
GE, 1
GN, 1
FR, 0, 1, 0, 0, 1.39, 0.
LD, 0, 101, 1, 1, 0., 0., 1.E–12
LD, 0, 201, 1, 1, 0., 0., 1.E–12
LD, 0, 301, 1, 1, 0., 0., 1.E–12
LD, 0, 401, 1, 1, 0., 0., 1.E–12
LD, 0, 501, 1, 1, 0., 0., 1.E–12
LD, 0, 601, 1, 1, 0., 0., 1.E–12
LD, 0, 801, 1, 1, 0., 0., 1.E–12
EX, 0, 701, 1,00, 1279. 46, 0.
RP, 0, 1361, 1001, 90., 0., 1., 1., 1000., 0.
EN
```

copy the complete tower 1 to the locations of the other unused towers. The command GW, 701, is tower 7. It is not skirted and it is driven by the EX command.

7.5 Antenna Monitor Readings

Perhaps the most useful information furnished by the NEC-2 output file is a prediction of the antenna monitor readings that will exist when the array is properly adjusted. This is especially important during the initial adjustment of a new array employing towers with heights greater than 90°.

By sampling the currents on each tower of the array, the antenna monitor gives a comparative indication of the magnitude ratio and phase of the tower current relative to that of the reference tower. Once properly set up, the antenna monitor oversees and provides visibility into the operation of the directional antenna.

When adjusting a new array without a NEC-2 analysis, however, the relationship between the radiated far fields and the antenna monitor readings are not yet established. Therefore, it is necessary to employ a cadre of field technicians, each stationed at a measuring point and equipped with a field strength meter and two-way radio, to "talk" the radiation pattern into spec compliance as the engineer makes adjustments on the phasing equipment in the transmitter building. When the array meets its pattern requirements, the antenna monitor readings (whatever they might be) are logged and become the onsite indicator of the array's proper performance.

Fortunately, the amount of field work and adjustment time can be greatly reduced by using information gained from a NEC-2 analysis. Because the amplitude and phase of the current on a tower are not constant from bottom to top, the height on the tower at which the current is sampled will determine the ratio and phase indication on the antenna monitor. If, on each tower, the antenna monitor sample is taken at that height on the tower where the ratio and phase of the tower current match the target field ratio and phase, then the antenna monitor will give indications closely approximating the radiated field ratios. That being the case, then during the adjustment process, once the monitor readings match the target values (regardless of how they are achieved), the pattern will very nearly coincide with the target pattern. Only a minimum amount of field work will then be required to verify the pattern and to make adjustments as might be caused by parasitic radiations or other causes.

7.5.1 Optimum Height for Sample Loops

Refer to the heading - CURRENTS AND LOCATIONS - in the NEC-2 output file SQR.OUT, as created in Chapter 6. Remember that the target field ratio phase for towers 1, 2, and 3 are 0°, 0°, and 0°, respectively. Also, remember that segments 1 through 20 are located on tower 1, segments 21 through 41 are located on tower 2, and segments 41 through 60 are on tower 3. We can determine the optimum height for the sample loops by finding the height on each tower where the phase of the tower current goes through the corresponding field ratio phase, which, in this example, is 0° for each tower.

A portion of the current distribution listing is shown in Output 7-1.

Output 7-1

```
                      - - - CURRENTS AND LOCATION - - -

                            DISTANCES IN WAVELENGTHS

SEG.TAG  COORD. OF SEG. CENTER    SEG.        - - - CURRENT (AMPS) - - -
NO. NO.    X       Y       Z     LENGTH    REAL       IMAG.      IMAG.     PHASE
 6  101  0.0000  0.0000  0.0688  0.01250  1.4578E+01  1.2462E-01  1.4579E+01   0.490
 7  101  0.0000  0.0000  0.0813  0.01250  1.4130E+01  1.6974E-02  1.4130E+01   0.069
 8  101  0.0000  0.0000  0.0938  0.01250  1.3590E+01 -7.5816E-02  1.3590E+01  -0.320
 9  101  0.0000  0.0000  0.1063  0.01250  1.2962E+01 -1.5409E-01  1.2963E+01  -0.681

26  201  0.5303  0.5303  0.1719  0.03125 -2.2479E-01 -3.1555E-01  3.8743E-01 -125.466
27  201  0.5303  0.5303  0.2031  0.03125 -2.1244E-03 -1.2591E-01  1.2593E-01  -90.967
28  201  0.5303  0.5303  0.2344  0.03125  2.1494E-01  5.0307E-02  2.2075E-01   13.173
29  201  0.5303  0.5303  0.2656  0.03125  4.1792E-01  2.0794E-01  4.6679E-01   26.453

46  301  0.5303 -0.5303  0.1719  0.03125 -2.2479E-01 -3.1555E-01  3.8743E-01 -125.466
47  301  0.5303 -0.5303  0.2031  0.03125 -2.1244E-03 -1.2591E-01  1.2593E-01  -90.967
48  301  0.5303 -0.5303  0.2344  0.03125  2.1494E-01  5.0307E-02  2.2075E-01   13.173
49  301  0.5303 -0.5303  0.2656  0.03125  4.1792E-01  2.0794E-01  4.6679E-01   26.453
```

Notice that within segments 1 through 20 (tower 1), the phase of the current goes through 0 between segments 7 and 8. We could interpolate between these segments for an exact height but for all practical purposes we can say that the phase is 0 at the center of segment 7 because at that height the phase is only +0.069°. The height of the center of segment 7 is given by the table as 0.0813 λ = 16.25 meters, or 53.31 feet. Thus on tower 1 the sample loop should be mounted at a height of approximately 53 feet 4 inches to give an antenna monitor indication representative of the field ratio.

In the case of tower 2, which contains segments 21 through 40, the phase of the current goes through 0° between segments 27 and 28. But notice here that the phase changes radically from −91° on segment 27 to +13° on segment 28. Therefore, it is imperative that the correct height be determined by interpolating between the two segments. Carrying out an interpolation shows that the current goes through 0° at 0.2304 λ. Thus the desired height for the current sample loop on tower 2 is 0.2304 λ = 46.05 meters, or 151 feet, 1.0 inch.

Tower 3 is the same height as tower 2 and seeks the same phase, so the results are the same as those for tower 2. The sample loop on tower 3 should be mounted at a height of 151 feet, 1 inch.

If all three towers were of the same height, then the analysis would lead to mounting the sample loops at the same height on each tower, regardless of the phase of each field ratio.

The interpolation may be carried out on the current magnitudes in addition to the phase. However, a word of caution is in order. With small field ratios, the round-off error and other uncertainties inherent in NEC-2 may yield significant error in the second and greater decimal place. For that reason, it is recommended that the sample loop be positioned based on phase and not magnitude.

7.5.2 Arbitrary Height for Sample Loops

There are occasions when existing sample loops must be used, or perhaps it is desired to forego an interpolation, in which case the antenna monitor indications for the correctly adjusted array can be predicted even though the samples are taken at an arbitrary height.

If, in this example, the sample loops were arbitrarily mounted at the same height on each tower, then the antenna monitor readings would

Table 7-1 Expected Antenna Monitor Readings

Tower	Expected Indication	Field Ratio
1	1.0 @ 0.0°	1.0 @ 0.0°
2	0.24 @ −88.0°	0.05 @ 0.0°
3	0.24 @ −88.0°	0.05 @ 0.0°

be quite different from the field ratios, but they would still be usable when initially adjusting the array.

Consider mounting the sample loops at a height of 133 feet on each of the three towers. On tower 1 this height is segment 17, where the current is 5.21A @ −2.97°. On towers 2 and 3 this height is segment 27 and 47, respectively, where the current is 1.26A @ −90.97° on both towers. The antenna monitor gives readings normalized to the reference tower (1 in this case) so to correctly set up the array, the network components should be adjusted such that the antenna monitor reads as shown in Table 7-1.

This is very useful information because the monitor indications are so different from the field ratio. It is unlikely that one would have anticipated their value during the tune-up process. The NEC-2 analysis thus eliminates a considerable amount of trial and error during the adjustment process.

7.5.3 Base Current Samples

Should the designer of this array elect to monitor the base current using current transformers located at the output of the antenna matching network, the expected monitor readings for the correctly adjusted array can be anticipated by noting the current at the feed points, as shown in the SQR.OUT file, a partial listing of which appears in Table 7-2.

Table 7-2 Antenna Input Parameters

Tag	Segment	Feed Point Current	
		Real	Imaginary
101	1	1.53306E+01	9.49276E-01
201	21	−1.15348E+00	−1.28349E+00
301	41	−1.15348E+00	−1.28349E+00

Where tag 101, segment 1 is the feed point to tower 1; tag 201, segment 21 is the feed to tower 2; and tag 301, segment 41 is the feed to tower 3. The expected monitor readings are obtained by normalizing the base currents listed in Table 7-2 to the current going to tower 1; the monitor readings to be expected when the array is properly adjusted are given in Table 7-3.

Again the NEC-2 analysis is very beneficial because the expected monitor readings are substantially different from the target field ratios.

Another word of caution is in order at this point. Shunt reactance across the drive point will alter the drive point impedance and thus the drive point current. The drive point current shown under the heading "Antenna Input Parameters" is the result of the applied voltage and the effect of the tower impedance as paralleled by any shunt reactance that has been included in the model. Thus the current listed for a given tag and segment under the heading - ANTENNA INPUT PARAMETERS - is the sum of the tower current and the current through the modeled shunt reactance. At the same time, the current listed under the - CURRENTS AND LOCATION - heading for the same tag and segment combination reflects only the tower current and does not include the current through the modeled shunt reactance.

Thus, when predicting the antenna monitor readings created from samples of the base current taken at the output of the tuning unit, one must read the appropriate tag and segment currents under the heading - ANTENNA INPUT PARAMETERS - as opposed to the currents listed under the heading - CURRENTS AND LOCATIONS - even though the tag and segment numbers are the same at both listings.

Moreover, if the NEC-2 model does not accurately duplicate the actual physical shunting reactance, then the currents predicted by the

Table 7-3 Expected Antenna Monitor Readings-Base Current Monitoring

Tower	Expected Indication	Field Ratio
1	1.0 @ 0.0°	1.0 @ 0.0°
2	0.112 @ −135.49°	0.05 @ 0.0°
3	0.112 @ −135.49°	0.05 @ 0.0°

NEC-2 analysis will not be consistent with the actual currents and the predicted monitor readings based on the drive point currents will be in error.

Notwithstanding modeling by measurement, it is not likely that one will be able to accurately duplicate the actual physical shunting reactance when modeling an array. Therefore, basing the initial antenna monitor readings on the base current ratios is not as accurate as basing them on the base voltage ratios or on current samples taken from monitor loops mounted on the tower.

Once the array has been adjusted to meet the specifications, however, then the base drive current samples are an excellent reference to monitor for any changes that might affect the array's operation.

7.5.4 Base Voltage Samples

If it is preferable not to use tower-mounted current sampling loops; the base voltage ratios are the better choice of base parameters to use for determining the initial antenna monitor readings. The base voltage determines the current distribution on the tower; thus, it must be set to the correct value regardless of shunt reactance. The NEC-2 analysis defines the voltage ratios; thus, it provides an excellent indication of the predicted monitor readings when the monitor inputs are voltage samples.

For this example, the base voltages are read from the output file, as shown in Table 7-4. The voltages shown in the table, normalized to tower 1, give the expected monitor readings shown in Table 7-5.

Table 7-4 Antenna Input Parameters

Tag	Segment	Voltage (Volts)			
		Real	**Imaginary**	**Magnitude**	**Phase**
101	1	616.21	436.76	755.30	35.33
201	21	−218.4	142.29	260.66	146.92
301	41	−218.4	142.29	260.66	146.92

Table 7-5 Expected Antenna Monitor Readings-Base Voltage Monitoring

Tower	Expected Indication	Field Ratio
1	1.0 @ 0.0°	1.0 @ 0.0°
2	0.345 @ 111.59°	0.05 @ 0.0°
3	0.345 @ 111.59°	0.05 @ 0.0°

Again, it is not likely that one would have anticipated these monitor readings during the tune-up process. The NEC-2 analysis thus eliminates a considerable amount of trial and error during the adjustment process.

7.6 Drive Point Impedance

The drive point impedances are listed in the SQR.OUT file under - ANTENNA INPUT PARMETERS -, as shown in the partial listing of Table 7-6. Thus the calculated drive point impedances are:

Tower	Impedance
1	41.8 + j25.9
2	23.3 − j149.2
3	23.3 − j149.2

7.6.1 Drive Point Impedance When Using a Network

Consider now the instance where matching networks are used to transform each of the above impedances to 50 + j0. To do that, the SQR.NEC file is copied and renamed NET.NEC and modified to add the networks.

Table 7-6 Antenna Input Parameters

Tag	Segment	Impedance (Ohms)	
		Real	Imaginary
101	1	4.17986E+01	2.59012E+01
201	21	2.32693E+01	−1.49249E+02
301	41	2.32693E+01	−1.49249E+02

Listing 7-3

```
CM EXAMPLE 2 - NET.NEC
CE  3-tower square pattern with matching networks
GW, 100, 1, 999., 999., 999., 999., 999., 999.01, .001
GW, 101, 20, 0., 0., 0., 0., 0., 49.9675, 0.1456
GW, 200, 1, –999., 999., 999., –999., 999., 999.01, .001
GW, 201, 20, 105.997, 105.997, 0., 105.997, 105.997, 124.9188, 0.1456
GW, 300, 1,999., –999., 999., 999., –999., 999.01, .001
GW, 301, 20, 105.997, –105.997, 0., 105.997, –105.997, 124.9188, 0.1456
GE, 1
GN, 1
FR, 0, 1, 0, 0, 1.5, 0.
NT, 100, 1, 101, 1, 0., –0.0124152, 0., –0.0218835, 0., –0.0000115
NT, 200, 1, 201, 1, 0., 0.1278266, 0., –0.0292313, 0., –0.0000181
NT, 300, 1, 301, 1, 0., 0.1278266, 0., –0.0292313, 0., –0.0000181
EX, 0, 100, 1, 00, 42.8561, –700.6906
EX, 0, 200, 1, 00, –43.7796, 39.3502
EX, 0, 300, 1,00, –43.7796, 39.3502
RP, 0, 1361, 1001, 90., 0., 1., 1., 1000., 0.
EN
```

For each network we must add a dummy wire to which we connect the input of that network. These dummy wires are tag 100, tag 200, and tag 300 in Listing 7-3. Notice that the dummy wires are located far away and are very short to minimize the effect they might have on the array radiation.

The output of the networks are connected to the base of each tower on the segment where the original drive voltage had been placed.

The matching networks are designed using the usual T-network procedures. The network Y-parameters are then calculated as described in Section 5.2.1 and the NT commands are added to the input file.

In this particular case, the complex base impedances were transformed to $50\,\Omega$ resistive with an arbitrary $+90°$ phase shift. The base drive voltages, which have been calculated to give the desired pattern, are translated from the tower base to the input of the matching networks by recalling that the phase shift within the network refers to current phase shift not voltage phase shift. The modified input file is as shown in Listing 7-3.

Run Listing 7-3 and name the output file NET.OUT, then the network parameters are listed in the NET.OUT output file under the heading - NETWORK DATA -, as shown in the partial listing of Output 7-2.

Output 7-2

- - - NETWORK DATA - - -
- - ADMITTANCE MATRIX ELEMENTS (MHOS) - -

- FROM -		- TO -		(ONE,ONE)		(ONE,TWO)		(TWO,TWO)	
TAG	SEG.	TAG	SEG.						
NO.	NO.	NO.	NO.	REAL	IMAG.	REAL	IMAG.	REAL	IMAG.
100	1	101	2	0.000E+00	−1.2415E−02	0.000E+00	−2.1884E−02	0.000E+00	−1.1500E−05
200	22	201	23	0.000E+00	1.2783E−01	0.000E+00	−2.9231E−02	0.000E+00	−1.8100E−05
300	43	301	44	0.000E+00	1.2783E−01	0.000E+00	−2.9231E−02	0.000E+00	−1.8100E−05

- - - STRUCTURE EXCITATION DATA AT NETWORK CONNECTION POINTS - - -

TAG	SEG.	VOLTAGE (VOLTS)		CURRENT (AMPS)		IMPEDANCE		ADMITTANCE		POWER
NO.	NO.	REAL	IMAG.	REAL	IMAG.	REAL	IMAG.	REAL	IMAG.	WATTS
101	2	6.1625E+2	4.3650E+2	1.5328E+1	9.4493E−1	4.1800E+1	2.5900E+1	1.7287E−2	−1.071E−2	.929E+3
201	23	−2.184E+2	1.420E+2	−1.152E+0	−1.283E+0	2.333E+1	−1.492E+2	1.023E−3	6.541E−3	3.473E+1
301	44	−2.184E+2	1.420E+2	−1.152E+0	1.283E+0	2.333E+1	−1.492E+2	1.023E−3	6.541E−3	3.473E+1
100	1	4.285E+1	−7.006E+2	3.864E−4	2.363E−5	−7.303E+0	−1.813E+6	−2.224E−12	5.514E−7	−5.472E−7
200	22	−4.377E+1	3.935E+1	−2.170E−5	−2.414E−5	1.039E+2	−1.813E+6	3.160E−11	5.514E−7	5.475E−8
300	43	−4.377E+1	3.935E+1	−2.170E−5	−2.414E−5	1.018E+2	−1.813E+6	3.096E−11	5.514E−7	5.364E−8

- - - ANTENNA INPUT PARAMETERS - - -

TAG	SEG.	VOLTAGE		CURRENT		IMPEDANCE		ADMITTANCE		POWER
NO.	NO.	REAL	IMAG.	REAL	IMAG.	REAL	IMAG.	REAL	IMAG.	WATTS
100	1	4.2856E+1	−7.0069E+2	8.5332E−1	−1.4017E+1	4.9986E+1	1.4356E−2	2.0005E−2	−5.7457E−6	4.929E+3
200	22	−4.3779E+1	3.9350E+1	−8.7735E−1	7.8918E−1	4.9882E+1	1.8797E−2	2.0047E−2	−7.5543E−6	3.473E+1
300	43	−4.3779E+1	3.9350E+1	−8.7735E−1	7.8918E−1	4.9882E+1	1.8797E−2	2.0047E−2	−7.5544E−6	3.473E+1

The voltage at the tower base is shown as the network output voltage at tags 101, 201, and 301 under the heading - STRUCTURE EXCITATION DATA AT NETWORK CONNECTION POINTS - in the NET.OUT output file. Under the same heading, the voltage at the input to the matching network is shown at tag 100, tag 200, and tag 300.

Finally, the results of the impedance transformation is shown under the heading - ANTENNA INPUT PARAMETERS - where the input impedance is shown as 49.99 + j0.01 for tower 1 and 49.88 + j0.02 for towers 2 and 3.

7.7 Exercises

7.1. Modify Listing 7-2 shown in Section 7.4.2 to convert the array to the directional mode by adding a spider connecting the bottom end of the skirts to the towers. Confirm the change by viewing the results with NVCOMP.EXE.

7.2. Create a NEC-2 input file by further modifying Listing 7-2 to change the drive voltage from the nondirectional mode to the directional mode using drive voltages as follows:

Tower	Voltage
1	$-191.38 + j475.31$
2	$-851.97 - j573.01$
3	$1594.97 + j426.46$
4	$-780.83 + j1439.34$
5	$-935.25 - j48.85$
6	$854.38 - j1604.54$
7	$-167.64 - j2163.19$
8	$-1564.52 - j1330.29$

Do a bnec.exe run using the modified input file and confirm that the power to the array is 5000 watts.

7-3. If the monitor system uses current transformers to monitor the tower feed point currents, what will be the antenna monitor indications when using tower 3 as the reference tower?

7-4. Use the tower feed point voltages to determine the expected antenna monitor readings when the array is adjusted correctly. Compare those results with those obtained when monitoring the base currents in exercise 7-3. Which is most reliable? Why?

Model by Measurement

8.1 Objective

One of the objects of a NEC-2 analysis is to calculate a close approximation of an array's driving point impedances when the array elements are in the active condition. In this instance, the active condition is defined as the condition that exists when the elements are driven by the currents and phases that yield the desired pattern. In association with that objective, it is generally believed that if the array elements are modeled such that their calculated self-impedances match the measured self-impedances of the elements of the physical array under passive conditions (i.e., with no drive currents applied) then, because the components involved comprise a linear system, those models will prevail under active conditions. Consequently, towers so modeled may be used in the array calculations to obtain a better estimate of the active drive point impedances.

A common practice, then, is to attempt to adjust the parameters of the tower models such that the calculated self-impedances match, or nearly match, the measured self-impedance of the physical towers. This process is referred to as "modeling by measurement" and is the subject of this chapter.

Unfortunately, the impedance as calculated by NEC-2 is probably the least acceptable parameter being determined by a NEC-2 analysis. Although the calculated impedance is quite adequate to use in designing the antenna-matching networks, in many cases it falls short of the accuracy needed to predict the antenna monitor readings from the calculated base drive currents. This is due not only to physical modeling errors caused by simplifying the model (round wire approximations, unequal radii at segment junctions, small loops, etc.) but also to inherent shortcomings within the NEC-2 computer code, such as the compromised means to mathematically represent the source voltage and the simplified representations of current flow in the conductors.

The data plotted in Figure 8-1 is similar to that in a paper titled "A Study of AM Tower Base Impedance" given by J. B. Hatfield at the

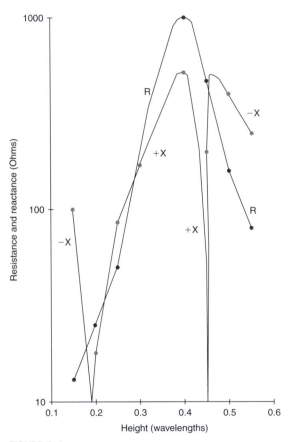

FIGURE 8-1

Typical measured self-impedance of an isolated tower.

42nd Annual IEEE Broadcast Symposium, September 17, 1992. At the time of this writing, a copy of that paper and other useful information is available at *http://www.hatdaw.com/downloads.html*. The graph is presented here to show the manner in which the self-impedance of an isolated tower varies with height and to serve as a reference point when considering the graphs in the following sections.

8.2 Adjusting the Model

Although it might not be essential to have an exact match between the calculated and measured self-impedance, there are occasions where some analysts may find it desirable to make parameter adjustments during calculations so as to force an acceptable comparison with measured data. The key word here is "force" because in many instances analysts have used artificial means (such as varying tower height) to create a match in the belief that it was beneficial. In reality, the only change may be to eliminate a "wrong answer" in favor of a "more satisfactory wrong answer." It is important, therefore, that all adjustments be logical and that they be made with discretion.

Reasonable adjustments normally concern only discretionary parameters or parameters that must be estimated because they cannot be measured conveniently. These may include the number and length of wire segments used in the NEC-2 calculations, the assumed equivalent radius of a triangular tower, the assumed effective radius and shunt reactance of the base insulator, the stray capacity and inductance associated with the measuring apparatus, parasitic effects, losses, and so forth. It is not wise to adjust such fundamental parameters as tower height to force the calculated data to agree with measured data because such adjustments might change the current distribution on the towers and distort the conclusions that may be drawn from the analysis. Moreover, the adjustment of fundamental parameters does not appear to make a significant contribution to the final results of an array analysis, so the value of such adjustments appears questionable.

Finally, realistic adjustments are divided into two categories—those associated with the modeled tower and those associated with the measuring apparatus. The latter include such things as test lead inductance and clip lead resistance. Adjustments associated with the tower will, of course, be included in the modeled array. Adjustments associated with the measuring apparatus must be removed when the model tower is incorporated into the array analysis.

The sections in this chapter demonstrate how several parameters might affect the self-impedance of a radiator. It is important to realize that the data displayed by the charts show general trends of a single isolated tower and should not be interpreted as being specific values applicable to any particular configuration or array situation.

8.2.1 Number of Segments

Figures 8-2(a), (b), and (c) show the self-impedance of an isolated tower of fixed height as calculated by NEC-2 using various number of segments ranging from 20 to 100. For all three figures, the tower height is fixed at approximately a quarter wavelength; G = 50 meters at a wavelength of 199.87 meters (1500 KHz). The figures show the results for towers of three different radii.

Figure 8-2(a) illustrates the impedance versus the number of segments for a typical broadcast tower having an equivalent radius of 0.29 meter. This corresponds to a triangular tower with a 24-inch face. It is

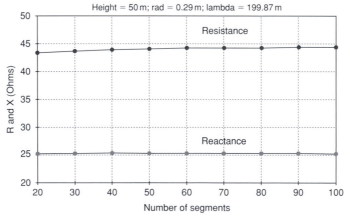

FIGURE 8-2(a)

Segmentation on a typical tower.

quite evident from this figure that increasing the number of segments beyond 20 has little effect on the calculated impedance.

Another interesting revelation from this figure is that the guidelines for tower modeling as issued in Chapter 3 are not hard-and-fast rules. The world doesn't suddenly come to an end if the guidelines are violated. For example, it is recommended in Chapter 3 that the ratio of segment length to radius be greater than 8; that is, $\Delta/a > 8$ unless the EK command is used, in which case the ratio Δ/a should be >2. The data in this figure shows that with 20 segments, $\Delta/a = 8.62$, which is within the guideline. At 100 segments, however, the ratio Δ/a has fallen to only 1.72. Notwithstanding the fact that the EK command was not used in the calculation, the results appear reasonably consistent, although there is some minor slope to the curve.

In comparison, Figure 8-2(b) is a similar plot representing the impedance of a very thin conductor comparable to a guy wire. The conductor radius in this example is 0.00635 meter (0.25 inch), corresponding to a half-inch diameter cable. With this small radius, the ratio of segment length to radius stays well above the guideline throughout the 20- to 100-segment range. At 20 segments, $\Delta/a = 394$ and at 100 segments $\Delta/a = 79$. As shown in Figure 8-2(b), both resistance and reactance are constant to the naked eye.

Figure 8-2(c) looks at the other extreme. Here all parameters remain unchanged except for radius, which has been increased to 1.83 meters, corresponding to a very thick wire with a radius of 6 feet. At 20 segments, the ratio $\Delta/a = 1.37$ and at 100 segments, the ratio Δ/a is only 0.27. At the fewer number of segments, from 20 to 60 for example, the ratio changes from $\Delta/a = 1.37$ to $\Delta/a = 0.45$ and the curve is reasonably well behaved but with significant slope. Beyond 60 segments, both resistance and reactance fall rapidly as Δ/a falls from 0.45 to 0.27.

Figure 8-2(c) also shows the improvement gained by using the EK command. All parameters were unchanged except that the EK command was added to the input code. Notice that the behavior of both the resistance and reactance are improved noticeably when the EK command is used.

In view of the guidance offered by these figures, using 20 segments per tower for broadcast work seems to be a reasonable choice.

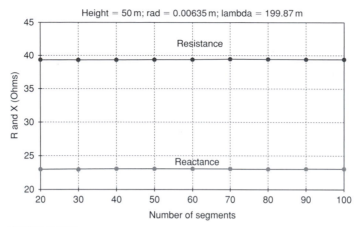

FIGURE 8-2(b)

Segmentation on a thin wire.

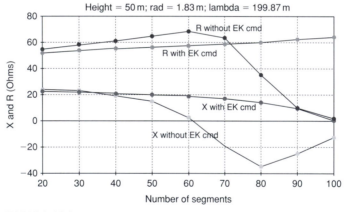

FIGURE 8-2(c)

Segmentation on a thick wire.

As a final comment on this subject, it is worthwhile to know that the dependency of the calculated impedance on the ratio of Δ/a is imposed by the numerical solutions employed in NEC-2 and are not a physical characteristic of the tower proper. As mentioned earlier, NEC-2 results are close approximations rather than exact solutions. In this particular instance, using the EK command changes the assumption that the current flows as a thin filament on the wire axis to one that has the current flowing axially over the complete wire surface. The latter gives a more realistic solution but requires more computer effort, which is not a serious handicap to modern computers. It is important to recognize, however, that both processes involve assumptions and both have limitations.

8.2.2 Tower Diameter

Figure 8-3(a) shows the effect on drive point impedance when the tower diameter is varied. The plot for short towers (G = 54°) shows

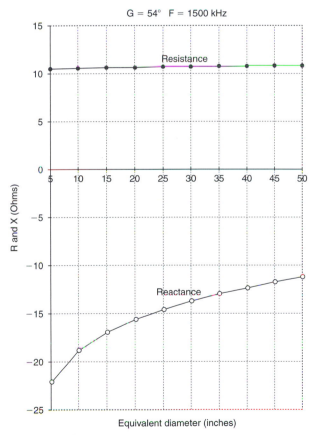

FIGURE 8-3(a)

Impedance versus tower diameter: G = 54°.

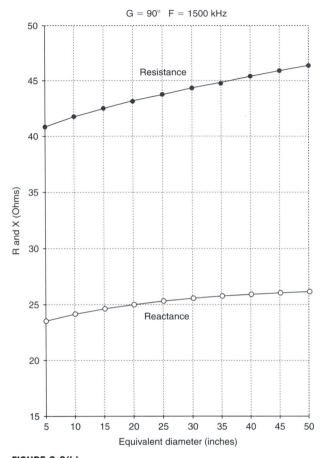

FIGURE 8-3(b)

Impedance versus tower diameter: G = 90°.

very little change in the resistive component as diameter is varied but there is significant change in the reactive component. With the resistance remaining near constant and the reactance decreasing, the effective Q of the antenna decreases, resulting in an increased bandwidth. This supports the notion that "fat" antennas have a broader bandwidth.

At G = 90°, changing the tower diameter has only a minimal effect on drive point impedance but at the taller heights, changing tower diameter changes the drive point impedance significantly.

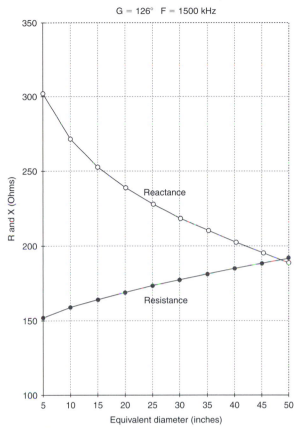

FIGURE 8-3(c)

Impedance versus tower diameter: G = 126°.

Notice that at G = 126°, the reactive component of imped-ance decreases by approximately 50 percent as the tower diameter increases. At the same time, the resistive component rises almost 30 percent.

The change in the resistive component is even greater, albeit in the opposite direction, as the tower height climbs to 180°. The resistive component falls to less one-third its thin value and the reactive compo-nent reduces to two-thirds its thin value.

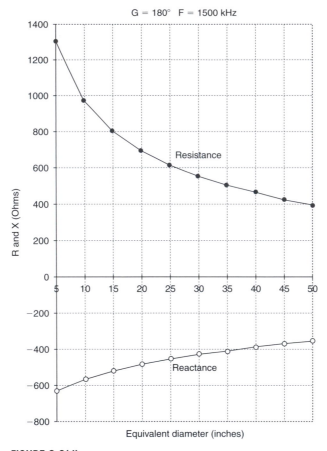

FIGURE 8-3(d)

Impedance versus tower diameter: G = 180°.

Thus, it may be concluded that tower diameter is more significant for tall towers than it is for shorter ones.

8.2.3 Segment and Radius Taper

The GC command in the NEC-2 input file permits both the radius and the segment length to be tapered from one end of the wire to the

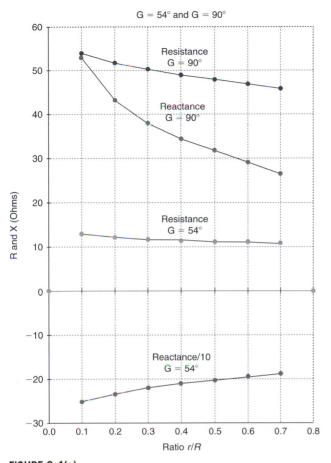

FIGURE 8-4(a)

Impedance versus taper: G = 54° & G = 90°.

other. That this feature can be used as a matching tool is shown in Figure 8-4.

These figures show the effect of tapering the segment length over the tower height which has been divided into 20 segments with a ratio of (segment N length/segment N-1 length) = 1.1. In addition, the tower radius is tapered in 20 segments from a starting radius of R at the base of the tower to radius r at the top.

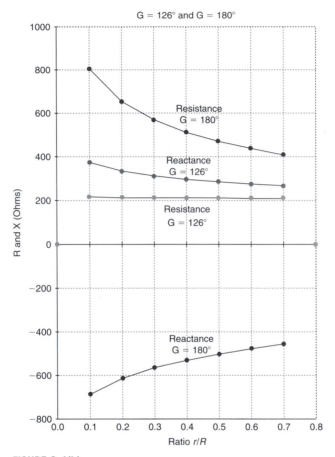

FIGURE 8-4(b)

Impedance versus taper: G = 126° & G = 180°.

Again, the effect of this variation is rather minor for the short tower (G = 54°) but grows to be quite significant on the taller towers.

8.2.4 Base Capacity

The base insulator and the tower itself present an effective capacity from tower bottom to ground.

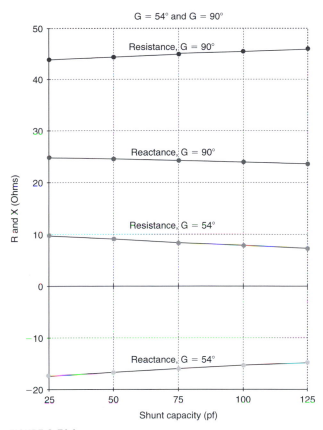

FIGURE 8-5(a)

Impedance versus base capacity: G = 54° & G = 90°.

Figure 8-5 shows how this capacity affects drive point impedance. On the taller towers, it appears that it is almost a necessity that this capacity be included in the model. The shorter towers, G = 54° and G = 90°, in Figure 8-5(a) show almost no change as the base capacity varies from 25 pf to 125 pf. On the other hand, with G = 180° in Figure 8-5(b), the resistive component of the drive point impedance changes from more than 400 ohms to 200 ohms as the base capacity is increased from 25 pf to 125 pf.

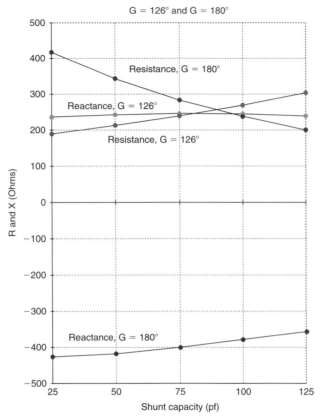

FIGURE 8-5(b)

Impedance versus base capacity: G = 126° & G = 180°.

For all tower heights, the change in the reactive component of the base drive impedance is only small to moderate.

8.2.5 Drive Segment Radius

The drive segment is essentially a model of the base insulator in tower configurations shown in Figures 3-1(c), (d), and (e). As such, some latitude is permissible in defining the radius of that segment.

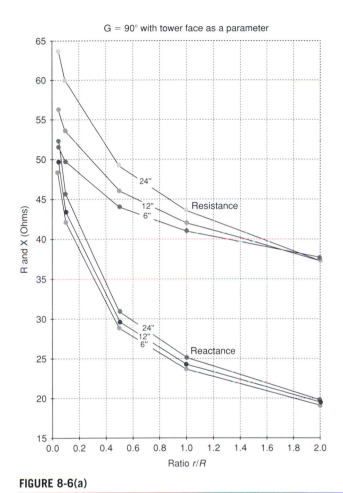

FIGURE 8-6(a)

Impedance versus drive segment radius with tower face as a parameter: G = 90°.

Figure 8-6 shows impedance versus the drive segment radius (r) expressed as a ratio with the radius of the main radiator (R). And as it turns out, the nature of NEC-2 is such that the drive point impedance is quite sensitive to the radius of that segment. Unfortunately, it is not always possible to select a drive segment radius to simultaneously match both the measured resistance and reactance. It appears that shorter towers are more likely to match resistance and taller towers are more likely to match reactance.

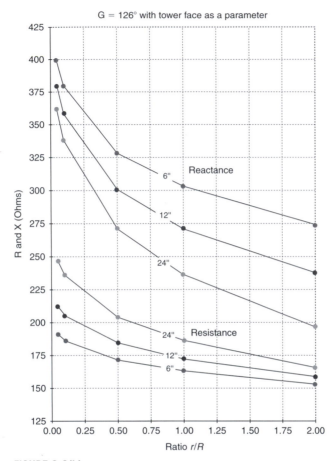

FIGURE 8-6(b)

Impedance versus drive segment radius with tower face as a parameter: G = 126°.

8.3 Exercise

8-1. Using a triangular tower whose height is 66° with a 12″ face and operating at 1070 kHz with the configuration shown in Chapter 3, Figure 3-1(c), show how the calculated drive point impedance varies as the length of the drive segment is changed from 1 meter to 10 meters in 1-meter increments. The radius of the drive segment is 40 percent of the radius of the tower proper.

Top-Loaded and Skirted Towers

9

9.1 General Considerations

You may have noticed that the top skirt shown in Figure 7-5 and included in Listing 7-2 used an exaggerated spacing between the skirt and the tower. This was necessary because a thick-wire tower model was used and to comply with the requirement that the spacing be at least several radii, it was necessary to exaggerate the spacing. However, to overcome such inconvenience and to make the tower model more realistic, the usual practice when modeling top hats, skirts, and so on is to use the lattice tower model, where the wires are all rather thin and thus can accommodate a closer spacing of conductors.

Another consideration to keep in mind when modeling closely spaced conductors is to keep the adjacent segments aligned as closely as possible. For instance, a top-skirt wire extending down five segments on the tower should itself contain five segments, and those segments should be aligned as closely as practical with the segments on the tower.

Also, when you want to examine the current distribution on a lattice tower, you must remember that the total current distribution on a lattice tower model is the vector sum of the current distributions on each tower leg. Therefore all legs of a tower must be included to determine the total current distribution. It is also important to recognize that the current in the horizontal girth wires should not be included in the current distribution.

121

Fortunately, it is not difficult to write a postprocessing computer program to read the NEC-2 output file and to determine the current distribution on a lattice tower according to these requirements.

9.2 Top Loading

Adding a "top hat" to a tower modifies the current distribution on the tower by terminating the top of the tower in a capacity, as opposed to leaving the top of the tower open. This causes the current at the top of the tower to increase from a near 0 value to a value determined by the amount of terminating capacity. When this is done, the current distribution along the entire height of the tower is changed, thus providing the means to achieve a more desirable drive point impedance or to modify the vertical angle of radiation.

From a mathematics viewpoint, the ideal top hat would be a horizontal disc because the capacity of a disc can be easily calculated. Unfortunately, the mechanical problems associated with implementing such a disc in the MF band make compromise necessary. The usual practice is to use a section of the upper set of guy wires as a down-sloping top hat. This does pose a limitation on how much top loading can be used, however. The current flowing in the guy wire top hat is made up of both a horizontal component and a downward vertical component. The horizontal component makes no contribution to the desired vertically polarized radiated field and the downward vertical component of current causes some measure of tower shielding. About 30° is generally taken as the practical limit for extending a foreshortened broadcast tower.

9.2.1 Estimating the Size of the Top Hat

In theory, the size of the top hat can be estimated by considering the tower to be an open transmission line, and calculating the effective capacity of the missing phantom section. But unfortunately, if that capacity is to be created using sections of the upper guy wires, there is no convenient way to determine how long the guy wire should be to create that capacity. Therefore, a starting point would be to make the guy wire section the length needed to make the overall length of tower plus guy wire equal to the desired tower height. A NEC-2 run can then determine the effect of that length and adjustments can be made as necessary.

9.2.2 Determining the Degree of Top Loading

The effect of the top load can be estimated by recognizing that the current maximum occurs at a fixed distance from the top of an unloaded tower. This is generally taken to be 90° but the finiteness of the physical tower modifies this somewhat.

Refer to Figure 9-1, in which the lower curve shows the current distribution on a 90° tower. Here the maximum current occurs at 9°, which is 81° below the top of the tower, as opposed to the generally assumed 90°.

Continuing now with the example in which we seek to load a 60° tower to an effective height of 90°, we start by generating a NEC-2 input file that models the 60° tower complete with the guy wire

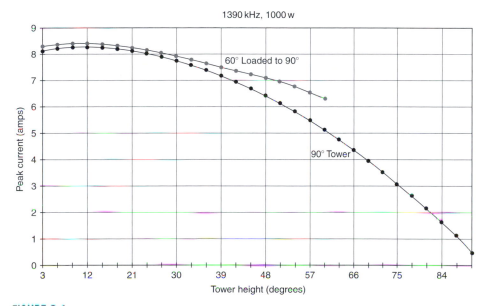

FIGURE 9-1

Current distribution, 60° tower loaded to 90°.

Listing 9-1

```
CM      TL.NEC Example 9-1 – 1390 kHz, 60° loaded to 90°
CM      with 3 guys & ring
CE      Lattice triangular tower model, 1m face, 1000W
GW, 101, 1, 0., 0., 0., 0., 0., 1.7973 0.019
GW, 102, 1, 0., 0., 1.7973, 0.5774, 0., 1.7973, 0.019
GW, 102, 1, 0., 0., 1.7973, −0.2887, 0.5, 1.7973, 0.019
GW, 102, 1, 0., 0., 1.7973, −0.2887, −0.5, 1.7973, 0.019
GW, 102, 1,0.5774, 0., 1.7973, −0.2887, 0.5, 1.7973, 0.019
GW, 102,1,−0.2887,0.5,1.7973,−0.2887,−0.5,1.7973,0.019
GW, 102, 1,−0.2887, −0.5, 1.7973, 0.5774, 0., 1.7973, 0.019
GW, 103,1,0.5774,0.,1.7973,0.5774,0.,3.5946,0.019
GW, 103, 1, −0.2887, 0.5, 1.7973, −0.2887, 0.5,3.5946, 0.019
GW, 103,1,−0.2887,−0.5,1.7973,−0.2887,−0.5,3.5946,0.019
GW, 103, 1,0.5774, 0., 3.5946, −0.2887, 0.5, 3.5946, 0.019
GW, 103, 1, −0.2887, 0.5, 3.5946, −0.2887, −0.5, 3.5946, 0.019
GW, 103, 1, −0.2887, −0.5, 3.5946, 0.5774, 0., 3.5946, 0.019
GM, 000, 18, 0., 0., 0., 0., 0., 1.7973, 103., 1., 103., 6.
GW, 104, 7, 0.5774, 0., 35.946, 8.8962, 0., 27.0505, 0.01
GW, 104, 7, −0.2887, 0.5, 35.946, −4.4481, 7.7043, 27.0505, 0.01
GW, 104, 7, −0.2887, −0.5, 35.946, −4.4481, −7.7043, 27.0505, 0.01
GW, 104, 7, 8.8962, 0., 27.0505, −4.4481, 7.7043, 27.0505, 0.01
GW, 104, 7, −4.4481, 7.7043, 27.0505, −4.4481, −7.7043, 27.0505, 0.01
GW, 104, 7, −4.4481, −7.7043, 27.0505, 8.8962, 0., 27.0505, 0.01
GE, 1
GN, 1
FR, 0, 1, 0, 0, 1.39, 0.
EX, 0, 101, 1, 00, 393.8827, 0.
PL, 1, 1, 0, 0
XQ
```

sections as its top hat. Such NEC-2 input file code is shown as TL.NEC in Listing 9-1.

A lattice tower model is used with wire tag 101 being the single-feed wire of the lattice tower configuration shown in Figure 3-1(e). Wire tag 102 makes up six segments of the spider and girth ring. Wire tag 103 is the standard section composed of three legs and a three-wire top girth. The GM command stacks eighteen standard sections to reach the tower height of 35.946 meters. Wire tag 104 creates the top load with the guys extending from the top of the tower down and outward to the 27.0505-meter level. The last three segments labeled tag 104 create the ring at the bottom of the top load wires.

Figure 9-2 shows the NVCOMP.EXE display of the modeled tower.

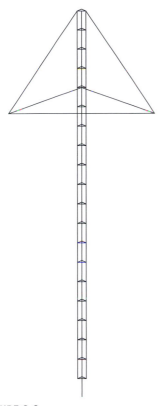

FIGURE 9-2

NVCOMP.EXE view of top-loaded tower.

The output file generated by this code reveals the current distribution for the top-loaded tower. This is shown by the top curve of Figure 9-1. At the lower levels, the current distribution is seen to be much like that of the full-sized 90° tower. The current magnitude peaks at 9° on the top-loaded 60° tower just as it does on the 90° tower, suggesting that there is an effective height of 81° above the 9° height. But in reality, the top-loaded 60° tower has only 51 physical degrees above the current maximum. Thus, the top-hat loading is adding 81° − 51° = 30° of phantom tower height to the 60° tower.

It is interesting to notice here that the current distribution on the 60° tower begins to deviate from that of the 90° tower as the top of the 60° tower is approached. This is caused by the interaction of the currents on the down-sloping top-load wires and the currents on the physical tower.

9.3 Skirted Towers

In addition to using a tower skirt to electrically shorten a tower for the purpose of detuning, the skirt is sometimes used to alter the current distribution on the tower and thus modify the vertical radiation pattern. Consider the case where it is desired to use a single tower for AM operation at 1430 kHz and also to support an FM antenna. The FM application requires a 500-foot tower but such a tall tower at 1430 kHz produces an undesirable radiation pattern with much of the radiation going into a high-angle lobe. See Figure 9-3.

To mitigate this problem, a 90° skirt can be placed at the top of the 500-foot tower to electrically shorten the tower to an effective 318 feet. The input file to perform this modification is shown as SKRT.NEC in Listing 9-2.

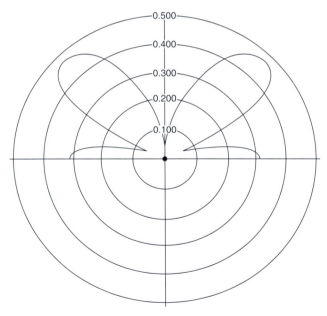

FIGURE 9-3

Vertical radiation pattern of 500-foot tower at 1430 kHz.

Listing 9-2

```
CM SKRT.NEC
CM FEEDING 152m TOWER AT 1430 kHz WITH 1KW
CE 90° SKIRT, VERTICAL PATTERN
GW, 101, 1, 0., 0., 0., 0., 0., 2., 0.0159
GW, 101, 1, 0., 0., 2., 0.6159, 0., 2., 0.0159
GW, 101, 1, 0., 0., 2., −0.308, 0.5334, 2., 0.0159
GW, 101, 1, 0., 0., 2., −0.308, −0.5334, 2., 0.0159
GW, 101, 1, 0.6159, 0., 2., −0.308, 0.5334, 2., 0.0159
GW, 101, 1, −0.308, 0.5334., 2., −0.308, −0.5334., 2., 0.0159
GW, 101, 1, −0.308, −0.5334, 2., 0.6159, 0., 2., 0.0159
GW, 102, 1, 0.6159, 0., 2., 0.6159, 0., 7., 0.0159
GW, 102, 1, −0.308, 0.5334, 2., −0.308, 0.5334, 7., 0.0159
GW, 102, 1, −0.308, −0.5334, 2., −0.308, −0.5334, 7., 0.0159
GW, 102, 1, 0.6159, 0., 7., −0.308, 0.5334, 7., 0.0159
GW, 102, 1, −0.308, 0.5334, 7., −0.308, −0.5334, 7., 0.0159
GW, 102, 1, −0.308, −0.5334, 7., 0.6159, 0., 7., 0.0159
GM, 0, 29, 0., 0., 0., 0., 0., 5., 102., 1., 102., 6.
GW, 103, 1, 0.6159, 0, 152., 1.6159, 0., 152., 0.0159
GW, 103, 1, −0.308, 0.5334, 152., −0.808, 1.3994, 152., 0.0159
GW, 103, 1, −0.308, −0.5334, 152., −0.808, −1.3994, 152., 0.0159
GW, 103, 10, 1.6159, 0., 152., 1.6159, 0., 102., 0.0127
GW, 103, 10, −0.808, 1.3994, 152., −0.808, 1.3994, 102., 0.0127
GW, 103, 10, −0.808, −1.3994, 152., −0.808, −1.3994, 102., 0.0127
GW, 103, 1, 1.6159, 0., 102., −0.808, 1.3994, 102., 0.0127
GW, 103, 1, −0.808, 1.3994, 102., −0.808, −1.3994, 102., 0.0127
GW, 103, 1, −0.808, −1.3994, 102., 1.6159, 0., 102., 0.0127
GE, 1
GN, 1
FR, 0, 1, 0, 0, 1.43, 0.
EX, 0, 101, 1, 00, 1495.226, 0.
PL, 3, 1, 1, 0
RP, 0, 181, 1, 1001, −90., 0., 1., 1., 1000., 0.
EN
```

As usual for this type application, the lattice tower model is used. Wire tag 101 generates the feed wire; it also creates the spider and girth to connect the feed wire to the three legs of the tower. Wire tag 102 is a 5-meter standard section and the GM command stacks twenty-nine of these standard sections to achieve the desired height.

Wire tag 103 generates the skirt with the first three commands creating the horizontal support arms, each standing off 1 meter from the tower leg. The next three commands with tag 103 are the vertical skirt wires running from the horizontal support arms at the top of the tower down to the lower support arms located at the 102-meter level AGL.

Notice here that the vertical skirt wires are 50 meters in length so they have been assigned ten segments each to match the length and alignment of the segments on the tower. The last three commands with tag 103 make up a ring at the bottom end of the skirt.

This input code also includes the PL command to generate a separate output file for plotting the vertical radiation pattern as generated by the RP command. The PL file as saved must be altered to accommodate the particular plotting arrangement that will be used.

See Appendix A for more detail on both the RP and PL commands. Figure 9-4 shows an NVCOMP.EXE view of the upper portion of the tower that contains the skirt wires.

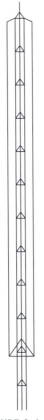

FIGURE 9-4

NVCOMP.EXE view of 500-foot tower with 90° top skirt.

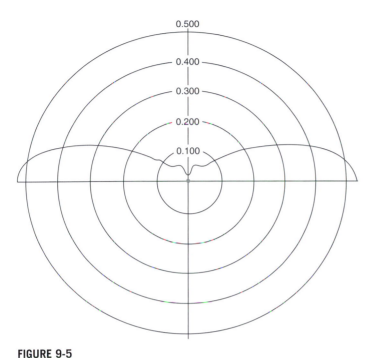

FIGURE 9-5

Vertical radiation pattern of 500-foot tower using 90° top skirt at 1430 kHz.

Figure 9-5 is a plot of the vertical radiation pattern as generated by the skirted tower. It is interesting to compare this figure with Figure 9-3 to appreciate the effect of the skirt.

9.4 Folded Monopole

Using skirts to create a folded monopole antenna permits a grounded tower to be used as an AM broadcast antenna. Also, using a grounded tower as a folded monopole eliminates the need for isocouplers or other devices to bring transmission lines and lighting wires across a base insulator. In addition, a folded monopole is an effective way to raise the radiation resistance of a short tower. The latter is illustrated in the following example.

Consider the case of a 170-foot (51.816 meters) triangular tower with a 12-inch face operating at 1000 watts on 1070 kHz. The tower is only 66° at the operating frequency and if used as such, NEC-2 will calculate a drive point impedance of only 14 – j79. If, however, the short tower is converted to a folded monopole by adding a full-length skirt and a single-drive wire from the bottom of the skirt to ground, then NEC-2 calculates the drive point impedance to be 97 – j249. The NEC-2 input file shown as FLMO.NEC in Listing 9-3 generates the data on this folded monopole.

Wire tag 101 is the feed wire connecting the skirt's bottom ring to ground. Wire tag 102 is the grounded standard section starting at ground level and running up 10 feet (3.048 meters). The first three commands describe the three tower legs and the next three commands describe the top girth on the standard section. Following that, the GM command stacks sixteen standard sections to reach the height of 51.816 meters. Finally, wire tag 103 creates the full-length skirt using

Listing 9-3

```
CM FLMO.NEC
CM Single 51.816 meter tower at 1070 kHz, 1000 watts
CM 3-WIRE FULL SKIRT SPACED 1 METER FED AT 1.524 METERS
CE
GW, 101, 1, 1.176, 0., 3.048, 1.176, 0., 0., 0.0127
GW, 102, 1, 0.176, 0., 0., 0.176, 0., 3.048, 0.0127
GW, 102, 1, −0.088, 0.1524, 0., −0.088, 0.1524, 3.048, 0.0127
GW, 102, 1, −0.088, −0.1524, 0, −0.088, −0.1524, 3.048, 0.0127
GW, 102, 1, 0.176, 0., 3.048, −0.088, 0.1524, 3.048, 0.0127
GW, 102, 1, −0.088, 0.1524, 3.048, −0.088, −0.1524, 3.048, 0.0127
GW, 102, 1, −0.088, −0.1524, 3.048, 0.176, 0., 3.048, 0.0127
GM, 0, 16, 0., 0., 0., 0., 0., 3.048, 102., 1., 102., 6.
GW, 103, 1, 0.176, 0., 51.816, 1.176, 0., 51.816, 0.0127
GW, 103, 1, −0.088, 0.1524, 51.816, −0.588, 1.0184, 51.816, 0.0127
GW, 103, 1, −0.088, −0.1524, 51.816, −0.588, −1.0184, 51.816, 0.0127
GW, 103, 16, 1.176, 0., 51.816, 1.176, 0., 3.048, 0.00635
GW, 103, 16, −0.588, 1.0184, 51.816, −0.588, 1.0184, 3.048, 0.00635
GW, 103, 16, −0.588, −1.0184, 51.816, −0.588, −1.0184, 3.048, 0.00635
GW, 103, 1, 1.176, 0., 3.048, −0.588, 1.0184, 3.048, 0.00635
GW, 103, 1, −0.588, 1.0184, 3.048, −0.588, −1.0184, 3.048, 0.00635
GW, 103, 1, −0.588, −1.0184, 3.048, 1.176, 0., 3.048, 0.00635
GE, 1
GN, 1
FR, 0, 1, 0, 0, 1.07, 0.
EX, 0, 101, 1, 00, 1211.59, 0.
XQ
EN
```

FIGURE 9-6

NVCOMP.EXE view of lower portion of folded monopole.

three 1-meter supporting arms at the top of the tower, three skirt wires, and three wires making up the ring at the bottom of the skirt. The skirt wires each have sixteen segments to match those on the tower.

Figure 9-6 shows the NVCOMP.EXE display of the lower portion of the skirted tower, including the feed wire.

The 97-ohm resistive component of the monopole can be transformed to near 50 ohms by placing a shorting spider at a selected height on the skirt. Because NEC-2 can accept connections only at the end of a segment, the shorting height used in the analysis is limited to the heights of the segment ends. Choosing a height of 5 segments up the skirt places a short at 18.288 meters and the resulting drive point impedance becomes 44 + j200. This calculated value is a starting place for the physical adjusting process. In practice, the shorting spider would be located a bit higher than this to get a drive point resistance closer to 50 Ω. Add the following three commands to Listing 9-3 to place this short at 18.288 meters.

```
GW, 103, 1, 0.176, 0., 18.288, 1.176, 0., 18.288, 0.0127
GW, 103, 1, −0.088, 0.1524, 18.288, −0.588, 1.0184, 18.288, 0.0127
GW, 103, 1, −0.088, −0.1524, 18.288, −0.588, −1.0184, 18.288, 0.0127
```

9.5 **Exercises**

9-1. Explain how the current moment of a skirted tower is calculated.

9-2. Explain how the current moment of a top-loaded tower is calculated.

System Bandwidth Analysis

10

10.1 Introduction

For the most part, conventionally designed directional antennas have considered operation only at the carrier frequency with little regard for bandwidth. More recently, however, the new modulation schemes raise questions concerning the actual bandwidth of a conventionally designed AM directional antenna, so it is useful to have a capability that provides some insight into that subject.

This chapter extends the application of NEC-2 to include the total system—antenna-matching networks, phasing networks, and other parts of the system including the transmission lines. The resulting analysis views the bandwidth of the total system plus the bandwidth at some intermediate points along the signal path.

The material in this chapter draws heavily from a paper the author submitted to *IEEE Transactions on Broadcasting*, in which the calculations were performed using NEC-4 rather than NEC-2. Although this difference might cause a minor variation in the numerical values displayed in the charts, the methods and procedures are identical in both codes and the conclusions reached will be the same.

10.2 System Definition

By definition, the antenna system consists of all networks and transmission lines beginning at the common point fed by the transmitter and **133**

Table 10-1 Array Parameters

Tower	Spacing	Bearing	Field Ratio	Phase	Height
1	0.°	0.°	0.88	−135	84°
2	72.4°	230.2°	1.00	0.°	84°
3	170.5°	305.8°	0.75	−29.4°	84°

continuing through the tower radiators. As you progress through this chapter, it will immediately be obvious that the system performance of a conventionally designed directional antenna system is well behaved at the carrier frequency: Everything that is supposed to be 50 Ω is, in fact, 50 Ω. Everything that is supposed to be j0 is indeed j0. But when viewed over the signal bandwidth, the system performance might vary surprisingly from the ideal.

In an attempt to seek a balance between being overly simple and excessively complicated, a three-tower array will be used as the vehicle to illustrate the concepts involved when analyzing the total system. The hypothetical system operates on a frequency of 850 kHz with a power of 5000 watts. The array parameters are given in Table 10-1.

The transmission line lengths are 725 feet, 468 feet, and 906 feet for towers 1, 2, and 3, respectively. Figure 10-1 is a simplified block diagram of the system.

10.2.1 Tower Models

This chapter provides another demonstration of modeling towers using the lattice tower model described in Chapter 3.

In creating the lattice tower model, the concrete tower base with four ground straps and the base insulator complete with spider and girth (as shown in Figure 10-2) are modeled using normal NEC-2 procedures.

Then a single tower section consisting of three upright legs with a three-wire top girth is modeled and repeated twenty-six times to stack twenty-seven 10-foot sections on end to complete the first tower.

Once the first tower is completely modeled, it is duplicated to generate the other two towers by using the GM command to translate the entire assembly to the proper locations. The details of how this is done are not repeated here since they have been covered previously.

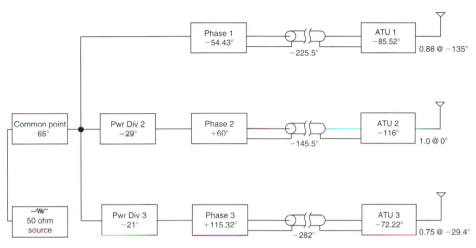

FIGURE 10-1

System block diagram.

FIGURE 10-2

NVCOMP.EXE view of lattice tower model.

There is, however, one item of interest in this tower geometry worth mentioning here. The wire simulating the base insulator and upon which the excitation is placed is 0.6731 meters long. Since it is desirable to have equal-length segments on both sides of the feed segment, a means to accomplish that goal is demonstrated on the tower section immediately above the insulator by dividing the section into three segments instead of the usual one, and then using the GC continuation command to taper the length of those three segments starting with 0.6731 meters (to equal that of the feed segment), and increasing with the ratio 1.4438:1 to approach 3.048 meters, which is the length of the tower sections above it. The following commands implement that segment taper on the three tower legs.

```
GW, 103, 3,0. 352, 0., 1.5875, 0.352, 0., 4.6355, .0
GC, 0, 0, 1.4438, 0.0191, 0.0191
GW, 103, 3, −0.176, 0.3048, 1.5875, −0.176, 0.3048, 4.6355, .0
GC, 0, 0, 1.4438, 0.0191, 0.0191
GW, 103, 3, −0.176, −0.3048, 1.5875, −0.176, −.3048, 4.6355, 0
GC, 0, 0, 1.4438, 0.0191, 0.0191
```

The GW wire specification in Appendix A contains information on using the GC continuation command, including a formula to calculate the segment ratio that will yield the desired starting segment length. It is a good idea to read that material at this time.

10.2.2 Tower Base Drive Voltages

The normalized base drive voltages necessary to create the desired pattern were calculated using the procedures described in Chapter 6 with the following results:

$$V'_1 = -0.0409 - j0.0916$$

$$V'_2 = 0.1218 - j0.2694$$

$$V'_3 = 0.2972 - j0.2690$$

The normalized base drive voltages were then scaled to obtain the full power drive of

$$V_1 = -30.41 - j670.33$$

$$V_2 = 90.56 - j200.30$$

$$V_3 = 220.97 - j200.00$$

These drives were placed in the NEC-2 input file and run to obtain the output file. This is where the effort would have normally ceased but in this instance, we will continue to include a study of the total system.

10.3 Bandwidth Analysis

The array characteristics as a function of frequency are easily obtained by making NEC-2 runs at the several frequencies of interest, in this case 850 kHz ± 20 kHz with intervals of 5 kHz. While a method is provided in the FR command for stepping the frequency through such a range, that method cannot be used for this analysis because the directional antenna system uses matching and phasing networks that are described in NEC-2 using NT commands. Each network is defined in the NT command by its frequency-sensitive Y-parameters and, unfortunately, NEC-2 does not scale the Y-parameters with frequency. Thus it will be necessary to specify a fixed frequency with the associated network commands written to that frequency, generate the required data, then change both the frequency and the network commands to a second frequency, generate that data, and so on.

In addition, it is important to note that NEC-2 requires that all network commands be grouped together so when one NT command is changed, all the unchanged network commands must be repeated to create a new and complete group. Moreover, be aware that NEC-2 considers transmission lines to be a special case of the network. Therefore, notwithstanding the fact that the TL commands are indeed scaled with frequency, they must nevertheless be included and repeated in each new group along with the NT commands.

10.3.1 Source Impedance of the Drive Voltage

The voltage source provided in NEC-2 by the EX command is a constant voltage with zero source impedance. During a normal NEC-2 design at the carrier frequency, where all networks and tower currents are designed and adjusted for the carrier frequency, source impedance of the drive voltage is not necessarily a factor. In practice over a bandwidth, however, when the load being driven by the voltage source varies with frequency, it causes the applied voltage to be a function of frequency depending on both the source impedance of the drive and the varying load impedance. This is especially noticeable when using NEC-2 to determine the various tower drive point impedances of an array over a bandwidth.

When driving a network or transmission line having a 50-ohm input, a 50-ohm voltage source can be created in NEC-2 by driving through a network containing a single 50-ohm series resistor, such as the one shown in Figure 5-2(b). However, a special frequency-sensitive impedance source replicating that of the output impedance of the antenna-tuning unit (ATU) is required to measure the bandwidth of the drive point impedance of an operating array's towers. This is necessary because the drive point impedance of the operating tower is a function of the drive voltage, which in itself is a function of the frequency-sensitive source impedance. This rather circular requirement can be met by driving each tower through its ATU with a 50-ohm-voltage source feeding the ATU. This yields both the frequency behavior of the ATU input impedance as read from the NEC-2 output file under the heading - ANTENNA INPUT PARAMETERS - as well as the tower drive point impedance, which is read from the same report under the heading - STRUCTURE EXCITATION DATA AT NETWORK CONNECTION POINTS -.

Figure 10-3(a) displays the effect that the source impedance can have in calculating the tower drive point resistance when driving the towers through their respective ATU. The figure shows tower 2 drive point resistance when the ATU is driven first with a drive source impedance of 0 ohms and then again when the ATU is driven using a drive source impedance of 50 ohms. Figure 10-3(b) shows the resistance seen looking into ATU 2 input when driving the ATU with a voltage of 0 source impedance, then driving it with a voltage having 50-ohm source impedance.

These curves were taken by simultaneously driving the inputs of the three ATUs with the voltages necessary to generate the desired field ratios at the carrier frequency and then varying the frequency as shown. The ATUs were driven first with the normal 0 source impedance of the NEC-2 EX command, then again with a 50-ohm source obtained with the EX command feeding the ATU through a 50-ohm network. The tower drive point impedance and the ATU input impedance were read from the NEC-2 output file.

In the interest of simplicity, only the results pertaining to the resistive part of tower 2 impedance are given in the illustrations of Figure 10-3(a) and 10-3(b). Figure 10-3(a) shows, the two sources give the same results at the carrier frequency of 850 kHz but as the frequency varies across the bandwidth, the results differ noticeably. Figure 10-3(a) also shows that driving the ATU with the zero source impedance causes

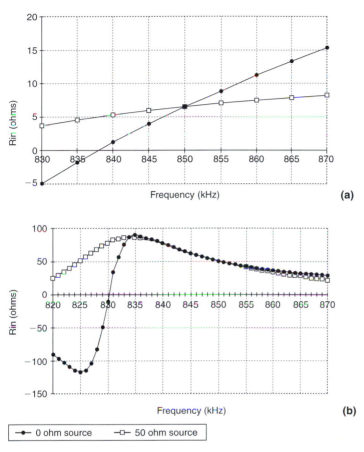

FIGURE 10-3

Effect of drive source impedance: (a) tower 2 drive point resistance, (b) antenna-tuning unit 2 input resistance.

the resistive part of the tower 2 impedance to go to 0 near 838 kHz. However, driving the ATU with the 50-ohm source impedance causes the resistive part of the tower 2 impedance to stay positive throughout the bandwidth.

Figure 10-3(b) shows the effect this has on the input impedance of the ATU. In this instance, the drive with 0 source impedance causes the ATU input resistance to go to 0 near 830 kHz while the drive with 50-ohm source impedance causes the ATU input resistance to remain positive throughout the bandwidth. Again, notice that both drive sources give the desired 50-ohm ATU input resistance at the 850 kHz carrier frequency.

10.3.2 Intermediate Data

The figures that follow display the NEC-2 calculated impedance data as it appears at the several network interfaces shown in Figure 10-1. The data were taken using a drive with a 50-ohm source impedance.

Procedure for Calculating Intermediate Data

To calculate the data that follows, the tower drive voltages necessary to create the desired field ratios were first calculated as described in Chapter 6. A NEC-2 run was made at the carrier frequency and the tower drive point impedances were thus determined. From that information, the complete system was designed as it appeared at the carrier frequency, including ATUs, phasing networks, power dividers, and so on.

Then, the drive voltages were translated back from the tower base to the input of the ATU to obtain the ATU input drive voltages that would create the desired field ratios. A NEC-2 run was made with the drive at the input to the ATU and the field ratios generated by the translated drive voltages were calculated and verified as being the target values. The ATU input impedances and the tower drive point impedances were then read from the NEC-2 output files thus created.

While holding the network component values constant but scaling reactance with frequency, additional NEC-2 runs were made with the frequency varied ±20 kHz in 5-kHz steps to generate the bandwidth performance as viewed at the tower bases and at the ATU inputs.

Following similar procedures, the ATU drive voltages were then translated back through the transmission lines to obtain the desired drive voltages at the transmission line inputs. There additional NEC-2 runs were made as before to obtain the transmission line input impedances versus frequency.

In turn, the voltages were translated back through each of the system's functional elements until the input to the common point-matching network was reached. At each voltage translation, the field ratios thus generated were calculated to confirm that the translated drive voltages did indeed produce the target field ratios.

In translating the voltages from network to network, it is important to remember that the network phase shifts refer to current phase shift. Therefore, the current is shifted backward to the input of the network, then that shifted current is used to calculate the voltage that must appear at the network input to create that current.

Tower Base Impedances

Figures 10-4(a) and (b) show the drive point impedance of the three towers when they are driven by their respective ATUs. Little comment

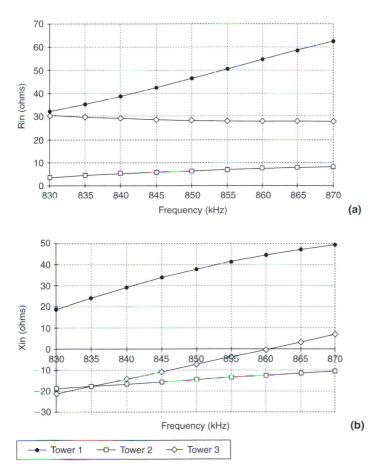

FIGURE 10-4

Tower drive point impedance when driven by ATU: (a) resistance, (b) reactance.

is needed here except to notice that the procedure described earlier was followed with the result that tower 2 shows a rather low resistance (slightly more than 6 ohms) at the carrier frequency.

ATU Input Impedances

Figures 10-5(a) and 10-5(b) show the input impedance to the three ATUs when they are driven with a 50-ohm source. Notice that all three ATUs

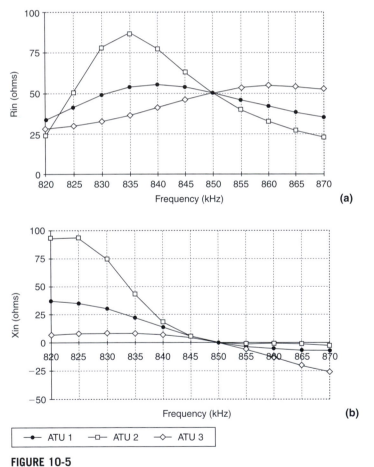

FIGURE 10-5

ATU input impedance: (a) resistance, (b) reactance.

show a 50 + j0 input impedance at the carrier frequency but ATU 2 varies significantly over the bandwidth.

Transmission Line Input Impedances

The curves showing the input impedance of the three transmission lines are given in Figures 10-6(a) and (b). In addition, Figure 10-6(c) has been included to show the voltage standing wave ratio (VSWR) of the transmission lines.

Figure 10-6(c) shows that the ratio for transmission lines 1 and 3 remain below 2:1 throughout the bandwidth but transmission line 2 exceeds 2:1 at the extremes and is up to 3.6:1 at the low-frequency end of the bandwidth. This is an item to be concerned with when selecting the type of transmission lines, although the need for this concern is not apparent when the design is limited to the carrier frequency. In this hypothetical system, tower 2 is the low-power tower so when the transmission line is selected to accommodate the highest power, it will also accommodate the power of tower 2 even with this higher VSWR. The inverse may be true in some instances, however.

Notice, too, in Figure 10-6(a) that the fairly low input impedance of ATU 1 has been transformed to approximately 90 ohms by transmission line 1. Also note in Figure 10-6(c) that although the terminating impedance of transmission line 1 has been transformed noticeably, the VSWR on transmission line 1 is reasonable; it does not exceed 1.8:1. This is a reminder that the VSWR is the same at all positions along a transmission line but that the impedance does, in fact, vary with position along the line.

Phasing Network Input Impedances

Figures 10-7(a) and (b) show the variation in the input impedance of the phasing networks and no comment is needed.

Power Divider Input Impedances

In designing the voltage buss for the power dividers, it was elected to set the buss voltage at the voltage required to accommodate the 50-ohm

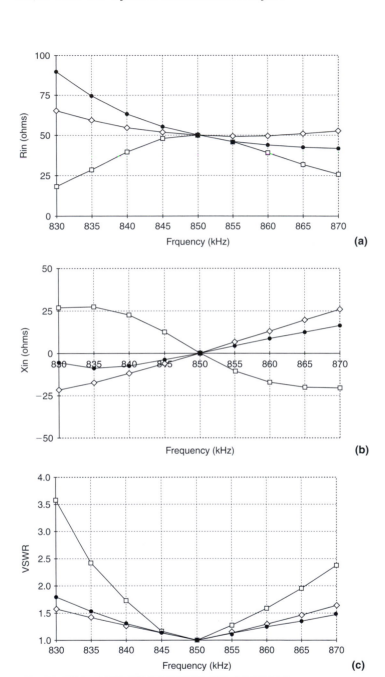

FIGURE 10-6

Transmission line input impedance: (a) resistance, (b) reactance, (c) VSWR.

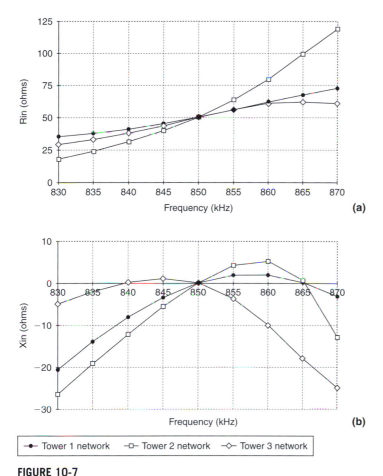

FIGURE 10-7

Phasing network input impedance: (a) resistance, (b) reactance.

impedance of the highest-power tower. With that voltage established, the input resistance of the power-dividing networks for the other two towers was defined. With all three paths paralleled, the resulting impedance was near 29 + j0 at the carrier frequency. Figure 10-8 shows how this impedance varies over the bandwidth.

Notice the smoothing effect that has occurred in paralleling the three paths. The rogue tower 2 has been somewhat subdued by its better-behaved companion towers.

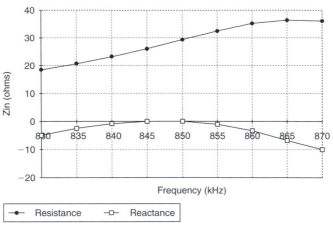

FIGURE 10-8

Power divider impedance.

10.3.3 **Total System Bandwidth Data**

A single voltage drive of arbitrary phase at the input to the common point-matching network drives the complete system. In this analysis, the drive is through a 50-ohm network to create a 50-ohm source impedance.

The Common Point Network

The common point-matching network transforms the 29-ohm parallel combination of the three tower paths to the conventional 50 ohms. The resulting input impedance behavior of this network is shown in Figure 10-9(a) and shows the design value of 50 + j0 impedance at the carrier frequency. Unfortunately, the common-point impedance fails to display the symmetry desired for digital transmissions so a phase-rotating network would be in order for that application.

Notwithstanding the antics of tower 2, the VSWR at the input to the common point–matching network remains reasonably symmetrical and below 1.5:1 over a ±15 kHz bandwidth, as shown in Figure 10-9(b).

Radiation Bandwidth

In the end, the question might be "How well does the system radiate over the bandwidth?" Some insight into that aspect of the analysis

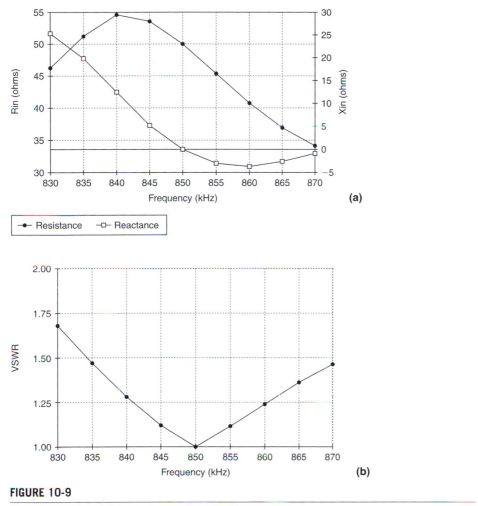

FIGURE 10-9

Common point: (a) impedance, (b) VSWR.

can be obtained by including an RP command in each frequency step. The parameters of this RP command are set to call for only one field calculation per frequency and for that calculation to occur at azimuth 59°, which is the peak of the main lobe of the radiation pattern.

The results are shown in Figure 10-10. Notice that radiation is fairly uniform, perhaps better than might be expected, with the field varying less than half a decibel over the total bandwidth.

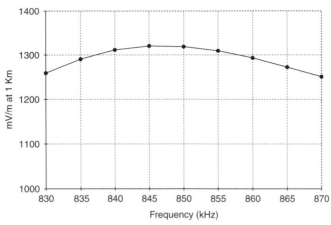

FIGURE 10-10

Field strength at 1 Km versus frequency.

10.4 Bandwidth Conclusions

- When doing a system analysis, it is important not only to simulate the system realistically but also to simulate the drive signal realistically. In this analysis, a 50-ohm source impedance was simulated to drive the 50-ohm interfaces and the drive to the tower bases was simulated by driving them through the 50-ohm input of their respective ATU network.

- Low-impedance towers can cause increased parameter variations. These variations must be examined to determine if they are problematic.

- The transmission lines become mismatched when the frequency varies from the carrier frequency. The length of the transmission line can be of concern when the mismatch causes undesirable impedance transformations.

- Parameter variations are often smoothed when the multiple paths to the individual towers are combined at the common point. Thus, the performance of the total system is often much better than may be suggested by viewing an ill-performing path to a particular tower.

Case Studies

11.1 Comparative Data

The data presented in this chapter is intended to demonstrate the assets and liabilities of NEC-2 in practical applications to AM broadcast directional arrays. In addition to comparing some calculated and measured data, this chapter gives a few general opinions and suggestions that may be useful to increase the utility of NEC-2 for broadcast work.

11.2 Case Study 1: Three-Tower Array

The measured data on this three-tower, 850-kHz, 5 Kw-array was furnished by Jack Sellmeyer of Sellmeyer Engineering, McKinney, Texas. The NEC-2 calculations were done by the author.

11.2.1 Array Description: Three-Tower Array

The array considered in this study has the parameters that are shown in Table 11-1.

11.2.2 Self-Impedance: Three-Tower Array

The towers were modeled using the simple single-pole configuration of Figure 3-1(c) with an estimated 20-pf capacity across the base insulator.   **149**

Table 11-1 Array Parameters

	Tower 1	Tower 2	Tower 3
Field Ratio	0.88	1.0	0.75
Phase	−135°	0°	−24.9
Spacing	0°	72.4°	170.5°
Bearing	0°	230.2°	305.8°
Tower Height (Al)	84°	84°	84°
Top of Insulator	3.5′	3.5′	11.5′

As the data will show, reasonable agreement was obtained with this simple tower model.

NEC-2 runs were made to determine the passive self-impedance of each tower both with the companion towers open at the base and with the companion towers shorted at the base. In time, the self-impedance of each tower was measured under conditions similar to those used in the NEC-2 analysis.

The calculated and measured self-impedances are tabulated in Table 11-2. While no attempt was made to modify the NEC-2 model to match the measured self-impedances, some analytical investigation was done in an attempt to learn more about the difference between measured and calculated self-impedances.

Table 11-2 shows that the self-impedance, as calculated with the companion towers open, are reasonably close to measured values except for tower 2. However, the self-impedance as calculated with the companion towers shorted differs significantly from the measured values.

Because towers 1 and 2 are closely spaced (72.4°) and tower 3 is further away (170.5°), we can expect the similarity that is shown in the impedances of towers 1 and 2 because the two towers are closely spaced and symmetrical in the tower layout. This similarity is quite obvious in the calculated results (20 + j8 and 21 + j9) and it is observable in the measured data (39 + j36 and 36 + j34).

We might also anticipate that the widely spaced tower 3 would measure close to its isolated self-impedance (38 + j40) either with the companion towers open or shorted, and it does that. It is not clear, however,

Table 11-2 Self-Impedance

	Tower 1	Tower 2	Tower 3
Companion Towers — Shorted			
Calculated	20 + j8	21 + j9	47 + j6
Measured	39 + j36	36 + j34	48 + j25
Companion Towers — Open			
Calculated	34 − j6	34 − j6	39 + j10
Measured	36 + j17	44 + j17	40 + j32

Table 11-3 Expected Monitor Readings

	Tower 1	Tower 2	Tower 3
Field Ratio	0.88 @ −135°	1.0 @ 0°	0.75 @ −24.9°
Base Current	12.2 @ −131.7°	14.9 @ 0.6°	0.5 @ −27.3°
Calculated Monitor Reading	0.82 @ −132.3°	1.0 @ 0°	0.71 @ -27.9°

why the closer spacing of towers 1 and 2 does not act to lower their measured impedance more dramatically when the companion towers are shorted, as it does in the calculated data. No reasonable model was found that duplicated those measured impedances.

11.2.3 Antenna Monitor Reading: Three-Tower Array

In this array, antenna monitor samples are taken from a toroid transformer at the output of the ATU. NEC-2 gives magnitude and phase of the current at that location. Thus, the expected antenna monitor readings can be estimated.

The current through a particular toroid can be normalized to the current through the reference tower toroid (which is tower 2 in this case) to yield the expected antenna monitor reading for that tower. In this instance, the data are shown in Table 11-3.

In the table, the expected monitor readings are listed along with the desired field ratios for reference.

Table 11-4 Array Drive Point Impedance

	Tower 1	Tower 2	Tower 3
Calculated	40 + j23	5 − j21	27 − j2
Measured	42 + j52	4 + j9	34 + j31

11.2.4 Array Data: Three-Tower Array

At initial tune-up of the array, the parameters were set such that the antenna monitor read the calculated values shown in Table 11-3 and the array drive point impedances were measured with results as shown in Table 11-4. Under these conditions, field pattern measurements revealed that only one specified radial was out of tolerance by about 7.5 percent. This out-of-tolerance condition was remedied by changing the phase of tower 3 by −7.5° (from a monitor reading of −27.9° to −35.4°).

The resistive component of the drive point impedance shows reasonable agreement between calculated and measured with the major deviation being the 7-ohm differential of tower 3. The calculated reactive component is consistently low, however, and appears to follow the trend shown in earlier chapters. If this trend to be low is accepted as a characteristic of NEC-2, then one might define a rule-of-thumb that arbitrarily adds a positive reactance to the calculated result. And, based not only on this example but on the results shown in previous chapters, that reactance can be in the order of +j30 for towers near 90°.

That rule-of-thumb is supported by the recognition that both the measured reactance and the reactance modeled at the tower base include the shunt reactance as imposed by the network of Figure 5-2(c). However, the measured values also included the series reactance leading to the base of the tower, whereas the model did not. The rule-of-thumb might be justified by considering that the +j30 rightfully adds the series reactance of the lead and any other series reactance that might appear in the measurement path. Applying that rule-of-thumb to this example yields the data shown in Table 11-5.

Designing to the calculated operating array drive point impedances even without the +j30 rule-of-thumb correction still led to networks

Table 11-5 Comparison of Adjusted Impedances

	Tower 1	Tower 2	Tower 3
Self-Impedance — Shorted			
Calculated + j30	20 + j38	20 + j39	47 + j36
Measured	39 + j36	36 + j34	48 + j25
Self-Impedance — Open			
Calculated + j30	34 + j24	34 + j24	39 + j40
Measured	36 + j17	44 + j17	40 + j32
Operating Array Z_d			
Calculated + j30	40 + j53	5 + j9	27 + j28
Measured	42 + j52	4 + j9	34 + j31

that were close enough to the final requirement so as to allow a tune-up free of local minima problems.

Although not absolutely essential, the correction factor appears to contribute a bit to make the calculated impedances better match the measured impedances and thus is a worthwhile addition.

11.2.5 Discussion: Three-Tower Array

Notwithstanding the lack of agreement between calculated and measured self-impedance, the calculated and measured array drive point impedances are in relatively good agreement. It is reasonable, then, to recognize that the drive point impedances are controlled more by the mutual coupling between radiators than they are by the modeling details of the individual radiators. That being the case, simple models might be used for the individual radiators and thus greatly simplify the NEC-2 input file.

11.2.6 NEC-2 Input File: Three-Tower Array

Listing 11-1 is the input file used to generate the data presented in this study.

Listing 11-1

```
CM     3TWR.NEC - 3 TOWER ARRAY WITH 2 WIRE LINEAR TOWER MODEL
CE     20pF insulator capacity
GW, 100, 1, 999., 0., 1., 999., 0., 1.1, .01
GW, 101, 3, 0., 0., 0., 0., 0., 4.38, 0.192
GW, 102, 20, 0., 0., 4.38, 0., 0., 83.36, 0.192
GW, 200, 1, 0., 999., 1.0, 0., 999., 1.1, .01
GW, 201, 3, -45.4, -54.5, 0., -45.4, -54.5, 4.38, 0.192
GW, 202, 20, -45.4, -54.5, 4.38, -45.4, -54.5, 83.36, 0.192
GW, 300, 1, -999., 0., 1.0, -999., 0., 1.1, .01
GW, 301, 3, 97.71, -135.48, 0., 97.71, -135.48, 6.34, 0.192
GW, 302, 20, 97.71, -135.48, 6.34, 97.71, -135.48, 85.80, 0.192
GE, 1
GN, 1,
EK,
FR, 0, 1, 0, 0, 0.85, 0.0
NT, 100, 1, 101, 1, 1.0E+10, 0.0, 0.0, 0.0, 0.0, 1.0676E-4
NT, 200, 1, 201, 1, 1.0E+10, 0.0, 0.0, 0.0, 0.0, 1.0676E-4
NT, 300, 1, 301, 2, 1.0E+10, 0.0, 0.0, 0.0, 0.0, 1.0676E-4
EX, 0, 101, 1, 00, -108.49, -548.77
EX, 0, 201, 1, 00, 84.41, -315.6
EX, 0, 301, 2, 00, 239.57, -142.52
RP, 0, 1, 361, 1001, 90., 0., 0., 1., 1000., 0.,
EN
```

11.3 Case Study 2: Six-Tower Array, Day Pattern

The following measured data on a six-tower, 1380-kHz array was furnished by Jack Sellmeyer of Sellmeyer Engineering in McKinney, Texas. The NEC-2 calculations were done by the author.

11.3.1 Array Description: Six-Tower Array, Day Pattern

The array discussed in this section has the parameters shown in Table 11-6 plus the following: frequency = 1380 kHz, power = 7000 watts, base insulator capacity = 20 pf.

11.3.2 Self-Impedance: Six-Tower Array, Day Pattern

The towers were modeled using the configuration shown in Figure 3-1(c) and taking 20 pf as the base insulator capacity.

Table 11-6 Six-Tower Array, Daytime Parameters

Tower	Ratio	Phase	Spacing	Bearing	Height
1	1.00	0.0°	0.0°	0.0°	90°
2	0.88	4.0°	170.0°	70.0°	90°
3	0.84	85.0°	192.0°	42.0°	90°
4	0.92	98.0°	90.0°	340.0°	90°
5	0.49	94.0°	192.0°	278.0°	90°
6	0.48	10.0°	170.0°	250.0°	90°

Table 11-7 Self-Impedance Companion Towers Shorted

Tower	Calculated + j30	Measured
1	77 + j78	69 + j71
2	70 + j88	71 + j66
3	71 + j88	74 + j66
4	77 + j79	73 + j52
5	71 + j88	70 + j63
6	70 + j88	70 + j63

The self-impedance with companion towers open was not calculated for this case history. However, the tower self-impedance with the companion towers shorted is given as a by-product of calculating the drive voltages, so that data is available without further effort. Therefore, the calculated self-impedance with companion towers shorted, along with the corresponding measured values, are shown in Table 11-7. The arbitrary +j30 applied by rule-of-thumb as discussed earlier, has been included in these calculated values.

11.3.3 Antenna Monitor Reading: Six-Tower Array, Day Pattern

As in the preceding case study, this array takes its antenna monitor samples from toroid transformers at the output of each ATU. Also, as before, the calculated base currents are taken from the NEC-2 output file and normalized to the reference tower to obtain the expected antenna monitor readings. These are shown in Table 11-8 along with the target field ratios for comparison.

11.3.4 Array Data: Six-Tower Array, Day Pattern

The initial adjustments set the array parameters to give the expected antenna monitor readings shown in Table 11-8. The array drive point impedances were then measured with the results shown in Table 11-9. The +j30 rule-of-thumb has been applied to the calculated values.

Table 11-9 gives a comparison of calculated and measured drive point impedances.

Table 11-8 Expected Monitor Readings

Tower	Peak Base Current	Expected Monitor Reading	Target Field Ratio
1	9.63 @ 6.47°	1.00 @ 0.0°	1 @ 0°
2	8.29 @ 9.99°	0.86 @ 3.5°	0.88 @ 4°
3	8.22 @ 86.5°	0.85 @ 80.0°	0.84 @ 85°
4	9.03 @ 97.1°	0.94 @ 90.6°	0.92 @ 98°
5	4.71 @ 95.5°	0.49 @ 89.0°	0.49 @ 94°
6	4.54 @ 15.1°	0.47 @ 8.6°	0.48 @ 10°

Table 11-9 Array Drive Point Impedance

Tower	Calculated + j30	Measured
1	77 + j61	80 + j51
2	73 + j76	80 + j73
3	16 + j53	19 + j47
4	−11 + j51	Not measured*
5	16 + j66	23 + j50
6	62 + j73	65 + j62

* Insufficient network adjusting range to compensate for the Operating Impedance Bridge.

11.3.5 Discussion: Six-Tower Array, Day Pattern

Field measurements were made with the initial array adjustments as above. Three out of four specified radials were above the standard pattern. In addition, two radials were abnormally low. Upon review, it was recognized that another station operating on 1430 kHz had a four-tower array located only 3.54 km from the six-tower array at a bearing of 156.3° and that array had not been included in the NEC-2 analysis. This four-tower array was almost directly in the main lobe of the six-tower's

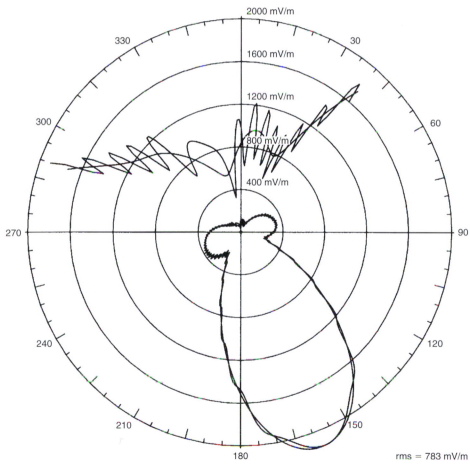

FIGURE 11-1

Effect of parasitic radiation from remote four-tower array, daytime pattern.

radiation pattern thus the re-radiation from the four-tower array was indeed significant.

The NEC-2 input file was modified to include all ten towers with the four towers of the 1430-kHz array terminated in the 1430-kHz conjugate drive point impedances as translated to the operating frequency of the six-tower array.

A theoretical pattern including all ten towers was plotted. This is shown as the undulating line in Figure 11-1 on the previous page.

The smooth line is the standard pattern of the six-tower array in the absence of the four-tower array. Notice that the undulating pattern is contained within the standard pattern of the six-tower array in all directions except for the northerly directions. From bearings of about 285° to 45°, the undulating pattern falls both above and below the six-tower standard pattern which suggests support for the measured field observations.

The pattern was "walked in" from these initial settings with a satisfactory adjustment being obtained on the second trial. Final monitor readings are listed in Table 11-10.

11.3.6 **NEC-2 Input File**

Listing 11-2 is the input file used to generate the six-tower NEC-2 data shown previously.

Table 11-10 Final Monitor Readings

Tower	Expected Monitor Reading	Final Monitor Reading	Target Field Ratio
1	1.00 @ 0.0°	1.00 @ 0.0°	1.00 @ 0.0°
2	0.86 @ 3.5°	0.85 @ 3.3°	0.88 @ 4.0°
3	0.85 @ 80.0°	0.86 @ 83°	0.84 @ 85°
4	0.94 @ 90.6°	0.95 @ 94°	0.92 @ 98°
5	0.49 @ 89.0°	0.50 @ 89°	0.49 @ 94°
6	0.47 @ 8.6°	0.48 @ 9.0°	0.48 @ 10°

Listing 11-2

```
CM    6TWR_D.NEC - 6 TOWER DAYTIME ARRAY WITH 3 WIRE LINEAR TOWER MODEL
CE
GW, 100, 1, 999., 0., 1., 999., 0., 1.1, .01
GW, 101, 3, 0., 0., 0., 0., 0., 3.5, 0.12
GW, 102, 3, 0., 0., 3.5, 0., 0., 7.0, 0.12
GW, 103, 20, 0., 0., 7.0, 0., 0., 57.42, 0.12
GW, 200, 1, 0., 999., 1.0, 0., 999., 1.1, .01
GW, 201, 3, 35.09, 96.4, 0.0, 35.09, 96.4, 3.5, 0.12
GW, 202, 3, 35.09, 96.4, 3.5, 35.09, 96.4, 7.0, 0.12
GW, 203, 20, 35.09, 96.4, 7.0, 35.09, 96.4, 57.42, 0.12
GW, 300, 1, –999., 0., 1.0, –999., 0., 1.1, .01
GW, 301, 3, 86.1, 77.53, 0.0, 86.1, 77.53, 3.5, 0.12
GW, 302, 3, 86.1, 77.53, 3.5, 86.1, 77.53, 7.0, 0.12
GW, 303, 20, 86.1, 77.53, 7.0, 86.1, 77.53, 57.42, 0.12
GW, 400, 1, 0., –999., 1.0, 0., –999., 1.1, .01
GW, 401, 3, 51.05, –18.58, 0.0, 51.05, –18.58, 3.5, 0.12
GW, 402, 3, 51.05, –18.58, 3.5, 51.05, –18.58, 7.0, 0.12
GW, 403, 20, 51.05, –18.58, 7.0, 51.05, –18.58, 57.42, 0.12
GW, 500, 1, 999., 999., 1.0, 999., 999., 1.1, .01
GW, 501, 3, 16.12, –114.73, 0.0, 16.12, –114.73, 3.5, 0.12
GW, 502, 3, 16.12, –114.73, 3.5, 16.12, –114.73, 7.0, 0.12
GW, 503, 20, 16.12, –114.73, 7.0, 16.12, –114.73, 57.42, 0.12
GW, 600, 1, –999., –999., 1.0, –999., –999., 1.1, .01
GW, 601, 3, –35.08, –96.4, 0.0, –35.08, –96.4, 3.5, 0.12
GW, 602, 3, –35.08, –96.4, 3.5, –35.08, –96.4, 7.0, 0.12
GW, 603, 20, –35.08, –96.4, 7.0, –35.08, –96.4, 57.42, 0.12
GE, 1
EK,
FR, 0, 1, 0, 0, 1.38, 0.0
GN, 1,
NT, 100, 1, 101, 3, 1.0E+10, 0.0, 0.0, 0.0, 0.0, 1.7342E–4
NT, 200, 1, 201, 3, 1.0E+10, 0.0, 0.0, 0.0, 0.0, 1.7342E–4
NT, 300, 1, 301, 3, 1.0E+10, 0.0, 0.0, 0.0, 0.0, 1.7342E–4
NT, 400, 1, 401, 3, 1.0E+10, 0.0, 0.0, 0.0, 0.0, 1.7342E–4
NT, 500, 1, 501, 3, 1.0E+10, 0.0, 0.0, 0.0, 0.0, 1.7342E–4
NT, 600, 1, 601, 3, 1.0E+10, 0.0, 0.0, 0.0, 0.0, 1.7342E–4
EX, 0, 101, 3, 00, 706.18, 378.14
EX, 0, 201, 3, 00, 529.99, 480.80
EX, 0, 301, 3,00, –183.86, 146.23
EX, 0, 401, 3,00, –174.02, –125.70
EX, 0, 501, 3, 00, –168.25, 60.03
EX, 0, 601, 3, 00, 221.91, 263.65
RP, 0, 1, 361, 1001, 90., 0., 0., 1., 1000., 0.,
EN
```

11.4 Case Study 3: Six-Tower Array, Night Pattern

The following measured data on a six-tower, 1380-kHz array was furnished by Jack Sellmeyer of Sellmeyer Engineering in McKinney, Texas, and is companion data to the six-tower daytime array discussed in Section 11.3. The NEC-2 calculations were made by the author.

11.4.1 Array Description: Six-Tower, Night Pattern

This array is the same array discussed in the previous section with the exception that this array is operating with the night-time pattern and power. Frequency = 1380 kHz, power = 250 watts. Insulator capacity continues to be 20 pf. The array parameters are given in Table 11-11.

11.4.2 Self-Impedance: Six-Tower Array, Night Pattern

Because this is the same physical tower plant and self-impedances are measured with no drive signals, the self-impedances are not changed from those presented in Section 11.3.2.

11.4.3 Antenna Monitor Readings: Six-Tower Array, Night Pattern

Expected monitor readings are calculated as done in the preceding study. The results are tabulated in Table 11-12.

Table 11-11 Array Description

Tower	Ratio	Phase	Spacing	Bearing	Height
1	1.00	0°	0°	0°	90°
2	0.88	0°	170°	70°	90°
3	0.59	80°	192°	42°	90°
4	0.70	98°	90°	340°	90°
5	0.47	98°	192°	278°	90°
6	0.48	10°	170°	250°	90°

Table 11-12 Expected Monitor Readings

Tower	Peak Base Current	Expected Monitor Readings
1	2.03A @ 5.65°	1.0 @ 0.0°
2	1.76A @ 5.22°	0.87 @ −0.43°
3	1.23A @ 80.61°	0.61 @ 75.0°
4	1.45A @ 95.95°	0.71 @ 90.3°
5	0.94A @ 99.76°	0.46 @ 94.1°
6	0.95A @ 15.2°	0.47 @ 9.50°

Table 11-13 Array Drive Point Impedance

Tower	Calculated + j30	Measured
1	68 + j60	68 + j51
2	63 + j73	67 + j72
3	4 + j45	−34 − j179*
4	−25 + j48	−21 + j44
5	16 + j67	24 + j61
6	61 + j79	65 + j69

* No explanation other than uncertainty of negative impedances

11.4.4 Array Data: Six-Tower Array, Night Pattern

During initial adjustments, the array parameters were set to give the expected antenna monitor readings shown in Table 11-12. With this adjustment, drive point impedances were measured as listed in Table 11-13, together with the calculated values for comparison. Following the rule-of-thumb established previously, a reactance of +j30 has been added to the calculated values with the results shown in Table 11-13.

11.4.5 Discussion: Six-Tower Array, Night Pattern

With the initial adjustment, the field strength at three of the twelve radials measured greater than the standard pattern with the worst

Table 11-14 Final Monitor Readings

Tower	Expected Monitor Reading	Final Monitor Reading	Target Field Ratio
1	1.0 @ 0.0°	1.0 @ 0.0°	1.0 @ 0.0°
2	0.87 @ −0.43°	0.86 @ −2.3°	0.88 @ 0.0°
3	0.61 @ 75.0°	0.60 @ 79.5°	0.59 @ 80.0°
4	0.71 @ 90.3°	0.72 @ 91.0°	0.70 @ 98.0°
5	0.46 @ 94.1°	0.50 @ 94.0°	0.47 @ 98.0°
6	0.47 @ 9.5°	0.40 @ 9.2°	0.48 @ 10.0°

being 34 percent high. Also, the field strength on another radial measured low, being approximately 66 percent of the standard value.

The pattern was "walked in" from these initial settings. Final monitor readings are listed in Table 11-14. The small changes that were necessary to the monitor readings could well be small shifts that moved the undulations caused by the re-radiation from the existing four-tower array, thus correcting the desired pattern as appropriate.

Being aware that the existing four-tower array influenced the day pattern, the nighttime theoretical pattern resulting from all ten towers was calculated and compared to the nighttime standard pattern. This is shown in Figure 11-2.

The undulations are most prominent in the third quadrant, but for the most part, the undulating pattern is contained within the standard pattern.

Detailed Measurements

To determine if the undulations actually occurred in the pattern as measured in the field, additional observations were made in the region of the 212° radial.

At a location 4.6 km out on the 212° radial, several field measurements were made transverse to the radial at 15-meter increments. This resulted in field measurements being made at approximately 0.2° increments, giving a detailed view of the measured pattern in that region. To obtain a comparison of measured and calculated data, a theoretical pattern was calculated at a distance of 4.6 km out the 212° radial. This gave the shape of the theoretical pattern in the vicinity of interest.

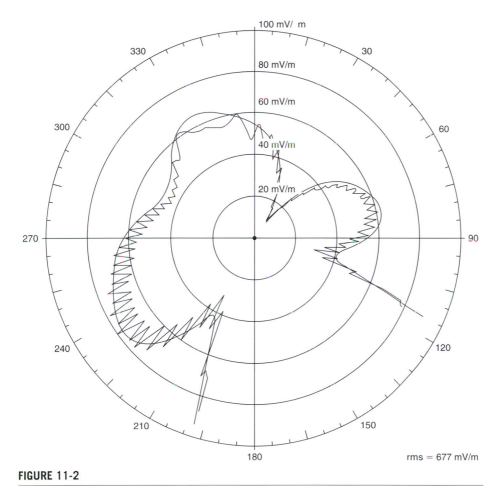

FIGURE 11-2

Effect of parasitic radiation from remote four-tower array, night pattern.

However, the calculated pattern was made assuming a perfectly conducting ground, whereas the measured data was over a finitely conducting ground. Therefore, to correctly superimpose the calculated pattern upon the measured pattern, the calculated data was scaled by the ratio of measured data and calculated data at the 212° radial. These results are plotted in Figure 11-3.

It appears that a partial cycle of undulation is indeed superimposed upon the undistorted pattern in this region, suggesting that the four-tower array does influence the radiation pattern of the subject six-tower array.

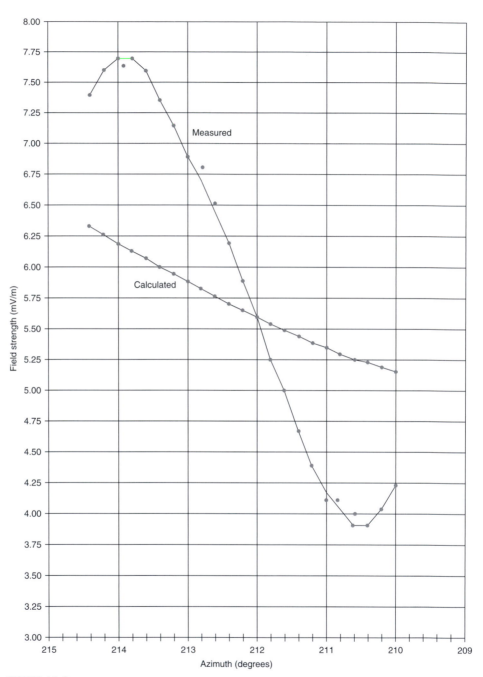

FIGURE 11-3

Detail of measured and calculated fields near the 212° radial.

11.4.6 NEC-2 Input File: Six-Tower Array, Night Pattern

Listing 11-3 is the NEC-2 input file used to generate the six-tower data.

Listing 11-3

```
CM 6TWR_N.NEC - 6 TOWER NIGHTTIME ARRAY WITH 3 WIRE LINEAR TOWER MODEL
CM Exciting towers with drive voltages to develop 250 watts.
CE
GW, 100, 1, 999., 0., 1., 999., 0., 1.1, .01
GW, 101, 3, 0., 0., 0., 0., 0., 3.5, 0.12
GW, 102, 3, 0., 0., 3.5, 0., 0., 7.0, 0.12
GW, 103, 20, 0., 0., 7.0, 0., 0., 57.42, 0.12
GW, 200, 1, 0., 999., 1.0, 0., 999., 1.1, .01
GW, 201, 3, 35.09, 96.4, 0.0, 35.09, 96.4, 3.5, 0.12
GW, 202, 3, 35.09, 96.4, 3.5, 35.09, 96.4, 7.0, 0.12
GW, 203, 20, 35.09, 96.4, 7.0, 35.09, 96.4, 57.42, 0.12
GW, 300, 1, –999., 0., 1.0, –999., 0., 1.1, .01
GW, 301, 3, 86.1, 77.53, 0.0, 86.1, 77.53, 3.5, 0.12
GW, 302, 3, 86.1, 77.53, 3.5, 86.1, 77.53, 7.0, 0.12
GW, 303, 20, 86.1, 77.53, 7.0, 86.1, 77.53, 57.42, 0.12
GW, 400, 1, 0., –999., 1.0, 0., –999., 1.1, .01
GW, 401, 3, 51.05, –18.58, 0.0, 51.05, –18.58, 3.5, 0.12
GW, 402, 3, 51.05, –18.58, 3.5, 51.05, –18.58, 7.0, 0.12
GW, 403, 20, 51.05, –18.58, 7.0, 51.05, –18.58, 57.42, 0.12
GW, 500, 1, 999., 999., 1.0, 999., 999., 1.1, .01
GW, 501, 3, 16.12, –114.73, 0.0, 16.12, –114.73, 3.5, 0.12
GW, 502, 3, 16.12, –114.73, 3.5, 16.12, –114.73, 7.0, 0.12
GW, 503, 20, 16.12, –114.73, 7.0, 16.12, –114.73, 57.42, 0.12
GW, 600, 1, –999., –999., 1.0, –999., –999., 1.1, .01
GW, 601, 3, –35.08, –96.4, 0.0, –35.08, –96.4, 3.5, 0.12
GW, 602, 3, –35.08, –96.4, 3.5, –35.08, –96.4, 7.0, 0.12
GW, 603, 20, –35.08, –96.4, 7.0, –35.08, –96.4, 57.42, 0.12
GE, 1
EK,
FR, 0, 1, 0, 0, 1.38, 0.0
GN, 1,
NT, 100, 1, 101, 3, 1.0E+10, 0.0, 0.0, 0.0, 0.0, 1.7342E–4
NT, 200, 1, 201, 3, 1.0E+10, 0.0, 0.0, 0.0, 0.0, 1.7342E–4
NT, 300, 1, 301, 3, 1.0E+10, 0.0, 0.0, 0.0, 0.0, 1.7342E–4
NT, 400, 1, 401, 3, 1.0E+10, 0.0, 0.0, 0.0, 0.0, 1.7342E–4
NT, 500, 1, 501, 3, 1.0E+10, 0.0, 0.0, 0.0, 0.0, 1.7342E–4
NT, 600, 1, 601, 3, 1.0E+10, 0.0, 0.0, 0.0, 0.0, 1.7342E–4
EX, 0, 101, 3, 00, 131.38, 74.06
EX, 0, 201, 3, 00, 104.47, 84.9
EX, 0, 301, 3, 00, –17.15, 8.01
EX, 0, 401, 3, 00, –22.14, –38.6
EX, 0, 501, 3, 00, –37.31, 9.2
EX, 0, 601, 3, 00, 44.19, 59.51
RP, 0, 1, 361, 1001, 90., 0., 0., 1., 1000., 0.,
EN
```

11.5 Case Study 4: Tall-Tower Array

The measured data shown in this study was furnished by Paul Carlier of FanField, Ltd, in the United Kingdom. The NEC-2 calculations were done by the author. The NEC-2 analysis was done after the fact with limited measured data furnished to contrast with the calculations.

11.5.1 Array Description: Tall Towers

This is a 500-kw high-power array operating at 1260 kHz with 121° towers. The array parameters are given in Table 11-15.

Each tower base insulator is shunted by a sample line isolation choke whose calculated inductance is 253.25 μH (X_L = j2005) plus a ring lighting transformer whose capacity, plus the stray capacity, was estimated to be 300 pf (X_c = −j421). Tower 2 uses a rain shield on the lighting transformer, so its total capacity was increased to 350 pf (X_c = −j361).

The tower 2 matching network is located inside the transmitter building, so the drive point impedance of tower 2 was actually measured at a point inside the building.

The towers were modeled using the simple single wire configuration of Figure 3-1(c). The parallel L-C combination at the base of towers 1 and 3 has a net calculated reactance of −j532.89 and the net base reactance at tower 2 is −j440.29.

11.5.2 Self-Impedance: Tall Towers

No self-impedance calculations were made on this array.

Table 11-15 Array Parameters					
Tower	**Ratio**	**Phase**	**Spacing**	**Bearing**	**Height**
1	0.54	135°	80°	−45°	121°
2	1.0	0.0°	0°	0°	121°
3	0.54	−135°	80°	135°	121°

Tower	Calculated Base Current	Expected Monitor Readings
Table 11-16 Expected Monitor Readings		
1	32.4A @ 110.3°	0.964 @ 110.3°
2	33.6A @ 0.0°	1.0 @ 0.0°
3	1.2A @ −95.1°	0.04 @ −95.1°

11.5.3 Antenna Monitor Readings: Tall Towers

The actual height of the sample loops and the associated antenna monitor readings were not included in the measured data furnished to this study. The NEC-2 output file indicates that the antenna monitor readings will closely indicate representative field values if the loops are placed a distance of 80 feet above ground. On the other hand, if it had been elected to use current transformers to monitor the current at the output of the matching network, the monitor readings would have been significantly different. Table 11-16 lists the expected monitor readings; although with relatively tall towers and only estimated values for the base shunting reactance, the calculated monitor readings are of questionable accuracy.

11.5.4 Array Data: Tall Towers

Because the operating impedance was measured through the long lead-in (into the transmitter building in the case of tower 2), the rule-of-thumb correction was modified to a calculated value determined by the estimated length of each lead-in including its lightning arrestor choke. This resulted in a correction of +j22 for towers 1 and 3 and a correction of +j53 for tower 2 instead of the general +j30. The resulting NEC-2 calculated drive point impedances as adjusted, together with measured values are as shown in Table 11-17.

Notice that the impedance of tower 3 and its associated shunt reactances formed a parallel resonant circuit, which resulted in the extremely high base impedance.

The base voltages were calculated by NEC-2 using the power budget as calculated for each tower of the operating array. The table lists peak values adjusted for 125 percent modulation.

Table 11-17 Array Drive Point Impedance

Tower	Calculated + Adjustment	Measured
1	63 + j212	60 + j206
2	370 + j418	360 + j474
3	10,566 + j2979	No data available*

* No measured data is available because the parameter value was beyond the range of the measuring instrument.

Table 11-18 Peak Base Voltages

Tower	Calculated	Measured
1	20,648 v	22 Kv
2	55,490 v	56 Kv
3	41,627 v	42 Kv

Listing 11-4

```
CM  TALL.NEC
CM  System data furnished by Paul Carlier, CM  3-towers, simple single wire model
CE
GW, 100, 1, 999., 999., 999., 999., 999., 999.01, .001
GW, 101, 20, 36.7474, −38.0531, 0., 36.7474, −38.0531, 80., 0.5828
GW, 200, 1, −999., 999., 999., −999., 999., 999.01, .001
GW, 201, 20, 0., 0., 0., 0., 0., 80., 0.5828
GW, 300, 1, 999., −999., 999., 999., −999., 999.01, .001
GW, 301, 20, −36.7474, 38.0531, 0., −36.7474, 38.0531, 80., 0.5828
GE, 1
GN, 1
FR, 0, 1, 0, 0, 1.26, 0.
NT, 100, 1, 101, 1, 1.0E+10, 0., 0., 0., 0., 1.8766E−3
NT, 200, 1, 201, 1, 1.0E+10, 0., 0., 0., 0., 2.2712E−3
NT, 300, 1, 301, 1, 1.0E+10, 0., 0., 0., 0., 1.8766E−3
EX, 0, 101, 1, 00, −7456.6, −5350.16
EX, 0, 201, 1, 00, 5121.53, 24124.05
EX, 0, 301, 1, 00, 12901.74, −13259.82
RP, 0, 1, 361, 1001, 90., 0., 1., 1., 1000., 0
EN
```

11.5.5 Discussion: Tall Towers

A complete set of descriptive data was not available for this case study so a number of assumptions and approximations were necessary in making this analysis. However, notwithstanding these shortcomings, it appears that the calculated results are a usable approximation of the actual results and gives a worthwhile demonstration of NEC-2's capability.

11.5.6 NEC-2 Input File: Tall Towers

The complete input file used in the calculations of this section is shown as Listing 11-4.

Supplemental Topics

12.1 Introduction

The previous chapters covered the basic topics that are essential to the design and analysis of MF directional antennas. This chapter adds a few subjects that may not be absolutely necessary, but they are interesting and add some insight to the analysis. Moreover, they are subjects that are not well documented elsewhere; thus, their presentation here fulfills an existing need.

12.2 Parallel Feeds: Network Combiners

When the triangular lattice tower configuration was discussed earlier, the voltage source exciting the tower was placed on a single wire and a spider configuration was used to connect that single-feed wire to each of the three the tower legs. This is a simple arrangement and gives usable results but it has been shown (see Burke and Poggio, "Computer Analysis of the Bottom-fed Fan Antenna," Report No. 173910, Lawrence Livermore National Labs, August, 1976) that NEC-2 gives a more accurate indication of the self-impedance of the tower when the drive voltage is made up of three separate and equal voltage sources with one source placed on each of the tower legs. See Figure 12-1.

This is equivalent to placing the three sources in parallel so the effective voltage remains the same as that of one source but the total

171

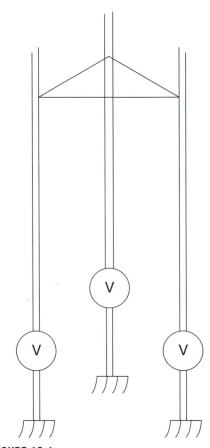

FIGURE 12-1

Multi-source drive on lattice tower.

current load is shared by the three sources. Thus, each voltage source sees an impedance that is approximately three times the self-impedance of the tower. Consequently, when the NEC-2 output file displays Impedance under the heading - ANTENNA INPUT PARAMETERS -, it will display three impedances—one for each of the voltage sources. The tower self-impedance must be calculated from the three impedances in parallel. However, since the three impedances will be very nearly equal, a practical self-impedance is simply one-third the value of one of the impedances.

For most modeling work, using three sources on each tower and handling them as described here does not pose a particular problem.

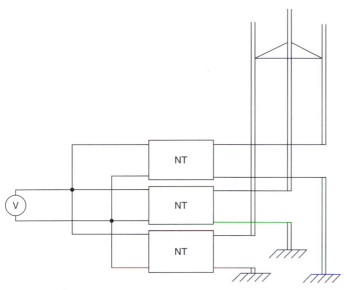

FIGURE 12-2

Drive splitting using networks.

There are instances, however, where it is desired to use the three sources per tower, and at the same time, it is necessary that there be a single drive point. A case in point might be that instance where it is desired to include the antenna-matching network in the model. In that case, three pass-through networks, as shown in Figure 5-2(a) in Chapter 5, may be created by using the NT commands to place all three inputs in parallel on a dummy feed segment containing the source voltage, and then terminating each network output on a separate tower leg. See Figure 12-2.

Because the networks are nonradiating, they will have no effect on the analysis if the dummy feed segment is placed in the far distance and made very short. Should there be reason to suspect that the dummy segment is influencing the result, however, then the LD command can be used to place a large resistance in series with the dummy segment.

12.3 New Structures: The NX Command

There are occasions where it may be desirable to analyze more than one structure set in a single NEC-2 run. An example of this is the case where it is desired to examine the effect that a parasitic tower may have on an array. A NEC-2 run can be made of the array without the parasitic tower, then another NEC-2 run can be made with the parasitic tower present, and then the two output files compared. However, to eliminate the need to make two separate NEC-2 runs, the comparison can be done in a single NEC-2 run by using the NX command.

When NEC-2 receives the NX command, it is directed to disregard the previously defined structure and to start an analysis of a new structure which will be defined according to the commands that follow. Thus, to make the comparison mentioned above, one would write the NEC-2 input file to describe the array without the parasitic tower. Then, following the EX command, the NX command would be written. The array description would then be copied and pasted following the NX command and the parasitic tower would be added to the array. The input file code would look similar to the following code.

```
COMMENTS
GW commands describing the array
Program control commands
RP to describe radiation pattern and to execute the run
NX
CE At least one comment is mandatory here
GW commands describing the array (same as first section)
GW command to add the parasitic tower
Program control commands (same as 1st section)
EN
```

When this input file is run by bnec.exe, the output file will contain two complete sets of output data—one set of data for the array without the parasitic tower, and another set of data for the array with the parasitic tower included.

It is important to recognize that the NX command is simple with only the letters NX written in the first two columns; nothing more. Also, be aware that it is mandatory that the NX command be followed by at least one comment. If there is only one comment, it is written with the CE command. If there is more than one comment, then only the last is written with the CE command, the others are written with CM commands as usual.

Please review the details of the NX command as given in Appendix A.

12.4 **Numerical Green's Function**

Copying and pasting the array data in the previous example is not the most efficient way to accomplish that task. It was used, however, to emphasize the function of the NX command. A more practical scheme is to use the Numerical Green's Function (NGF) to make a structure available without having to repeat the coding of that structure.

The Numerical Green's Function provides the user with the option to generate a structure and save it for later use in the same run, where it may be modified or added to without the expense of having to repeat the coding for the entire structure. This is particularly useful for a big structure that will be analyzed using several modified forms. An example of this is an eight-tower array in which a vehicle has been included in the model and it is desired to determine the effects of the vehicle at several locations.

Perhaps of more immediate application to the broadcaster is the ability of the Numerical Green's Function to take advantage of partial symmetry. In a single run, a structure must be perfectly symmetric for NEC-2 to use symmetry in the solution. Any unsymmetric segments, or ones that lie in the symmetry plane or on the axis of rotation, will prevent the use of symmetry in the analysis. However, partial symmetry may be exploited by creating and running the symmetric part of the model first and writing a NGF file. Then the NX command can be used to create a new structure that is composed of that saved in the NGF file plus the unsymmetric parts that are added to make up the complete structure. This feature is demonstrated in Section 12.5.2, which describes the GR command.

The NGF is used in two steps.

Step 1: The code for the structure to be saved as a NGF file is written as usual. Immediately after the GE command, the frequency, ground parameters, and loading must be set by writing the FR, GN, and LD commands. The EK or KH commands, if applicable, may also be included at that point. Other commands, such as EX and NT, do not affect the NGF and should not be included as part of the NGF file. After the NGF structure has been defined, a WG command is written to cause the NGF data to be saved to a file.

If desired, other commands may follow the WG command (such as to define an excitation and request field calculations) as in a normal run. The WG command should come before XQ, RP, NE, or NH. Also, the FR command must not specify multiple frequencies when a NGF is written.

Step 2: Use a NX command to create a new structure that will consist of the saved NGF data plus additions or modifications.

As explained earlier, the command immediately following NX must be a comment. Thereafter, the first geometry command following the CE command must be the GF command to recall the NGF structure that was saved in Step 1 and make it available for inclusion in the total structure. Subsequent structure data commands are then written to define the new structure to be added to the NGF structure.

All types of structure geometry data commands may be used, although GM, GR, GX, and GS will affect the new structure only, not that from the NGF file. While symmetry may have been used in writing the NGF file, it may not be used for the new structures that are used with the NGF file. For connections between the new structure and an NGF structure, the new segment ends must be made to coincide with the NGF segment ends, as would be done in a normal run.

Following the GE command, the program control commands may be used as usual, with the exception that FR and GN commands may not be used again. Recall that the parameters from the FR and GN commands were included in the NGF file. Therefore, following the NX command, those parameters are taken from the NGF file and cannot be changed.

LD commands may be used to load new segments but not segments in the NGF structure since those have already been included. If integers I3 and I4 on a LD command are blank, the command will load all new segments but not NGF segments. If I2, I3, and I4 select a specific NGF segment, the run will terminate with an error message. The effect of loading on NGF segments may be added by using an NT command, since NT (and TL) may connect to either new or NGF segments.

The lines that follow show the form of a NEC-2 input file that uses Numerical Green's Function.

```
COMMENTS
GW commands describing the NGF portion
GE
FR
GN
WG command to write the NGF file
NX create a new structure consisting of NGF plus additions
CE Comment
GF command to recall the NGF file
GW commands making the additions to NGF
GE
EX
RP
EN
```

12.5 Ground Screens

Ground screens can be implemented in NEC-2 in two ways: (1) using the GN command to specify a ground screen as one of two media and (2) using the GR command to literally create the ground screen as part of the structure.

12.5.1 The GN Command

The GN command specifies the nature of the ground used in the model and as such, the GN command has the capacity to specify a radial ground screen. But NEC-2 only models the ground screen's effect through an approximation; it does not physically model the wires. As a result, the GN command can only model the ground screen at the origin ($x = 0$ and $y = 0$). Therefore, its use is limited to a one-tower analysis. Also, the radial ground screen approximation may not be used with the Sommerfeld/Norton ground option, which is discussed later. Moreover, the ground screen identified by the GN command cannot be moved by the GM command to create a multitower array because the segments are not identified as geometry. Despite its limitations, however, the GN radial ground screen approximation is very convenient to use when only one tower is being analyzed.

It would be helpful to read the description of the GN command in Appendix A.

A simple NEC-2 input file that creates a ground screen is shown in Listing 12-1. For simplicity, it shows a ground screen over perfect ground, which is a rather impractical notion, but it serves this purpose adequately.

Listing 12-1

```
CM One tower using
CM the GN command to create a
CM ground screen over perfect ground
CE
GW 102 10 0. 0. 0. 0. 0. 50. .3
GE 1
FR 0 1 0 0 1.5
GN 1 120 0 0 0. 0. 50. .003 0. 0.
EX 0 102 1 00 308.12 199.17
RP 4 1 361 1001 90. 0. 1. 1. 1000. 0.
EN
```

Notice that in addition to displaying the ground-type flag, the GN command now specifies the number of radials in the ground screen (120), the length of the radials (50 meters), and the radius of the wire making up the radials (0.003 meters). Also, the RP command is written to indicate the presence of a ground screen by setting the first integer to 4 (in this case) as opposed to the usual 0. When this NEC-2 input file is run, the presence of the ground screen is noted in the output file just prior to the tabulation of the pattern data.

12.5.2 The GR Command

The GR command is used to advantage when a creating structure containing identical elements spaced symmetrically about the Z-axis. A good example is the ground screen that may consist of as many as 120 identical wire radials equally spaced about the base of the tower. In that case, instead of writing 120 GW commands, it is only necessary to describe one radial with the GW command(s) and then use the GR command to reproduce it 120 times equally spaced about the base of the tower.

Be aware that NEC-2 cannot model wires below the surface of the earth; therefore, the NEC-2 model must be compromised by spacing the wires a small distance above ground. Due consideration must be given the modeling rules, especially those that cause NEC-2 to assume a connection between segment and ground if the spacing is less than 10^{-3} times the length of the segment.

Listing 12-2 is a NEC-2 input file modeling a two-tower array with 120 radial ground screens at each tower. This example serves to demonstrate the GR command, the use of the NGF, and the NX command.

Listing 12-2

```
CM TwoTwr.nec
CM NEC-2's version of a two tower broadcast array employing
CM Green's Function to create the two 120 radial ground screens
CM over a finite ground.
CM
CE Create ground screens first -
GW 101 5 0. 0. .02 49. 0. .02 .003
GR 0 120
GM 100 1 0. 0. 0. 50. 0. 0. 101 1 101 600
GE 1
FR 0 1 0 0 1.5
GN 2 0 0 0 4. .001
WG
NX
CE Now add the two towers and execute the NEC-2 run
GF 1
GW 102 10 0. 0. .02 0. 0. 50.02 .3
GW 202 10 50. 0. .02 50. 0. 50.02 .3
GE 1
EX 0 102 1 00 308.12 199.17
EX 0 202 1 00 11.1 93.95
RP 0 1 361 1001 80. 0. 1. 1. 1000. 0.
EN
```

In summary, the file exploits the symmetry of the 120 radial ground screens by generating the screens separately and adding the towers after the screens are complete. Figure 12-3 demonstrates the principle.

Refer to Listing 12-2 to see that the two parts are generated and combined by generating one ground screen at the origin using the GR command to replicate the single radial that was described by the preceding GW command. Once created at the origin, the total ground screen is duplicated at a location 50 meters north by using the GM command. Following that, the GE, FR, and GN commands define the appropriate parameters. Then all are saved by writing them to a NGF file via the WG command.

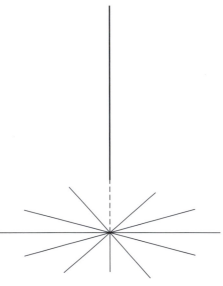

FIGURE 12-3

Monopole added to ground screen

Because NEC-2 cannot model wires underground, the ground screen in this example has been placed 0.02 meters above ground. Remember, however, that if the radials are placed too close to the ground, NEC-2 will try to connect the radial wires to ground and will reject the input with an error message. This is not a concern when using NEC-4 because the radial wires may be placed underground with that code.

The NX command then starts a new structure that will be created by recalling the two ground screens with the GF command and then adding a tower to each ground screen, as described by the next two GW commands.

Following the end of the geometry definition are the excitation and radiation pattern commands used in the conventional way.

When a finite ground is used, NEC-2 shows zero radiation at ground level, so the RP command must call for a pattern at some small angle above the horizon. In this example, theta has been arbitrarily specified as 80° (10° above the horizon), although that may be a bit large.

Refer to Appendix A to study the details of the commands used in this example. Notice especially that the number in the second field of the GR command specifies how many radials are to be created. This number is the total number of radials to be created including the one described by the GW command. For example, if a total of 120 radials is desired and one is described by the GW command, then 120 would be entered in the GR command, not 119. The total number of times that the structure can be repeated is limited by array dimensions in the NEC-2 program. In the NEC-2 files available on the Internet, the limit is 16 times. However, the program associated with this book, bnec.exe, has been modified to accept 120 radials, in keeping with the usual broadcast practice. If this modification causes bnec.exe to exceed the memory limits of the computer, use bnec3k.exe or download a suitable NEC-2 program from the Internet.

The GR command should never be used when there are segments on the Z-axis or crossing the Z-axis since overlapping segments would result. Placement of nonradiating networks or sources does not affect the use of the GR command, however.

The reader is encouraged to enter the NEC-2 input file of Listing 12-2 and to run the NEC-2 analysis. It is useful to know that the input file twotwr.nec takes almost 2 minutes to run using bnec.exe on a 2.7-GHz machine. Each radial in the ground screen has 5 segments and there are 120 radials in each ground screen, so the two ground screens have a total of 1200 segments. Then each of the two towers has 10 segments, so there are a total of 1220 segments in the model. This large number of segments exceeds the capability of NECMOM.EXE; thus, the calculated field ratios cannot be determined using the furnished software.

The output file will contain the equivalent of two regular NEC-2 output files—one for the NGF structure containing ground screens only and another containing ground screens plus towers. You are encouraged to study this output file carefully.

12.6 Finite Ground

For the most part, specifying a perfectly conducting ground for the NEC-2 analysis of a broadcast directional array simplifies the task and gives satisfactory results. The elaborate ground screens used with broadcast antennas and the fact that the surface impedance at the center of a ground screen is zero causes the calculated impedance and current distribution using the ground screen to be equivalent to that of a perfectly conducting ground. This encourages one to choose the simpler perfect ground rather than a finite ground for most broadcast analysis.

There are, however, occasions that make it necessary to model the system using a finite ground. This section introduces the subject of finite grounds but the coverage is by no means complete in itself.

NEC-2 uses two procedures in addressing a finite ground. The Reflection Coefficient Approximation (RCA) is simple and sufficiently accurate for those applications where horizontal conductors are not too near the ground. The Sommerfeld/Norton method is more accurate in general and has more application near the ground but it is less convenient to use and uses more computer time.

12.6.1 Reflection Coefficient Approximation

The Reflection Coefficient Approximation computes the radiated field over a real ground by including the field of the image structure as modified by a reflection coefficient determined by the surface impedance of the ground at the spectral point. The RCA can only be used with horizontal wires that are not too close to the ground, with reasonable results being obtained when those wires are more than 0.1 to 0.2 wavelengths above ground.

The use of the RCA is selected by setting I2 = 0 in the GN command and specifying the ground dielectric constant and conductivity. For example,

```
GN  0  0  0  0  10  .006
```

12.6.2 Sommerfeld/Norton Analysis

The more accurate Sommerfeld/Norton ground method uses exact solutions for fields in the presence of the specified ground and is more accurate for horizontal wires that are closer to the ground. It is less convenient to use, however, not only because it is more time consuming when running but also because it requires a look-up table that must be created prior to the NEC-2 run. Rather than make certain laborious calculations when the Sommerfeld/Norton method is used, NEC-2 looks to a grid of values in a look-up table of previously calculated results. It interpolates within the grid for values as required.

For most NEC-2 versions available on the Internet, it is necessary for the user to create the look-up table by running an auxiliary program named SOMNEC prior to making the NEC-2 calculation. SOMNEC accepts user input of relative dielectric constant, ground conductivity, and frequency and then writes an output as a binary file, which NEC-2 reads.

In the software associated with this book (see Appendix C), however, SOMNEC has been incorporated directly into the NEC-2 program, bnec.exe. It is not necessary for the user to create the look-up table file because bnec.exe calculates the values internally as needed.

When the Sommerfeld/Norton ground is used, the NEC-2 output file states that fact under the heading - ANTENNA ENVIRONMENT - in addition to listing the specified dielectric constant and conductivity.

The use of Sommerfeld/Norton is selected by setting I2 = 2 in the GN command and specifying the ground dielectric constant and conductivity.

For example,

GN 2 0 0 0 10 .006

Refer to the GN command in Appendix A for more information about the Sommerfeld/Norton ground.

NEC-2 Input File Statements

Notice

The input commands listed in this appendix have been taken from Naval Ocean Systems Center Technical Document 116 (TD 116), volume 2, *Numerical Electromagnetic Code (NEC) – Method of Moments, Part III: User's Guide*, revised 2 January 1980.

Contents

1.0 **Comment Commands**

The input file for a NEC-2 run must begin with one or more comment commands, which can contain a brief description and structure parameters for the run. The comment commands are printed at the beginning of the output file for identification only and have no effect on the computation. Any alphabetic and numeric characters can be used on these commands.

1.1 Comment (CM, CE)

The comment commands, like all other data commands, have a two-letter identifier in columns 1 and 2. The comment commands occur in two forms:

```
CM Comments go here
CE This is the last comment command
```

When a CM command is read, the contents of columns 3 through 80 are printed in the output file, and the next command is read as a comment line. When a CE command is read, columns 3 through 80 are printed in the output file, and reading of comments is terminated. The next command must be a geometry command. Thus, a CE command must always occur in a data file and may be preceded by as many CM commands as are needed to describe the run.

2.0 **Structure Geometry Commands**

Several geometry commands are provided to conveniently generate the array description. The format for the commands begins with a two letter identifier, which is followed by two fields of integer numbers. The remainder of the command is used as required for real number fields. In the following descriptions, the integer numbers are referred to as I1 and I2 and the real numbers as F1, F2, F3, . . ., as required.

2.1 Wire Arc Specification (GA)

Purpose

To generate a circular arc of wire segments.

GA,	I1,	I2,	F1,	F2,	F3,	F4
	ITG	NS	RADA	ANG1	ANG2	RAD

Parameters

Integers

ITG (I1) – Tag number assigned to all segments of the wire arc.

NS (I2) – Number of segments into which the arc will be divided.

Decimal Numbers

RADA (F1) – Arc radius (center is the origin and the axis is the Y-axis).

ANG1 (F2) – Angle of first end of the arc measured from the X-axis in a left-hand direction about the Y-axis (degrees).

ANG2 (F3) – Angle of the second end of the arc.

RAD (F4) – Wire radius.

Notes

- The segments generated by GA form a section of polygon inscribed within the arc.
- If an arc in a different position or orientation is desired, the segments may be moved with a GM command.
- Use of GA to form a circle will not result in symmetry being used in the calculation. It is a good way to form the beginning of the circle, to be completed by GR, however.
- See notes for GW.

2.2 End Geometry Input (GE)

Purpose

To terminate reading of geometry data commands and reset geometry data if a ground plane is used.

GE,   I1
         gpflag

Typical Broadcast Application

GE, 1

Parameters

Integers

gpflag –

   0 – Indicates no ground plane is present.

   1 – Indicates a ground plane is present. Structure symmetry is modified as required, and the current expansion is modified so that the currents on segments touching the ground (X-Y plane) are interpolated to their images below the ground (charge at base is zero).

   −1 – Indicates a ground is present. Structure symmetry is modified as required. Current expansion, however, is not modified. Thus, currents on segments touching the ground will go to zero at the ground.

Notes

■ The basic function of the GE command is to terminate reading of geometry data commands. In doing this, it causes the program to search through the segment data that have been generated by the preceding commands to determine which wires are connected for current expansion.

■ At the time that the GE command is read, the structure dimensions must be in units of meters.

- A positive or negative value of I1 does not cause a ground to be included in the calculation. It only modifies the geometry data as required when a ground is present. The ground parameters must be specified on a program control command following the geometry commands.
- When I1 is nonzero, no segment may extend below the ground plane (X-Y plane) or lie in this plane. Segments may end on the ground plane, however.
- If the height of a horizontal wire is less than 10^{-3} times the segment length, I1 equal to 1 will connect the end of every segment in the wire to ground. I1 should be -1 to avoid this disaster.
- As an example of how the symmetry of a structure is affected by the presence of a ground plane (X-Y plane), consider a structure generated with cylindrical symmetry about the Z-axis. The presence of a ground does not affect the cylindrical symmetry. If, however, this same structure is rotated off the vertical, the cylindrical symmetry is lost in the presence of the ground. As a second example, consider a dipole parallel to Z-axis that was generated with symmetry about its feed. The presence of a ground plane destroys this symmetry. The program modifies structure symmetries as follows when I1 is nonzero. If the structure was rotated about the X- or Y-axis by the GM command, all symmetry is lost (i.e., the no-symmetry condition is set). If the structure was not rotated about the X- or Y-axis, only symmetry about a plane parallel to the X-Y plane is lost. Translation of a structure does not affect symmetries.

2.3 Read NGF File (GF)

Purpose

To read a previously written NGF file.

```
GF,    I1
       PRT
```

Typical Broadcast Application

```
GF, 0
```

Parameters

Integers

PRT (I1)

> 0 – Indicates normal printing.

> 1 – Prints a table of the coordinates of the ends of all segments in the NGF.

Notes

GF must be the first command in the structure geometry section, immediately after CE. The effects of some other data commands are altered when a GF command is used.

2.4 Helix and Spiral Specification (GH)

Purpose

To generate a helix or spiral of wire segments.

```
GH,  I1,  I2,  F1,  F2,  F3,  F4,  F5,  F6,   F7
     ITG  NS    S   HL   A1   B1   A2   B2  RAD
```

Parameters

Integers

ITG (I1) – Tag number assigned to all segments of the helix or spiral.

NS (I2) – Number of segments into which the helix or spiral will be divided.

Decimal Numbers

S (F1) – Spacing between turns.

HL (F2) – Total length of the helix.

A1 (F3) – Radius in x at z = 0.

B1 (F4) – Radius in y at z = 0.

A2 (F5) – Radius in x at z = HL.

B2 (F6) – Radius in y at z = HL.

RAD (F7) – Radius of wire.

Notes

- Structure will be a helix if A2 = A1 and HL > 0.
- Structure will be a spiral if A2 = A1 and HL = 0.
- Unless it has been fixed in the codes in circulation, the use of HL = 0 for a flat spiral will result in division by zero in NEC-2. GH was an unofficial addition to NEC-2.
- HL negative gives a left-handed helix.
- HL positive gives a right-handed helix.

2.5 Coordinate Transformation (GM)

Purpose

To translate or rotate a structure with respect to the origin of the coordinate system or to generate new structures translated or rotated from the origin. See Special Note on next page.

GM	I1	I2	FI	F2	F3	F4	F5	F6	F7	F8	F9	F10
	ITGI	NRPT	ROX	ROY	ROZ	XS	YS	ZS	ITI	ISI	IT2	IS2

Typical Broadcast Application

GM, 100, 1, 0., 0., 0., 45., 32., 0., 101., 1., 101., 6.

Parameters

Integers

ITGI (I1) – Tag number increment.

NRPT (I2) – The number of new structures to be generated.

Decimal Numbers

ROX (Fl) – Angle in degrees through which the structure is rotated about the X-axis. A positive angle causes a right-hand rotation.

ROY (F2) – Angle of rotation about the Y-axis in degrees.

ROZ (F3) – Angle of rotation about the Z-axis in degrees.

XS (F4) – X coordinate as shifted from the origin.

YS (F5) – Y coordinate as shifted from the origin.

ZS (F6) – Z coordinate as shifted from the origin.

ITl (F7) – Tag number of the first segment to be moved or duplicated.

IS1 (F8) – Segment number of the first segment to be moved or duplicated.

IT2 (F9) – Tag number of the last segment to be moved or duplicated.

IS2 (F10) – Segment number of the last segment to be moved or duplicated.

Notes

- If NRPT is zero, the structure is moved by the specified rotation and translation, leaving nothing in the original location. If NRPT is greater than zero, the original structure remains fixed and NRPT new structures are formed, each shifted from the previous one by the requested transformation.

- The tag increment ITGI is used when new structures are generated (NRPT greater than 0) to avoid duplication of tag numbers. Tag numbers of the segments in each new copy of the structure are incremented by ITGI from the tag on the previous copy or original. Tags of segments that are generated from segments having no tags (tag equal to 0) are not incremented. Generally, ITGI will be greater than or equal to the largest tag number on the original structure to avoid duplication of tags. For example, if the tag numbers 1 through 100 have been used, a GM command is read having NRPT equal to 2, then ITGI equal to 100 will cause the first copy of the structure to have tags from 101 to 200 and the second copy from 201 to 300. If NRPT is 0, the tags on the original structure will be incremented.

- The result of a transformation depends on the order in which the rotations and translation are applied. The order is first rotation about the x-axis, then rotation about the y-axis, then rotation about the z-axis and, finally, translation by (XS, YS, ZS). All operations refer to the fixed coordinate system axes. If a different order is desired, separate GM commands may be used.

- All segments that are to be moved by a GM command must appear BEFORE the GM command appears.

- **Special Note:** The NEC-2 program (bnec.exe) used in this book has been modified to accept the command format shown before so as to make the GM command more useful for broadcast applications. The usual versions of NEC-2 use a GM command format as follows:

GM, ITGI, NRPT, ROX, ROY, ROZ, XS, YS, ZS, ITS

In this format, the last field (ITS) is interpreted differently depending on the version of NEC-2. In some versions, ITS is interpreted as the tag number assigned to that portion of the structure to be moved. In others, ITS is input as a decimal number of the form Seg1.Seg2, where all segments between Seg1 and Seg2 are moved. In yet other versions, all segments from ITS to the end of the structure are moved.

2.6 Geometry Print Control (GP)

Purpose

To suppress printing of segmentation information. Must precede the GE command.

GP blank

Parameters

None.

2.7 Generate Cylindrical Structure (GR)

Purpose

To reproduce a structure while rotating about the Z-axis to form a complete cylindrical array and to set flags so that symmetry is used in the solution.

GR,   I1,   I2
        TINC   NUM

Parameters

Integers

TINC (I1) – Tag number increment.

NUM (I2) – Total number of times that the structure is to occur in the cylindrical array.

Decimal Numbers

The decimal number fields are not used.

Notes

- The tag increment (I1) is used to avoid duplication of tag numbers in the reproduced structures. In forming a new structure for the array, all valid tags on the previous copy or original structure are incremented by (I1). Tags equal to 0 are not incremented.
- The GR command should never be used when there are segments on the Z-axis or crossing the Z-axis because overlapping segments would result.
- The GR command sets flags so the program uses cylindrical symmetry in solving for the currents. If a structure modeled by N segments has M sections in cylindrical symmetry (formed by a GR command with I2 equal to M), the number of complex numbers in

matrix storage and the proportionality factors for matrix fill time and matrix factor time are:

	Matrix Storage	Fill Time	Factor Time
No symmetry	N^2	N^2	N^3
M symmetric sections	N^2/M	N^2/M	N^3/M^2

The matrix factor time represents the optimum for a large matrix factored in core. Generally, somewhat longer times will be observed.

- If the structure is added to or modified after the GR command in such a way that cylindrical symmetry is destroyed, the program must be reset to a no-symmetry condition. In most cases, the program is set by the geometry routines for the existing symmetry. The following operations automatically reset the symmetry conditions.
  - Addition of a wire by a GW command destroys all symmetry.
  - Generation of additional structures by a GM command, with NRPT greater than 0, destroys all symmetry.
  - A GM command acting on only part of the structure (having ITS greater than 0) destroys all symmetry.
  - A GX or GR command will destroy all previously established symmetry.
  - If a structure is rotated about either the X- or Y-axis by use of a GM command and a ground plane is specified on the GE command, all symmetry will be destroyed. Rotation about the Z-axis or translation will not affect symmetry. If a ground is not specified, symmetry will be unaffected by any rotation or translation by a GM command, unless NRPT or ITS on the GM command is greater than 0.
- Symmetry will also be destroyed if lumped loads are placed on the structure in an unsymmetric manner. In this case, the program is not automatically set to a no-symmetry condition but must be set by a data command following the GR command. A GW command

with NS blank will set the program to a no-symmetry condition without modifying the structure. The command must specify a nonzero radius, however, to avoid reading a GC command.

- Placement of nonradiating networks or sources does not affect symmetry.
- When symmetry is used in the solution, the number of symmetric sections (I2) is limited by array dimensions.
- The GR command produces the same effect on the structure as a GM command if I2 on the GR command is equal to (NRPT + 1) on the GM command and if ROZ on the GM command is equal to 360/(NRPT + 1) degrees. If the GM command is used, however, the program will not be set to take advantage of symmetry.

2.8 Scale Structure Dimensions (GS)

Purpose

To scale all dimensions of a structure by a constant.

GS,   blank,   blank,   F1

Parameters

Integers

The integer fields are not used.

Decimal Numbers

(F1) – All structure dimensions, including wire radius, are multiplied by F1.

Note

At the end of geometry input, structure dimensions must be in units of meters. Hence, if the dimensions have been input in other units, a GS command must be used to convert to meters.

2.9 Wire Specification (GW, GC)

Purpose

To generate a string of segments to represent a straight wire.

GW,	I1,	I2,	F1,	F2,	F3,	F4,	F5,	F6,	F7
	ITG	NS	XW1	YW1	ZW1	XW2	YW2	ZW2	RAD

This command defines a string of segments with radius RAD. If RAD is 0 or blank, a second command is read to set parameters to taper the segment lengths and radius from one end of the wire to the other. The format for the second command (GC), which is read only when RAD is 0, is:

GC,	blank,	blank,	F1,	F2,	F3
			RDEL	RAD1	RAD2

Typical Broadcast Application

GW, 201, 20, 45.0, 33.1, 0., 45.0, 33.1, 50., 0.
GC, 0, 0, 1.1, 0.5, 0.5

Parameters of GW Command

Integers

ITG (I1) – Tag number assigned to all segments of the wire.

NS (I2) – Number of segments into which the wire will be divided.

Decimal Numbers

XW1 (F1) – X coordinate of wire end 1.

YW1 (F2) – Y coordinate of wire end 1.

ZW1 (F3) – Z coordinate of wire end 1.

XW2 (F4) – X coordinate of wire end 2.

YW2 (F5) – Y coordinate of wire end 2.

ZW2 (F6) – Z coordinate of wire end 2.

RAD (F7) – Wire radius, or 0 for tapered segment option.

Parameters of Optional GC Command

RDEL (F1) – Ratio of the length of a segment to the length of the previous segment in the string.

RAD1 (F2) – Radius of the first segment in the string.

RAD2 (F3) – Radius of the last segment in the string.

The ratio of the radii of adjacent segments is:

$$RRAD = (RAD2/RAD1)^{1/(NS-1)}$$

If the total wire length is L, the length of the first segment is

$$S1 = L(1\text{-RDEL}) / (1\text{-RDEL}^{NS})$$

or

$$S1 = L / NS \text{ if RDEL=1.}$$

Notes

- The tag number is for later use when a segment must be identified, such as when connecting a voltage source or lumped load to the segment. Any number except 0 can be used as a tag. When identifying a segment by its tag, the tag number and the number of the segment in the set of segments having that tag are given. Thus, the tag of a segment does not need to be unique. If no need is anticipated to refer back to any segments on a wire by tag, the tag field may be left blank. This results in a tag of 0, which cannot be referenced as a valid tag.
- If two wires are electrically connected at their ends, then identical coordinates should be used for the connected ends to ensure that the wires are treated as connected for current interpolation. If wires intersect away from their ends, the point of intersection must occur at segment ends within each wire for interpolation to occur. Generally, wires should intersect only at their ends unless the location of segment ends is accurately known.
- The only significance of differentiating end 1 from end 2 of a wire is that the positive reference direction for current will be in the direction from end 1 to end 2 on each segment making up the wire.

- As a rule of thumb, segment lengths should be less than 0.1 wavelength at the desired frequency. Somewhat longer segments may be used on long wires with no abrupt changes, while shorter segments, 0.05 wavelength or less, may be required in modeling critical regions of an antenna.
- If input is in units other than meters, then the units must be scaled to meters through the use of a Scale Structure Dimensions (GS) command (see page 208).

2.10 Reflection in Coordinate Planes (GX)

Purpose

To form structures having planes of symmetry by reflecting part of the structure in the coordinate planes, and to set flags so that symmetry is used in the solution.

```
GX   I1   I2
     TNI  XYZ
```

Parameters

Integers

TNI (I1) – Tag number increment.

XYZ (I2) – This integer is divided into three independent digits, in columns 8, 9, and 10, which control reflection in the three orthogonal coordinate planes. A 1 in column 8 causes reflection along the X-axis (reflection in Y, Z plane); a 1 in column 9 causes reflection along the Y-axis; and a 1 in column 10 causes reflection along the Z-axis. A 0 or blank in any of these columns causes the corresponding reflection to be skipped.

Decimal Numbers

The decimal number fields are not used.

Notes

- Any combination of reflections along the X, Y, and Z-axes may be used. For example, 101 for (I2) will cause reflection along axes X and Z, and 111 will cause reflection along axes X, Y, and Z. When combinations of reflections are requested, the reflections are done in reverse alphabetical order. That is, if a structure is generated in a single octant of space and a GX command is then read with I2 equal to 111, the structure is first reflected along the Z-axis; the structure and its image are then reflected along the Y-axis; and, finally, these four structures are reflected along the X-axis to fill all octants. This order determines the position of a segment in the sequence and, hence, the absolute segment numbers.

- The tag increment I1 is used to avoid duplication of tag numbers in the image segments. All valid tags on the original structure are incremented by I1 on the image. When combinations of reflections are employed, the tag increment is doubled after each reflection. Thus, a tag increment greater than or equal to the largest tag on the original structure will ensure that no duplicate tags are generated. For example, if tags from 1 through 100 are used on the original structure with I2 equal to 011 and a tag increment of 100, the first reflection, along the Z-axis, will produce tags from 101 through 200; and the second reflection, along the Y-axis, will produce tags from 201 through 400, as a result of the increment being doubled to 200.

- The GX command should never be used when there are segments located in the plane about which reflection would take place or when segments cross this plane. The image segments would then coincide with or intersect the original segments, and such overlapping segments are not allowed. Segments may end on the image plane, however.

- When a structure having plane symmetry is formed by a GX command, the program will make use of the symmetry to simplify solution for the currents. The following table shows the number of complex numbers in matrix storage and the proportionality factors for matrix fill time and matrix factor time for a structure modeled by N segments.

Number of Symmetry Planes	Matrix Storage	Fill Time	Factor Time
0	N^2	N^2	N^3
1	$N^2/2$	$N^2/2$	$N^3/4$
2	$N^2/4$	$N^2/4$	$N^3/16$
3	$N^2/8$	$N^2/8$	$N^3/64$

The matrix factor time represents the optimum for a large matrix factored in core. Generally, somewhat longer times will be observed.

- If the structure is added to or modified after the GX command in such a way that symmetry is destroyed, the program must be reset to a no-symmetry condition. In most cases, the program is set by the geometry routines for the existing symmetry. The following operations automatically reset the symmetry condition.
  - Addition of a wire by a GW command destroys all symmetry.
  - Generation of additional structures by a GM command, with NRPT greater than 0, destroys all symmetry.
  - A GM command acting on only part of the structure (having ITS greater than 0) destroys all symmetry.
  - A GX command or GR command will destroy all established symmetry. For example, two GR commands with I2 equal to 011 and 100, respectively, will produce the same structure as a single GX command with I2 equal to 111; however, the first case will set the program to use symmetry about the Y-Z plane only while the second case will make use of symmetry about all three coordinate planes.
  - If a ground plane is specified on the GE command, symmetry about a plane parallel to the X-Y plane will be destroyed. Symmetry about other planes will be used, however.
  - If a structure is rotated about either the X- or Y-axis by use of a GM command and a ground plane is specified on the GE command, all symmetry will be destroyed. Rotation about the Z-axis or translation will not affect symmetry. If a ground is not specified, no rotation or translation will affect symmetry conditions unless NRPT on the GM command is greater than zero.
  - Symmetry will also be destroyed if lumped loads are placed on the structure in an unsymmetric manner. In this case, the program is not automatically set to a no-symmetry condition but must be set by a data command following the GX command. A GW command with NS blank will set the program to a no-symmetry condition without modifying the structure. The command must specify a nonzero radius, however, to avoid reading a GC command.
- Placement of sources or nonradiating networks does not affect symmetry.

2.11 Surface Patch (SP)

Purpose

To input parameters of a single surface patch.

SP,	I1,	I2,	F1,	F2,	F3,	F4,	F5,	F6
	blank	NS	X1	Y1	Z1	X2	Y2	Z2

If NS is 1, 2, or 3, a second command is read in the following format:

SC,	I1,	I2,	F1,	F2,	F3,	F4,	F5,	F6
	blank	see Notes	X3	Y3	Z3	X4	Y4	Z4

Parameters

Integers

blank (I1) is not used.

NS (I2) – Selects the patch shape.

0 – (default) arbitrary patch shape

1 – rectangular patch

2 – triangular patch

3 – quadrilateral patch

Decimal Numbers

Arbitrary shape (NS = 0).

X1 (F1) – X coordinate of patch center.

Y1 (F2) – Y coordinate of patch center.

Z1 (F3) – Z coordinate of patch center.

X2 (F4) – Elevation angle above the X-Y plane of outward normal vector (degrees).

Y2 (F5) – Azimuth angle from X-axis of outward normal vector (degrees).

Z2 (F6) – Patch area (square of units used).

Rectangular, triangular, or quadrilateral patch (NS = 1, 2, or 3).

   X1 (F1) – X coordinate of corner 1.

   Y1 (F2) – Y coordinate of corner 1.

   Z1 (F3) – Z coordinate of corner 1.

   X2 (F4) – X coordinate of corner 2.

   Y2 (F5) – Y coordinate of corner 2.

   Z2 (F6) – Z coordinate of corner 2.

   X3 (Fl) – X coordinate of corner 3.

   Y3 (F2) – Y coordinate of corner 3.

   Z3 (F3) – Z coordinate of corner 3.

For the quadrilateral patch only (NS = 3).

   X4 (F4) – X coordinate of corner 4.

   Y4 (F5) – Y coordinate of corner 4.

   Z4 (F6) – Z coordinate of corner 4.

Note

For more detail on the use of surface patches, see NOSC Technical Document 116, *Numerical Electromagnetic Code (NEC) – Method of Moments, Part III: User's Guide*, available on the Internet at *www. ntis.gov*.

2.12 Multiple Patch Surface (SM)

Purpose

To cover a rectangular region with surface patches.

SM,	I1,	I2,	F1,	F2,	F3,	F4,	F5,	F6,	blank
.	NX	NY	X1	Y1	Z1	X2	Y2	Z2	.

A second command with the following format must immediately follow an SM command:

SC,	I1,	I2,	F1,	F2,	F3,	F4,	F5,	F6,	blank
.			X3	Y3	Z3				.

Parameters

Integers

NX, NY (I1, I2) – The rectangular surface is divided into NX patches from corner 1 to corner 2 and NY patches from corner 2 to corner 3.

Decimal Numbers

X1, Y1, Z1 (F1, F2, F3) – X,Y,Z coordinates of corner 1.

X2, Y2, Z2 (F4, F5, F6) – X,Y,Z coordinates of corner 2.

X3, Y3, Z3 (F1, F2, F3) – X,Y,Z coordinates of corner 3.

Note

For more detail on the use of surface patches see NOSC Technical Document 116, *Numerical Electromagnetic Code (NEC) – Method of Moments, Part III: User's Guide,* available on the Internet at *www. ntis.gov*.

3.0 **Program Control Commands**

The program control commands follow the structure geometry commands. They set electrical parameters for the model, select options for the solution procedure, and request data computation.

There is no fixed order for the program control commands. The desired parameters and options are set first, followed by requests for calculations. Parameters that are not set in the input data are given default values. The one exception to this is the excitation command (EX), which must be set by the user.

Computation of currents may be requested by an XQ command. RP, NE, or NH commands cause calculation of the currents and radiated or near fields on their first occurrence. Subsequent RP, NE, or NH commands cause computation of fields using the previously calculated currents. Any number of near-field and radiation-pattern requests may be grouped together in a data file. An exception to this occurs when multiple frequencies are requested by a single FR command. In this case, only a single NE or NH command and a single RP command will remain in effect for all frequencies.

All parameters retain their values until changed by subsequent data commands. Hence, after parameters have been set and currents or fields computed, selected parameters may be changed and the calculations repeated. For example, if a number of different excitations are required at a single frequency, the file could have the form FR, EX, XQ, EX, XQ, ... If a single excitation is required at a number of frequencies, the commands EX, FR, XQ, FR, XQ, ... could be used.

The program control commands are explained on the following pages. The format of all program commands has four integers and six floating-point numbers. Not all are used on every command.

3.1 Coupling Calculation (CP)

Purpose

To request the calculation of the maximum coupling between segments identified as TAG1, SEG1 and TAG2, SEG2.

CP,	I1,	I2,	I3,	I4
	TAG1 _	SEG1 _	TAG2 _	SEG2

Parameters

> TAG1 (I1) & SEG1 (I2) – Specify segment number SEG1 in the set of segments having tag TAG1. If TAG1 is blank or 0, then SEG1 is the absolute segment number.
>
> TAG2 (I3) & SEG2 (I4) – Same as above.

Notes

- Up to five segments may be specified on 2-1/2 CP commands. Coupling is computed between all pairs of these segments. When more than two segments are specified, the CP commands must be grouped together. A new group of CP commands replaces the old group.
- CP does not cause the program to proceed with the calculation but only sets the segment numbers. The specified segments must then be excited (EX command) one at a time in the specified order and the currents computed (XQ, RP, NE, or NH command). The excitation must use the applied-field voltage-source model. When all of the specified segments have been excited in the proper order, the couplings will be computed and printed. After the coupling calculation, the set of CP commands is cancelled.
- When using NEC-2, CP will not return the correct values for segments containing network or transmission line connections. NEC-4 does not suffer this limitation.

3.2 Extended Thin-Wire Kernal (EK)

Purpose

To control use of the extended thin-wire kernel approximation. Without an EK command, the program will use the standard thin-wire kernel.

```
EK,  I1
     ITMP1
```

Typical Broadcast Application

```
EK
```

Parameters

Integers

ITMP1 (I1) – Blank or zero to initiate use of the extended thin-wire kernel, −1 to return to standard thin-wire kernel.

3.3 End of Run (EN)

Purpose

To indicate to the program the end of all execution.

EN

Typical Broadcast Application

EN

Parameters

None.

3.4 Excitation (EX)

Purpose

To specify the excitation for the structure. The excitation can be voltage sources on the structure, an elementary current source, or a plane-wave incident on the structure.

EX, I1, I2, I3, I4, F1, F2, F3, F4, F5, F6

Typical Broadcast Application

EX, 0, 101, 1, 00, 325.478, 176.932

Parameters

Integers

(I1) – Determines the type of excitation that is used.

    0 – Voltage source (applied-E-field source).

    1 – Incident plane wave, linear polarization.

    2 – Incident plane wave, right-hand (thumb along the incident k vector) elliptic polarization.

    3 – Incident plane wave, left-hand elliptic polarization.

    4 – Elementary current source.

    5 – Voltage source (current-slope-discontinuity).

Remaining integers depend on excitation type.

a. If I1 is a voltage source of type 0 or 5, then

    (I2) – Tag number of the source segment. This tag number, along with the number to be given in (I3), uniquely defines the source segment. Blank or 0 in field (I2) implies that the Source segment will be identified by using the absolute segment number in the next field.

    (I3) – Equal to m, specifies the mth segment of the set of segments whose tag numbers are equal to the number set by the previous parameter. If the previous parameter is 0, the number in (I3) must be the absolute segment number of the source.

(I4) – Columns 19 and 20 of this field are used separately. The options for column 19 are:

0 – No action.

1 – Maximum relative admittance matrix asymmetry for source segments and network connections will be calculated and printed.

The options for column 20 are:

0 – No action

1 – The input impedance at voltage sources is always printed directly before the segment currents in the output. By setting this flag, the impedance of a single source segment in a frequency loop will be collected and printed in a table (in a normalized and unnormalized form) after the information at all frequencies has been printed. Normalization to the maximum value is a default, but the normalization value can be specified (refer to F3 under voltage source below). When there is more than one source on the structure, only the impedance of the last source specified will be collected.

b. If I1 is an incident plane wave of type 1, 2, or 3:

(I2) – Number of theta angles desired for the incident plane wave.

(I3) – Number of phi angles desired for the incident plane wave.

(I4) – 0 – no action

1 – maximum relative admittance matrix asymmetry for network connections will be calculated and printed.

c. If I1 is an elementary current source of type 4:

(I2) and (I3) – Blank.

(I4) – Identical to that listed under b.

Floating-Point Options

a. Voltage source (I1 = 0 or 5).

(F1) – Real part of the voltage in volts.

(F2) – Imaginary part of the voltage in volts.

(F3) – If a second digit (1) is placed in I4 (see above), this field can be used to specify a normalization constants for the impedance printed in the optional impedance table. Blank in this field produces normalization to the maximum value.

(F4), (F5), and (F6) – blank.

b. Incident plane wave (I1 = 1, 2, or 3). The incident wave is characterized by the direction of incident $^\wedge k$ wave polarization in the plane normal to $^\wedge k$.

(F1) – Theta in degrees. Theta is defined in standard spherical coordinates.

(F2) – Phi in degrees. Phi is the standard spherical angle defined in the X-Y plane.

(F3) – Eta in degrees. Eta is the polarization angle defined as the angle between the theta unit vector and the direction of the electric field for linear polarization or the major ellipse axis for elliptical polarization.

(F4) – Theta angle stepping increment in degrees.

(F5) – Phi angle stepping increment in degrees.

(F6) – Ratio of minor axis to major axis for elliptic polarization (major axis field strength – 1 V/m).

c. Elementary current source (I1 = 4). The current source is characterized by its Cartesian coordinate position, orientation, and its magnitude.

(F1) – X position in meters.

(F2) – Y position in meters.

(F3) – Z position in meters.

(F4) – alpha in degrees. alpha is the angle the current source makes with the X-Y plane.

(F5) – beta in degrees. beta is the angle the projection of the current source on the X-Y plane makes with the X-axis.

(F6) – "Current moment" of the source. This parameter is equal to the product current times length in amp meters.

Notes

- In the case of voltage sources, excitation commands can be grouped to specify multiple sources. The maximum number of voltage sources that may be specified is determined by dimension statements in the program.
- The applied-E-field voltage source is located on the segment specified.
- The current-slope-discontinuity source is located at the first end, relative to the reference direction, of the specified segment, at the

junction between the specified segment and the previous segment. This Junction must be a simple two-segment junction, and the two segments must be parallel with equal lengths and radii.

- A current-slope-discontinuity voltage source may lie in a symmetry plane. An applied-field voltage source may not lie in a symmetry plane since a segment may not lie in a symmetry plane. An applied-field voltage source may be used on a wire crossing a symmetry plane by exciting the two segments on opposite sides of the symmetry plane, each with half the total voltage, taking account of the reference directions of the two segments.

- An applied-field voltage source specified on a segment that has been impedance-loaded, through the use of an LD command, is connected in series with the loads. An applied-field voltage source specified on the same segment as a network is connected in parallel with the network port. For the specific case of a transmission line, the source is in parallel with both the line and the shunt load. Applied-field voltage sources should be used in these cases since loads and network connections are located on, rather than between, segments.

- Only one incident plane wave or one elementary current source is allowed at a time. Also, plane-wave or current-source excitation is not allowed with voltage sources. If the excitation types are mixed, the program will use the last excitation type encountered.

- When a number of theta and phi angles are specified for an incident plane-wave excitation, the theta angle changes more rapidly than phi.

- The current element source illuminates the structure with the field of an infinitesimal current element at the specified location. The current element source cannot be used over a ground plane.

3.5 Frequency (FR)

Purpose

To specify the frequency(s) in megahertz.

FR,	I1,	I2,	I3,	I4,	F1,	F2
	IFRQ	NFRQ	blank	blank	FMHZ	DELFRQ

Typical Broadcast Application

FR, 0, 1, 0, 0, 0.87, 0.

Parameters

Integers

IFRQ (I1) – Determines the type of frequency stepping, which is

   0 – Linear stepping.

   1 – Multiplicative stepping.

NFRQ (I2) – Number of frequency steps. If this field is blank, one is assumed.

(I3) and (I4) – Blank.

Floating Point

FMHZ (F1) – Frequency in megahertz.

DELFRQ (F2) – Frequency stepping increment. If the frequency stepping is linear, this quantity is added to the frequency each time. If the stepping is multiplicative, this is the multiplication factor.

(F3) through (F6) – Blank.

Notes

- If a frequency command does not appear in the data file, a single frequency of 299.8 MHz is assumed. Since the wavelength at

299.8 MHz is 1 meter, the geometry is in units of wavelengths for this case.

- Frequency commands may not be grouped together. If they are, only the information on the last command in the group will be used.
- After an FR command with NFRQ greater than 1, an NE or NH command will not initiate execution but an RP or XQ command will. In this case, only one NE or NH command and one RP command will be effective for the multiple frequencies.
- After a frequency loop for NFRQ greater than 1 has been completed, it will not be repeated for a second execution request. The FR command must be repeated in that case.

3.6 Additional Ground Parameters (GD)

Purpose

To specify the ground parameters of a second medium, which is not in the immediate vicinity of the antenna. This command may only be used if a GN command has also been used. It does not affect the field of surface patches.

GD,	I1,	I2,	I3,	I4,	F1,	F2,	F3,	F4
	blank	blank	blank	blank	EPSR2	SIG2	CLT	CHT

Typical Broadcast Application

GD, 0, 0, 0, 0, 6.0, 1.0E-3, 40., 0.

Parameters

Integers

All integer fields are blank.

Floating Point

EPSR2 (F1) – Relative dielectric constant of the second medium.

SIG2 (F2) – Conductivity in mhos/mecer of the second medium.

CLT (F3) – Distance in meters from the origin of the coordinate system to the join between medium 1 and 2. This distance is either the radius of the circle where the two media join, or the distance out the plus X-axis to where the two media join in a line parallel to the Y-axis. Specification of the circular or linear option is on the RP command.

CHT (F4) – Distance in meters (positive or 0) by which the surface of medium 2 is below medium 1.

Notes

- The GD command can only be used in a data file where the GN command has been used since the GN command is the only way to specify the ground parameters in the vicinity of the antenna (see GN command write-up). However, a number of GD commands may be used in the same data file with only one GN command.

- GD commands may not be grouped together. If they are, only the information on the last command of the group is retained.
- When a second medium in specified, a flag must also be set on the radiation pattern (RP) data command in order to calculate the patterns including the effect of the second medium. Refer to the radiation-pattern command write-up for details.
- Use of the GD command does not require recalculation of the matrix or currents.
- The parameters for the second medium are used only in the calculation of the far-fields. It is possible then to set the radius of the boundary between the two media equal to 0 and thus have the far-fields calculated by using only the parameters of medium 2. The currents for this case will still have been calculated by using the parameters of medium 1.
- When a model includes surface patches, the fields due to the patches will be calculated by using only the primary ground parameters. Hence, a second ground medium should not be used with patches.

3.7 Ground Parameters (GN)

Purpose

To specify the relative dielectric constant and conductivity of ground in the vicinity of the antenna. In addition, a second set of ground parameters for a second medium can be specified, or a radial wire ground screen can be modeled using a reflection coefficient approximation.

GN,	I1,	I2,	I3,	I4,	F1,	F2,	F3,	F4,	F5,	F6
	IPERF	NRADL	blank	blank	EPSE	SIG	P1	P2	P3	P4

Typical Broadcast Application

GN,1

Parameters

Integers

IPERF (I1) – Ground-type flag. The options are:

- −1 – Nullifies ground parameters previously used and sets free-space condition. The remainder of the command is left blank in this case.
- 0 – Finite ground, reflection coefficient approximation.
- 1 – Perfectly conducting ground.
- 2 – Finite ground, Sommerfeld/Norton method.

NRADL (I2) – Number of radial wires in the ground screen approximation; blank or 0 implies no ground screen.

(I3) and (I4) – Blank.

Floating Point

EPSE (F1) – Relative dielectric constant for ground in the vicinity of the antenna. Leave blank in case of a perfect ground.

SIG (F2) – Conductivity in mhos/meter of the ground in the vicinity of the antenna. Leave blank in the case of a perfect ground. If SIG is input as a negative number, the complex dielectric constant is set to EPSR − j |SIG|.

Options for Remaining Floating Point Fields (F3–F6)

a. For the case of an infinite ground plane, F3 through F6 are blank.

b. Radial wire ground screen approximation (NRADL ≠ 0). The ground screen is always centered at the origin, that is, (0, 0, 0) and lies in the X-Y plane.

   P1 (F3) – The radius of the screen in meters.
   P2 (F4) – Radius of the wires used in the screen in meters.
   P3 (F5) – blank.
   P4 (F6) – blank.

c. Second medium parameters (NRADL = 0) for medium outside the region of the first medium (cliff problem). These parameters alter the far-field patterns but do not affect the antenna impedance or current distribution.

   P1 (F3) – Relative dielectric constant of medium 2.
   P2 (F4) – Conductivity of medium 2 in mhos/meter.
   P3 (F5) – Distance in meters from the origin of the coordinate system to the boundry between medium 1 and 2. This distance is either the radius of the circle where the two media join, or the distance out the positive X-axis to where the two media join in a line parallel to the Y-axis. Specification of the circular or linear option is on the RP command.
   P4 (F6) – Distance in meters (positive or 0) by which the surface of medium 2 is below medium 1.

Notes

- When the Sommerfeld/Norton method is used, many NEC-2 codes require an input-data file that is generated by the program SOMNEC for the specific ground parameters and frequency. SOMNEC is integrated into bnec.exe, however, and is run transparently when needed. The file generated by SOMNEC depends only on the complex dielectric constant. NEC-2 compares the complex dielectric constant from the file with that determined by the GN command parameters and frequency. If the relative difference exceeds 10^{-3}, an error message is printed. Once the SOMNEC data file has been read for the first use of the Sommerfeld/Norton method, the data is retained until the end of the run. Subsequent data, including new data sets following NX commands, may use the SOMNEC data file if the ground parameters and frequency remain unchanged. Other ground options may be intermixed with the Sommerfeld/Norton option.

- The parameters of the second medium can also be specified on another data command whose mnemonic is GD. With the GD command, the parameters of the second medium can be varied and only the radiated fields need to be recalculated. Furthermore, if a radial wire ground screen has been specified on the GN command, the GD command is the only way to include a second medium. See the write-up of the GD command for details.

- GN commands may not be grouped together. If they are, only the information on the last command will be retained.

- Use of a GN command after any form of execute dictates structure matrix regeneration.

- Only the parameters of the first medium are used when the antenna currents are calculated; the parameters associated with the second medium are not used until the calculation of the far-fields. It is possible then to calculate the currents over one set of ground parameters (medium 1), but to calculate the far-fields over another set (medium 2) by setting the distance to the start of medium 2 to 0. Medium 1 can even be a perfectly conducting ground specified by IPERF = 1.

- When a radial-wire ground screen or a second medium is specified, it is necessary to indicate their presence by the first parameter on the RP command in order to generate the proper radiation patterns.

- When a ground plane is specified, this fact should also be indicated on the GE command. Refer to the GE command for details.

- When a model includes surface patches, the fields due to the patches will be calculated by using only the primary ground parameters. Hence, a second ground medium should not be used with patches. The radial-wire ground screen approximation also is not implemented for patches.

3.8 Interaction Approximation Range (KH)

Purpose

To set the minimum separation distance for use of a time-saving approximation in filling the interaction matrix.

KH,	I1,	I2,	I3,	I4,	F1
	blank	blank	blank	blank	RKH

Parameters

Integers

None.

Decimal Numbers

RKH (F1) - The approximation is used for interactions over distances greater than RKH wavelengths.

Notes

- If two segments or a segment and a patch are separated by more than RKH wavelengths, the interaction field is computed from an impulse approximation to the segment current. The field of a current element located at the segment center is used. No approximation is used for the field due to the surface current on a patch since the time for the standard calculation is very short.
- The KH command can be placed anywhere in the data file following the geometry commands (with FR, EX, LD, etc.) and affects all calculations requested following its occurrence. The value of RKH may be changed within a data set by use of a new KH command.

3.9 Loading (LD)

Purpose

To specify the impedance loading on one segment or a number of segments. Series and parallel RLC circuits can be generated. In addition, a finite conductivity can be specified for segments.

LD,	I1,	I2,	I3,	I4,	F1,	F2,	F3
	LDTYP	LDTAG	LDTAGF	LDTAGT	ZLR	ZLI	ZLC

Typical Broadcast Application

LD, 0, 101, 1, 1, 0., 2.5E–6, 0.,

Parameters

Integers

LDTYP (I1) – Determines the type of loading used. The options are:

-    -1 – short all loads (used to nullify previous loads).
          The remainder of the command is left blank.
-    0 – series RLC, input ohms, henries, farads.
-    1 – parallel RLC, input ohms, henries, farads.
-    2 – series RLC, input ohms/meter, henries/meter, farads/meter.
-    3 – parallel RLC, input ohms/meter, henries/meter, farads/meter.
-    4 – impedance, input resistance and reactance in ohms.
-    5 – wire conductivity, mhos/meter.

LDTAG (I2) – Tag number; identifies the wire section(s) to be loaded by its (their) tag numbers. The next two parameters can be used to further specify certain segment(s) on the wire section(s). Blank or 0 here implies that absolute segment numbers are being used in the next two parameters to identify segments. If the next two parameters are blank or 0, all segments with tag LDTAG are loaded.

LDTAGF (I3) – Equal to m specifies the *m*th segment of the set of segments whose tag numbers equal the tag number specified in the previous parameter. If the previous parameter (LDTAG) is 0, LDTAGF then specifies an absolute segment number. If both LDTAG and LDTAGF are 0, all segments will be loaded.

LDTAGT (I4) – Equal to *n* specifies the *n*th segment of the set of segments whose tag numbers equal the tag number specified in the parameter LDTAG. This parameter must be greater than or equal to the previous parameter. The loading specified is applied to each of the *m*th through nth segments of the set of segments having tags equal to LDTAG. Again, if LDTAG is zero, these parameters refer to absolute segment numbers. If LDTAGT is left blank, it is set equal to the previous parameter (LDTAGF).

Floating Point – Input for the Various Load Types

a. Series **RLC** (LDTYP = 0)
   ZLR (F1) – Resistance in ohms; if none, 0 or leave blank.
   ZLI (F2) – Inductance in henries; if none, 0 or leave blank.
   ZLC (F3) – Capacitance in farads; if none, 0 or leave blank.

b. Parallel **RLC** (LDTYP = 1).
   Floating point inputs same as in item a.

c. Series **RLC** (LDTYP = 2) input, parameters per unit length.
   ZLR – Resistance in ohms/meter; if none, 0 or leave blank.
   ZLI – Inductance in henries/meter; if none, 0 or leave blank.
   ZLC – Capacitance in farads/meter; if none, 0 or leave blank.

d. Parallel **RLC** (LDTYP = 3), input parameters per unit length, floating point input same as in item c.

e. Impedance (LDTYP = 4).
   ZLR – Resistance in ohms.
   ZLI – Reactance in ohms.

f. Wire conductivity (LDTYP = 5).
   ZLR – Conductivity in mhos/meter.

Notes

- Loading commands can be input in groups to achieve a desired structure loading. The maximum number of loading commands in a group is determined by dimensions in the program.
- If a segment is loaded more than once by a group of loading commands, the loads are assumed to be in series (impedances added), and a comment is printed in the output alerting the user to this fact.
- When resistance and reactance are input (LDTYP = 4), the impedance does not automatically scale with frequency.
- Loading commands used after any form of execute, require the regeneration of the structure matrix.
- Since loading modifies the interaction matrix, it will affect the conditions of plane or cylindrical symmetry of a structure. If a structure is geometrically symmetric and each symmetric section is to receive identical loading, then symmetry may be used in the solution. The program is set to use symmetry during geometry input by inputting the data for one symmetric section and completing the structure with a GR or GX command. If symmetry is used, the loading on only the first symmetric section is input on LD commands. The same loading will be assumed on the other sections. Loading should not be specified for segments beyond the first section when symmetry is used. If the sections are not identically loaded, then during geometry input the program must be set to a no-symmetry condition to permit independent loading of corresponding segments in different sections.

3.10 Near Fields (NE, NH)

Purpose

To request calculation of near electric fields in the vicinity of the antenna (NE) or to request near magnetic fields (NH). Use NE or NH as appropriate.

NE/NH	I1,	I2,	I3,	I4,	F1,	F2,	F3,	F4,	F5,	F6
	NEAR	NRX	NRY	NRZ	XNR	YNR	ZNR	DXNR	DYNR	DZNR

Parameters

Integers

NEAR (I1) – Coordinate system type. The options are:
  0 – Rectangular coordinates will be used.
  1 – Spherical coordinates will be used.

Remaining integers depend on coordinate type.

a. Rectangular coordinates (NEAR = 0).
  NRX, NRY, NRX (I2, I3, I4) – Number of points desired in the X, Y, and Z directions, respectively. X changes the most rapidly, then Y, and then Z. The value 1 is assumed for any field left blank.

b. Spherical coordinates (NEAR = 1).
  (I2, I3, I4) – Number of points desired in the r, phi, and theta directions, respectively. r changes the most rapidly, then phi, and then theta. The value 1 is assumed for any field left blank.

Floating Point Fields

Their specification depends on the coordinate system chosen.

a. Rectangular coordinates (NEAR = 0).
  XNR, YNR, ZNR (F1, F2, F3) – The (X, Y, Z) coordinate position (F1, F2, F3), respectively, in meters of the first field point.

  DXNR, DYNR, DZNR (F4, F5, F6) – Coordinate stepping increment in meters for the X, Y, and Z coordinates (F4, F5, F6), respectively. In stepping, X changes most rapidly, then Y, and then Z.

b. Spherical coordinates (NEAR = 1).
   (F1, F2, F3) – The (r, phi, theta) coordinate position (Fl, F2, F3),
      respectively, of the first field point. r is in meters, and phi and
      theta are in degrees.
   (F4, F5, F6) – Coordinate stepping increments for r, phi, and theta
      (F4, F5, F6), respectively. The stepping increment for r is in
      meters and for phi and theta, it is in degrees.

Notes

- When only one frequency is being used, near-field commands may
  be grouped together in order to calculate fields at points with various coordinate increments. For this case, each command encountered produces an immediate execution of the near-field routine
  and the results are printed. When automatic frequency stepping
  is being used (i.e., when the number of frequency steps [NFRQ]
  on the FR command is greater than one), only one NE or NH command can be used for program control inside the frequency loop.
  Furthermore, the NE or NH command does not cause an execution
  in this case. Execution will begin only after a subsequent radiation-
  pattern command (RP) or execution command (XQ) is encountered (see write-ups on both of these commands).
- The time required to calculate the field at one point is equivalent
  to filling one row of the matrix. Thus, if there are N segments in the
  structure, the time required to calculate fields at N points is equivalent to the time required to fill an N x N interaction matrix.
- The near electric field is computed by whichever form of the
  field equations selected for filling the matrix, either the thin-wire
  approximation or extended thin-wire approximation. At large distances from the structure, the segment currents are treated as
  infinitesimal current elements.
- If the field calculation point falls within a wire segment, the point
  is displaced by the radius of that segment in a direction normal to
  the plane containing each source segment and the vector from that
  source segment to the observation segment. When the specified
  field-calculation point is at the center of a segment, this convention

is the same as is used in filling the interaction matrix. If the field point is on a segment axis, that segment produces no contribution to the H-field or the radial component of the E-field. If these components are of interest, the field point should be on or outside of the segment surface.

3.11 Networks (NT)

Purpose

To generate a two-port nonradiating, network connected between any two segments in the structure. The characteristics of the network are specified by its short-circuit admittance matrix elements. For the special case of a transmission line, a separate command is provided for convenience, although the mathematical method is the same as for networks. Refer to the TL command.

NT,	I1,	I2,	I3,	I4,	F1,	F2,	F3,	F4,	F5,	F6
	TAG1	SEG1	TAG2	SEG2	Y11R	Y11I	Y12R	Y12I	Y22R	Y22I

Typical Broadcast Application

NT, 100, 1, 101, 1, 0.01, −0.01, 1.0E−10, 0., 1.0E+10, 0.

Parameters

Integers

TAG1 (I1) – Tag number of the segment to which port 1 of the network is connected. This tag number along with the number to be given in (I2), which identifies the position of the segment in a set of equal tag numbers, uniquely defines the segment for port 1. Blank or 0 here implies that the segment will be identified, using the absolute segment number in the next location (I2).

SEG1 (I2) – Equal to m, specifies the mth segment of the set of segments whose tag numbers are equal to the number set by the previous parameter. If the previous parameter is 0, the number in (I2) is the absolute segment number corresponding to end 1 of the network. A minus one in this field will nullify all previous network and transmission line connections. The rest of the command is left blank in this case.

TAG2 (I3) – Used in exactly the same way as (I1) and (I2) in order to specify the segment corresponding to port 2 of the network connection.

SEG2 (I4) – As above.

Floating Point

The six floating-point fields are used to specify the real and imaginary parts of three short-circuit admittance matrix elements $(1, 1), (1, 2)$, and $(2, 2)$, respectively. The admittance matrix is symmetric so it is unnecessary to specify element $(2, 1)$.

Y11R (F1) – Real part of element $(1, 1)$ in mhos.

Y11I (F2) – Imaginary part of element $(1, 1)$ in mhos.

Y12R (F3) – Real part of element $(1, 2)$ in mhos.

Y12I (F4) – Imaginary part of element $(1, 2)$ in mhos.

Y22R (F5) – Real part of element $(2, 2)$ in mhos.

Y22I (F6) – Imaginary part of element $(2, 2)$ in mhos.

Notes

- Network commands may be used in groups to specify several networks on a structure. All network commands for a network configuration must occur together with no other commands (except TL commands) separating them. When the first NT command is read following a command other than an NT or TL command, all previous network and transmission line data are destroyed. Hence, if a set of network data is to be modified, all network data must be input again in the modified form. Dimensions in the program limit the number of networks that may be specified. In the present NEC-2 deck, the number of two-port networks (including transmission lines) is limited to thirty, and the number of different segments having network ports connected to them is limited to thirty.
- One or more network ports can be connected to any given segment. Multiple network ports connected to one segment are connected in parallel.
- If a network is connected to a segment that has been impedance loaded (i.e., through the use of the LD command), the load acts in series with the network port.
- A voltage source specified on the same segment as a network port is connected in parallel with the network port.

- Segments can be impedance-loaded by using network commands. Consider a network connected from the segment to be loaded to some other arbitrary segment, as shown in Figure 5.2(c) on page 55. The admittance matrix elements are $Y_{11} = 1/Z_1$, $Y_{12} = 0$, and $Y_{22} = $ infinity (computationally, a very large number such as 10^{10}). The advantage of using this technique for loading Ls is that the load can be changed without causing a recalculation of the structure matrix as required when LD commands are used. Furthermore, in some cases a higher degree of structure matrix symmetry can be preserved because the matrix elements are not directly modified by networks, as they are when using the LD commands. (Consider, for instance, a loop with one load where the loop is rotationally symmetric until the load is placed on it.) The disadvantage of the NT command form of loading is that the user must calculate the load admittance, and this value does not automatically scale with frequency. Obviously, in the above schematic, replacing the short with an impedance would load two segments. At a segment at which a voltage source is specified, the effect of loading by the LD and NT commands differs, however, since the network is in parallel with the voltage source while the load specified by an LD command is in series with the source.
- Use of network commands (NT) after any form of execute requires the recalculation of the current only.
- NT and TL commands do not affect structure symmetry.

3.12 Next Structure (NX)

Purpose

To signal the end of data for one structure and the beginning of data for the next.

NX

Parameters

NX appears in the first two columns, and the rest of the command is blank.

Note

The command that directly follows the NX command must be a comment command; CM or CE.

3.13 Print Control for Charge on Wires (PQ)

Purpose

To control the printing of charge densities on wire segments.

PQ,	I1,	I2,	I3,	I4
	IPTFLQ	IPTAQ	IPTAQF	IPTAQT

Parameters

Integers

IPTFLQ (I1) – Print control flag

-1 – Suppress printing of charge densities. This is the default condition.

0 (or blank) – Print charge densities on segments specified by the following parameters. If the following parameters are blank, charge densities are printed for all segments.

IPTAQ (I2) – Tag number of the segments for which charge densities will be printed.

IPTAQF (I3) – Equal to m specifies the mth segment of the set of segments having tag numbers of IPTAQ. If IPTAQ is 0 or blank, then IPTAQF refers to an absolute segment number. If IPTAQF is left blank, then charge density is printed for all segments.

IPTAQT (I4) – Equal to n, specifies the nth segment of the set of segments having tag numbers of IPTAQ. Charge densities are printed for segments having tag number IPTAQ starting at the mth segment in the set and ending at the nth segment. If IPTAQ is zero or blank, then IPTAQF and IPTAQT refer to absolute segment numbers. If IPTAQT refer to absolute segment numbers. If IPTAQT is left blank, it is set equal to IPTAQF.

Floating Point

Floating-point fields are not used.

3.14 Data Storage for Plotting (PL)

Purpose

To write selected output data into a predesignated file for later plotting.

PL,	I1,	I2,	I3,	I4
	IPLP1	IPLP2	IPLP3	IPLP4

Parameters

Integers

IPLP1 (I1) – Data type to be written into auxiliary file:

> 0 – No action.
> 1 – Wire currents.
> 2 – Near fields.
> 3 – Far-field patterns.
> 4 – Impedance, SWR.
> 5 – Admittance, SWR.

Remaining integers depend on data type(IPLP1):

a. Wire Currents (IPLP1 = 1).

IPLP2 (format) = 0 – No action
= 1 – Use real and imaginary format
= 2 – Use magnitude and phase format

IPLP3 (patch I components) = 0 – No action
= 1 – Ix
= 2 – Iy
= 3 – Iz
= 4 – Ix, Iy, Iz

(all measured in magnitude and phase)

b. Near-Fields (IPLP1 = 2)

IPLP2 (format) = 0 – No action.
= 1 – Use real and imaginary format.
= 2 – Use magnitude and phase format.

IPLP3 (components) = 0 – No action.

                                                     = 1 – X component.

                                                     = 2 – Y component.

                                                     = 3 – Z component.

                                                     = 4 – X, Y, Z component.

                                                     = 5 – Total field (magnitude only)

IPLP4 (coordinates) = 1 – X coordinate

                                                   = 2 – Y coordinate

                                                   = 3 – Z coordinate

c. Far-Field Patterns (IPLP1 = 3).

IPLP2 (Angle to be stored) = 1 – Theta or Z

                                                     = 2 – Phi

                                                     = 3 – Rho

IPLP3 (E-field component) = 0 – No action

                                                   = 1 – E(Theta)

                                                   = 2 – E(Phi)

                                                   = 3 – E(Rho)

(all in magnitude and phase)

IPLP4 (Power pattern) = 0 – No action

                                                   = 1 – Vertical gain in dB.

                                                   = 2 – Horizontal gain in dB.

                                                   = 3 – Total gain in dB.

                                                   = 4 – Vertical, horizontal, and total gain
                                                        in dB.

Notes

1. The PL command may be used anywhere between the GE and XQ commands.
2. A PL command with IPLP1 = 0 will suspend any previous PL specs.
3. All the data requested is written out to a prenamed file.

3.15 Print Control (PT)

Purpose

To control the printing of currents on wire segments. Current printing can be suppressed or limited to a few segments, or special formats for receiving patterns can be requested.

PT,	I1,	I2,	I3,	I4
	IPTFLG	IPTAG	IPTAGF	IPTAGT

Parameters

Integers

IPTFLG (I1) – Print control flag; specifies the type of format used in printing segment currents. The options are:

> −2 - All currents printed. This it a default value for the program if the command is omitted.
>
> −1 - Suppress printing of all wire segment currents.
>
> 0 - Current printing will be limited to the segments specified by the next three parameters.
>
> 1 - Currents are printed by using a format designed for a receiving pattern. Only currents for the segments specified by the next three parameters are printed.
>
> 2 - Same as for 1 above; in addition, however, the current for one segment will be normalized to its maximum, ant the normalized values along with the relative strength in dB will be printed in a table. If the currents for more than one segment are being printed, only currents from the last segment in the group appear in the normalized table.
>
> 3 - Only normalized currents from one segment are printed for the receiving pattern case.

IPTAG (I2) – Tag number of the segments for which currents will be printed.

IPTAGF (I3) – Equal to *m*, specifies the *m*th segment of the set of segments having the tag numbers of IPTAG, at which printing of currents starts. If IPTAG is 0 or blank, then IPTAGF refers to an absolute segment number. If IPTAGF is blank, the current is printed for all segments.

IPTAGT (I4) – Equal to *n* specifies the *n*th segment of the set of segments having tag numbers of IPTAG. Currents are printed for segments having tag number IPTAG starting at the *m*th segment in the set and ending at the *n*th segment. If IPTAG is 0 or blank, then IPTAGF and IPTAGT refer to absolute segment numbers. In IPTAGT is left blank, it is set to IPTAGF.

Note

For suppressing current print – PT, –1, 1, 1, 1

3.16 Radiation Pattern (RP)

Purpose

To specify radiation pattern sampling parameters and to cause program execution. Options for a field computation include a radial-wire ground screen, a cliff, or surface-wave fields.

RP,	I1,	I2,	I3,	I4,	F1,	F2,	F3,	F4,	F5,	F6
	MOD	NTH	NPH	XNDA	THETS	PHIS	DTH	DPH	RFLD	GNOR

Typical Broadcast Application

RP, 0, 1, 361, 1001, 90., 0., 1., 1., 1000., 0.

Parameters

Integers

MOD (I1) – This integer selects the mode of calculation for the radiated field. Some values of (I1) will affect the meaning of the remaining parameters in the command. Options available for I1 are:

> 0 – Normal mode. Space-wave fields are computed. An infinite ground plane is included if it has been specified previously on a GN command; otherwise, antenna is in free space.

> 1 – Surface wave propagating along ground is added to the normal space wave. This option changes the meaning of some of the other parameters on the RP cart as explained below, and the results appear in a special output format. Ground parameters must have been input on a GN command.

The following options cause calculation of only the space wave but with special ground conditions. Ground conditions include a two-medium ground (cliff) where the media join in a circle or a line, and a radial-wire ground screen. Ground parameters and dimensions must be input on a GN or GD command before the RP command is read. The RP command only selects the option for inclusion in the field calculation. (Refer to the GN and GD commands for further explanation.)

2 – Linear cliff with antenna above upper level. Lower medium parameters are as specified for the second medium on the GN cart or on the GD command.

3 – Circular cliff centered at origin of coordinate system: with antenna above upper level. Lower medium parameters are as specified for the second medium on the GN command or on the GD command.

4 – Radial-wire ground screen centered at origin.

5 – Both radial-wire ground screen and linear cliff.

6 – Both radial-wire ground screen and circular cliff.

The field point is specified in spherical coordinates (*r*, sigma, theta) except when the surface wave is computed. For computing the surface-wave field (MOD (Il) = 1), cylindrical coordinates (phi, theta, z) are used to accurately define points near the ground plane at large radial distances. The RP command allows automatic stepping of the field point to compute the field over a region about the antenna at uniformly spaced points. The integers I2 and I3 and floating-point numbers Fl, F2, F3, and F4 control the field-point stepping.

NTH (I2) – Number of values of theta (e) at which the field is to be computed (number of values of z for ll = 1).

NPH (I3) – Number of values of phi (f) at which field is to be computed. The total number of field points requested by the command is NTH x NPH. If I2 or I3 is left blank, a value of 1 will be assumed.

XNDA (14) – This optional integer consists of four independent digits, each having a different function. The mnemonic XNDA is not a variable name in the program. Rather, each letter represents a mnemonic for the corresponding digit in I4. If I1 = 1, then I4 has no effect and should be left blank.

X (the first digit) – controls output format.

X = 0 – major axis, minor axis and total gain printed.

X = 1 – vertical, horizontal ant total gain printed.

N (second digit) – Causes normalized gain for the specified field points to be printed after the standard gain output. The number of field points for which the normalized gain can be printed is limited by an array dimension in the program. In the demonstration program, the limit is 600 points. If the number of field points exceeds this limit, the remaining points will be omitted from the normalized gain. The gain may be normalized to its maximum or to a value input in field F6. The type of gain that is normalized is determined by the value of N as follows:

N = 0 – No normalized gain.
  = 1 – Major axis gain normalized.
  = 2 – Minor axis gain normalized.
  = 3 – Vertical axis gain normalized.
  = 4 – Horizontal axis gain normalized.
  = 5 – Total gain normalized.

D (the third digit) – Selects either power gain or directive gain for both standard printing and normalization. If the structure excitation is an incident plane wave, the quantities printed under the heading "gain" will actually be the scattering cross section (a/λ^2) and will not be affected by the value of D. The column heading for the output will still read "power" or "directive gain," however.

D = 0 – Power gain.
  = 1 – Directive gain.

A – (the fourth digit) – Requests calculation of average power gain over the region covered by field points.

A = 0 – No averaging.
  = 1 – Average gain computed.
  = 2 – Average gain computed; printing of gain at the field points used for averaging is suppressed. If NTH or NPH is equal to one, average gain will not be computed for any value of A since the area of the region covered by field points vanishes.

Floating Point Numbers

THETS (F1) – Initial theta angle in degrees (initial z coordinate in meters if I1 = 1).

PHIS (F2) – Initial phi angle in degrees.

DTH (F3) – Increment for theta in degrees (increment for z in meters if I1 = 1).

DPH (F4) – Increment for phi in degrees.

RFLD (F5) – Radial distance (R) of field point from the origin in meters. RFLD is optional. If it is blank, the radiated electric field will have the factor exp(-jkR)/R omitted. If a value of R is specified, it should represent a point in the far-field region since near components of the field cannot be obtained with an RP command. (If I1 = 1, then RFLD represents the cylindrical coordinate phi in meters and is not optional. It must be greater than about one wavelength.)

GNOR (F6) – Determines the gain normalization factor if normalization has been requested in the I4 field. If GNOR is blank or 0, the gain will be normalized to its maximum value. If GNOR is not 0, the gain will be normalized to the value of GNOR.

Notes

- The RP command will initiate program execution, causing the interaction matrix to be computed and factored, and the structure currents to be computed if these operations have not already been performed. Hence, all required input parameters must be set before the RP command is read.
- At a single frequency, any number of RP commands may occur in sequence so that different field-point spacings may be used over different regions of space. If automatic frequency stepping is being used (i.e., NFRQ on the FR command is greater than 1), only one RP command will act as data inside the loop. Subsequent commands will calculate patterns at the final frequency.
- When both NTH and NPH are greater than 1, the angle theta (or Z) will be stepped faster than phi. When a ground plane has been specified, field points should not be requested below the ground (theta greater than 90 degrees or Z less than 0.)

3.17 Transmission Line (TL)

Purpose

To generate a transmission line between any two points on the struc-ture. Characteristic impedance, length, and shunt admittance are the defining parameters.

TL, I1, I2, I3, I4, F1, F2, F3, F4, F5, F6

Typical Broadcast Application

TL, 102, 1, 101, 1, 50., 62.0

Parameters

Integers

I1 and I2 – Tag and segment number to which end 1 is connected (see NT command).

I3 and I4 – Tag and segment number to which end 2 is connected (see NT command).

Floating Point

(F1) – The characteristic impedance of the transmission line in ohms. A negative sign in front of the characteristic impedance will act as a flag for generating the transmission line with a 180 degree phase reversal (crossed line) if this is desired.

(F2) – The length of transmission line in meters. If this field is left blank, the program will use the straight-line distance between the specified connection points.

The remaining four floating-point fields are used to specify the real and imaginary parts of the shunt admittances at end one and two, respectively.

(F3) – Real part of the shunt admittance in mhos at end 1.

(F4) – Imaginary part of the shunt admittance in mhos at end 1.

(F5) – Real part of the shunt admittance in mhos at end 2.

(F6) – Imaginary part of the shunt admittance in mhos at end 2.

Notes

- The rules for transmission line lines are the same as for network lines. All transmission line commands for a particular transmission line configuration must occur together with no other commands (except NT commands) separating than. When the first TL or NT command is read following a command other than a TL or NT command, all previous network or transmission line data are destroyed. Hence, if a set of TL commands is to be modified, all transmission line and network data must be input again in the modified form. Dimensions in the program limit the number of commands in a group that may be specified. In the NEC-2 demonstration deck, the number of two-port networks (specified by NT commands and TL commands) is limited to thirty, and the number of segments having network ports connected to them is limited to thirty.
- One or more networks (including transmission lines) may be connected to any given segment. Multiple network ports connected to one segment are connected in parallel.
- If a transmission line is connected to a segment that has been impedance-loaded (i.e., through the use of an LD command), the load acts in series with the line.
- Use of transmission line commands (TL) after any form of execute requires the recalculation of the current only and does not require recalculation of the matrix.
- NT and TL commands do not affect symmetry.

3.18 Write NGF File (WG)

Purpose

To write a NGF file for a structure.

WG

Typical broadcast Application

WG

Parameters

None.

3.19 Execute (XQ)

Purpose

To cause program execution at points in the data stream where execution is not automatic. Options on the command also allow for automatic generation of radiation patterns in either of two vertical cuts.

XQ, I1

Typical Broadcast Application

XQ

Parameters

Integers

(I1) Options controlled by (I1) are:

0 – No patterns requested (normal case).

1 – Generates a pattern cut in the X-Z plane, i.e., phi = 0 degrees and theta varies from 0 degrees to 90 degrees in 1-degree steps.

2 – Generates a pattern cut in the Y-Z plane, i.e., phi = 90 degrees theta varies from 0 degrees to 90 degrees in 1-degree steps.

3 – Generates both of the cuts described for the values 1 and 2.

The remainder of the command is blank.

Notes

- For the case of a single frequency step, four commands will automatically produce program execution (i.e., the program stops reading data and proceeds with the calculations requested to that point); the four commands are the execute command (XQ), the near-field commands (NE, NH), and the radiation-pattern command (RP). Thus, the only time the XQ command is mandatory, for the case of one frequency, is when only currents and impedances for the structure are desired. On the other hand, for the case of automatic frequency stepping, only the XQ command and the RP command cause execution. Thus, if only near-fields or currents are desired, the XQ command is mandatory to cause execution. Furthermore, the XQ command can always be used as a divider in the data after a command that produces an execute. For instance, if the user wished to put a blank XQ command after an RP command to more easily divide the data into execution groups, the XQ command would act as a do-nothing command.

- The radiation-pattern generation option of the XQ command must not be used when a radial-wire ground screen or a second medium has been specified. For these cases, the RP command is used where the presence of the additional ground parameters is indicated.

Error Messages

B

Notice

The error messages listed in this appendix have been taken from Naval Ocean Systems Center Technical Document 116 (TD 116), volume 2, *Numerical Electromagnetic Code (NEC) – Method of Moments, Part III: User's Guide*, revised 2 January 1980.

Error Messages

1. CHECK DATA, PARAMETER SPECIFYING SEGMENT POSITION IN A GROUP OF EQUAL TAGS CANNOT BE ZERO.
   This error results from an input data error and may occur at any point where a tag number is used to identify a segment. Execution terminated.

   Data on the NT, TL, EX, and PT commands should be checked.

2. CONNECT – SEGMENT CONNECTION ERROR FOR SEGMENT _.
   Possible causes: number of segments at a junction exceeds limit; segment lengths are zero; array overflow.

3. DATA FAULT ON LOADING COMMAND NO. =__ ITAG STEP1 =__ IS GREATER THAN ITAG STEP2 = __
   When several segments are loaded, the number of the second segment specified must be greater than the number of the first segment.

   Execution terminated.

4. EOF ON UNIT __NBLKS = __NEOF = __.
   An end of file has been encountered while reading data from the unit. NBLKS determines how many records are read from the unit. NEOF is a flag to indicate which call to BLCKIN-initiated thread. If NEOF = 777, this diagnostic is normal and execution will continue. Otherwise, an error is indicated and execution will terminate.

5. ERROR – ARC ANGLE EXCEEDS 360 DEGREES
   Error on GA command.

6. ERROR – B LESS THAN A IN ROM2.
   Program malfunction.

7. ERROR – FR/GN COMMAND IS NOT ALLOWED WITH NGF.

8. ERROR – CORNERS OF QUADRILATERAL PATCH DO NOT LIE IN A PLANE.
   The four corners of a quadrilateral patch (SP command) must lie in a plane.

9. ERROR – COUPLING IS NOT BETWEEN 0 AND 1,
   Inaccuracy in solution or error in data.

10. ERROR – GF MUST BE FIRST GEOMETRY DATA COMMAND.

11. ERROR IN GROUND PARAMETERS – COMPLEX DIELECTRIC CONSTANT FROM FILE IS REQUESTED.
    Complex dielectric constant from SOMNEC file does not agree with data from GN and FR commands.

12. ERROR – INSUFFICIENT STORAGE FOR INTERACTION MATRICES.IRESRV, IMAT. NEQ. NEQ2 =
    Array storage exceeded in NGF solution.

13. ERROR – INSUFFICIENT STORAGE FOR MATRIX.
    Array storage for matrix is not sufficient for out-of-core solution.

14. ERROR – NETWORK ARRAY DIMENSIONS TOO SMALL.
    The number of different segments to which transmission lines or network ports are connected exceeds array dimensions. Execution terminated.

15. ERROR – LOADING MAY NOT BE ADDED TO SEGMENTS IN NGF SECTION.

16. ERROR – NGF IN USE. CANNOT WRITE NEW NGF.

17. ERROR – THE NUMBER OF NEW SEGMENTS CONNECTED TO NGF SEGMENTS OR PATCHES EXCEEDS LIMIT.

18. FAULTY DATA COMMAND LABEL AFTER GEOMETRY
    SECTION.
    A command with an unrecognizable mnemonic has been
      encountered in the program control commands following
      the geometry commands.
    Execution terminated.

19. GEOMETRY DATA COMMAND ERROR.
    A geometry data command was expected, but the command
      mnemonic is not that of a geometry command.
    Execution terminated.
    After the GE command in a data file, the possible geometry mne-
      monics are GE, GM, GR, GS, GW, GX, SP, and SS. The GE com-
      mand must be used to terminate the geometry commands.

20. GEOMETRY DATA ERROR - - PATCH __ LIES IN PLANE OF
    SYMMETRY.

21. GEOMETRY DATA ERROR - - SEGMENT __ EXTENDS BELOW
    GROUND.
    When ground is specified on the GE command, no segment may
      extend below the XY plane.
    Execution terminated.

22. GEOMETRY DATA ERROR - - SEGMENT __ LIES IN GROUND
    PLANE.
    When ground is specified on the GE command, no segment
      should lie in the XY plane.
    Execution terminated.

23. GEOMETRY DATA ERROR - - SEGMENT __ LIES IN PLANE OF
    SYMMETRY.
    A segment may not lie in or cross a plane of symmetry about
      which the structure is reflected since the segment and its
      image will coincide or cross.
    Execution terminated.

24. IMPROPER LOAD TYPE CHOSEN. REQUESTED TYPE IS __.
    Valid load types (LDTYP on the LD command) are from 0
        through 5.

    Execution terminated.

25. INCORRECT LABEL FOR A COMMENT COMMAND.
    The program expected a comment command, with mnemonic
        CM or CE, but encountered a different mnemonic.

    Execution terminated.

    Comment commands must be the first commands in a data set,
        and the comments must be terminated by the CE mnemonic.

26. LOADING DATA COMMAND ERROR, NO SEGMENT HAS AN
    ITAG = __.
    ITAG specified on an LD command could not be found as a
        segment tag.

    Execution terminated.

27. NO SEGMENT HAS AN ITAG OF __.
    This error results from faulty input data and can occur at any
        point where a tag number is used to identify a segment.

    Execution terminated.

    Tag numbers on the NT, TL, EX, CP, PQ, and PT commands should
        be checked.

28. NOTE, SOME OF THE ABOVE SEGMENTS HAVE BEEN LOADED
    TWICE, thus the IMPEDANCES WERE ADDED.
    A segment or segments have been loaded by two or more LD
        commands. The impedances of the loads have been added in
        series. This is only an informative message.

    Execution continues.

29. NUMBER OF EXCITATION COMMANDS EXCEEDS STORAGE
    ALLOTTED.
    The number of voltage source excitations exceeds array
        dimensions.

Execution terminated.

The dimensions in the original NEC-2 file allow 10 voltage sources. Refer to Array Dimension Limitations to change the dimensions.

30. NUMBER OF LOADING COMMANDS EXCEEDS STORAGE ALLOTTED.

The number of LD commands exceeds array dimension.

Execution terminated.

The dimension in the original NEC-2 file allows 30 LD commands.

31. NUMBER OF NETWORK COMMANDS EXCEEDS STORAGE ALLOTTED.

The number of NT and TL commands exceeds array dimension.

Execution terminated.

The dimension in the original NEC-2 file allows 30 commands.

32. NUMBER OF SEGMENTS IN COUPLING CALCULATION (CP) EXCEEDS LIMIT.

Array dimension limit.

33. NUMBER OF SEGMENTS AND SURFACE PATCHES EXCEEDS DIMENSION LIMIT.

The sum of the number of segments and patches is limited by dimensions. The present limit is 300.

34. PATCH DATA ERROR.

Invalid data on SP, SM, or SC command; or SC command not found where required.

35. PIVOT (__) = __.

This will be printed during the Gauss Doolittle factoring of the interaction matrix or the network matrix when a pivot element less than 10E−10 is encountered, and it indicates that the matrix is nearly singular. The number in parentheses shows on which pass through the matrix the condition occurred. This is usually an abnormal condition, although execution will continue. It may result from coinciding segments or a segment of zero length.

36. RADIAL WIRE G.S. APPROXIMATION MAY NOT BE USED WITH SOMMERFELD GROUND OPTION.

37. RECEIVING PATTERN STORAGE TOO SMALL, ARRAY TRUNCATED.
    Routine: MAIN.

    The number of points requested in a receiving pattern exceeds array dimension. Execution will continue, but storage of normalized pattern will be truncated. This array dimension is 200 in the original NEC-2 file.

38. ROM2 - - STEP SIZE LIMITED AT Z =.

    Probably caused by a wire too close to the ground in the Sommerfeld/Norton ground method. Execution continues but results may be inaccurate.

39. SBF – SEGMENT CONNECTION ERROR FOR SEGMENT__.

    The number of segments at a junction exceeds dimension limit (30), or the connection numbers are not self-consistent.

40. SEGMENT DATA ERROR.

    A segment with zero length or zero radius was found.

    Execution terminated.

41. STEP SIZE LIMITED AT Z = __.

    The numerical integration to compute interaction matrix elements, using the Romberg variable interval width method, was limited by the minimum allowed step size. Execution will continue. An inaccuracy may occur but is usually not serious. May result from a thin wire or a wire close to the ground.

42. STORAGE FOR IMPEDANCE NORMALIZATION TOO SMALL, ARRAY TRUNCATED.

    The number of frequencies on FR command exceeds the array dimension for impedance normalization. An impedance beyond the limit will not be normalized. Execution continues. The limit is 50 in the original NEC file.

43. ERROR – NROW, NCOL =
    Array overflow or program malfunction.

44. TBF – SEGMENT CONNECTION ERROR FOR SEGMENT _.
    Same as error 39.

45. TRIO – SEGMENT CONNECTION ERROR FOR SEGMENT _.
    Same as error 39.

46. WHEN MULTIPLE FREQUENCIES ARE REQUESTED, ONLY ONE
    NEAR-FIELD COMMAND CAN BE USED. LAST COMMAND READ
    IS USED.
    Execution continues.

Software

1.1 Introduction

Basic NEC with Broadcast Applications uses public domain NEC-2 software available on the Internet. However, the fundamental concepts presented in this book are still valid regardless of the software programs used, so any method-of-moments software can be used with this book if the output file provides access to the calculated current distributions and other similar data. Most commercial software programs use the basic NEC-2 or NEC-4 engine and yield appropriate output data and therefore such programs are usable with this book. The postprocessing software must be tailored to the particular method-of-moments output file format, however.

1.2 Disk Content

The disk associated with this book contains the basic NEC-2 software and some postprocessing programs to perform tasks that are essential to broadcast applications. Also, as a convenience to the reader, the example program listings given in the text are included on the disk to relieve you of the task of typing them into your computer. Finally, the solutions to the exercises are also included on the disk.

1.3 Essential Software

Although additional software is indeed useful, the software included here is considered adequate to perform the basic design and analysis of an AM broadcast directional array. It includes the NEC-2 engine as modified for broadcast applications (bnec.exe), a geometry viewing program (NVCOMP.EXE), a postprocessing program to convert target field ratios to base drive voltages (NecDrv2.EXE), a postprocessing program to verify the field ratios created by a given set of base drive voltages (NECMOM.EXE), and an elementary pattern plotting program (WJGRAPS.EXE).

The postprocessing programs read the standard NEC-2 output file to retrieve source data that is subsequently processed to yield a desired result. In some instances these special-purpose programs require a defined NEC-2 input file discipline to yield the necessary source data. This file discipline is described in the text.

The most convenient way to use these programs is to place them in a common folder (perhaps named BasicNEC) and place that folder on your PATH variable in an Autoexec.BAT file. Doing that allows each job to be placed in a folder named for the job and the processing programs can be called directly from that job folder simply by typing the processing program name.

2.1 Software Installation

The software is installed manually as follows:

1. From the desktop, click START then RUN; enter "CMD" then click OK. A DOS window opens your hard drive (assumed to be C).

2. Change to the root folder by typing "CD\ <ENTER>".

3. Make a folder titled "BasicNEC" in the drive C root folder by typing "MD BasicNEC <ENTER>".

4. Change to the BasicNEC folder by typing "CD BasicNEC <ENTER>".

5. Make three subfolders by typing "MD NECfiles <Enter>" and "MD TextFiles <Enter>", then "MD Exercises <ENTER>".

6. Change to the NECfiles subfolder by typing "CD NECfiles <ENTER>".

7. Place the associated disk in CD drive D.

8. Copy the NEC files into the C:\NECfiles subfolder by typing "XCOPY D:\NECfiles*.* <ENTER>".

9. Change to the TextFiles subfolder on drive C by typing "CD.. <ENTER>" and then typing "CD TextFiles <ENTER>".

10. Copy the NEC input files into the TextFiles subfolder by typing "XCOPY D:\TextFiles*.* <ENTER>".

11. Change to the Exercises subfolder on drive C by typing "CD.. <ENTER>" and then typing "CD Exercises <ENTER>".

12. Copy the exercise files into the Exercises subfolder by typing "XCOPY D:\Exercises*.* /s <ENTER>".

13. Change to the drive C root folder by typing "CD\ <ENTER>".

14. Search for an AUTOEXEC.BAT file by typing "DIR AUTOEXEC.BAT".

15. If AUTOEXEC.BAT is found, prepare for editing by typing "EDIT AUTOEXEC.BAT". If no AUTOEXEC.BAT is found, go to step 19.

16. Add the following as the last line in the AUTOEXEC.BAT file "PATH C:\BasicNEC\NECfiles; %PATH%;" (Do not include the quotes.).

17. Save the modified file and close "EDIT".

18. Restart the computer to install the new path.

19. If no AUTOEXEC.BAT file can be found in step 14, then create one by typing "EDIT" to bring up the editor.

20. Type "PATH C:\BasicNEC\NECfiles; %PATH%; <ENTER>".

21. Save the file as C:\AUTOEXEC.BAT and close the editor.

22. Restart the computer to install the new path.

3.1 User Manual

3.1.1 bnec.exe

The NEC-2 computer program used in this book is a modified version of NEC2ds.zip, which is a free public domain program available on the Internet. At the time of this writing, NEC2dxs.zip can be downloaded free of charge at *http://www.si-list.net/swindex.html*.

NEC2dxs.zip contains executables and source code for a version of NEC-2 that has the Somnec interpolation table generator integrated into the NEC-2 executable. It has been compiled with the public domain GNU g77 compiler, thus it can be modified by the user. It is compatible for use with Win 95/98/Me/NT4/2000/XP operating systems as a 32-bit Windows application from a DOS console window. This public domain version was originally contributed by Ray Anderson WB6TPU <ray.anderson@xilinx.com> and further modified by Arie Voors, <4NEC2@gmx.net>, Neede, The Netherlands.

The unzipped version is on the CD included with this book. It has been modified and renamed bnec.exe but is referred to by the general term NEC-2. It has been modified slightly to make the GM command input format more useful to the broadcaster by providing the capability to specify both the starting and ending segments of a move. In addition, bnec.exe has been changed to protect the input file from accidental erasure should the output file be named with the same name and extension as the input file. The arrays have also been dimensioned to accommodate a ground screen that uses up to 120 radials.

IMPORTANT: If the larger arrays of bnec.exe exceed the memory capability of the computer, use bnec3k.exe. This program is equivalent to bnec.exe except that it has been compiled with smaller dimensioned arrays; therefore, it does not have the ability to model 120 radial ground screens.

It is important to know that the GM command as modified by bnec.exe is not compatible with the usual unmodified NEC2dxs programs. The GM command is, however, compatible with the NEC-4 file format; therefore, the input files generated during the study of this book are, for the most part, usable with both bnec.exe and NEC-4 should the reader elect to get the license for NEC-4.

When bnec.exe is run, it issues a call for the path and name of the input file plus the name that the user wishes to assign to the output file. There are no other communications with the user while NEC-2 runs. Bnec.exe stores its output in a file that it places in the computer's currently active folder. The user must recall the output file to read, print, or otherwise use it.

The output file is most conveniently viewed using WordPad. A satisfactory hard copy of the output file can be printed in the portrait orientation by changing the font of the entire file to size 6. The font can be changed to size 8 if the file is printed in the landscape orientation.

3.2 NVCOMP.EXE

NVCOMP.EXE was created by Glenn Stumpff (gstumpff@yahoo.com) and at the time of this writing is contained in the software package designated as NVNEW.ZIP on the Internet at *http://www.si-list.net/swindex.html*.

The package contains an enhanced version of David de Schweinitz's NV program. These enhancements include support for GA, GH, GM, GX, and GR commands as well as support for VGA graphics. It has the capability to output a PCX or BMP image file to the current folder and it also works with NEC-4 input files.

Assuming that NVCOMP.EXE is included in the PATH variable and the NEC-2 input file to be viewed is in the current folder, then to use the program it is only necessary to type NVCOMP followed by the name of the NEC-2 input file to be viewed. An image of the array will appear on the screen with control guides listed on the right screen edge. The control guides are explained as follows in the order of probable use.

SHIFT AXIS – Pressing 2 moves the total image down.

Pressing 4 moves the image left.

Pressing 6 moves the image right.

Pressing 8 moves the image up.

Pressing 0 returns the image to the origin.

CHANGE SCALE – Pressing Page Up zooms out.

Pressing Page Down zooms in.

ROTATE IMAGE – The arrow keys rotate the image. The current angles are displayed under the headings PHI and THETA.

HIGHLIGHT WIRE – When the image is first displayed, wire 1 is highlighted. The highlighted wire can be changed pressing + or − on the numerical keypad.

WIRE PARAMETERS – The parameters of the highlighted wire are displayed along the bottom of the screen. The wire number is listed along with its tag, segment, end 1 coordinates, end 2 coordinates, and wire radius.

CHANGE COLOR – Pressing various keys cycles colors of the image through a fixed color set.

Pressing B changes background color.

Pressing L changes line colors.

Pressing S changes the color of the highlighted wire.

Pressing X, Y, or Z changes the color of the X-, Y-, or Z-axis. To make an axis invisible, give it the same color as the background.

NVCOMP.EXE has the capability to save an image in a file using either the PCX or BMP image formats. If VGA mode 12 is in use, a PCX file of the displayed NEC-2 geometry will be written in the current folder when "C" (or "c") is pressed. The file will be given the default name NECGEO.PCX. This capability is currently only available if NVCOMP succeeds in autodetecting video mode 12. (If you don't see the "C FOR PCX" instruction on the lower right screen, the option isn't available because the computer is not in mode 12.)

NVCOMP will create a BMP file of the displayed NEC-2 geometry when "T" (or "t") is pressed. The file will be given the default name NEC00000.BMP if you press "T" once since first running NVCOMP. If you press "T" a second time, the file will be given the default name NEC00001.BMP, and then NEC00002.BMP if you press "T" again, and so on. As before, this capability is only available if NVCOMP succeeds in autodetecting video mode 12. Also, if you don't see the "C FOR PCX" and "T for BMP" instruction on the lower right side of the screen, the option isn't available because the computer is not in mode 12.

The primary purpose of having differently named BMP files with every press of "T" is for use of this output feature with the capability of NVCOMP to display multiple geometries stored in a single NEC-2 file.

3.3 NecDrv2.EXE

NecDrv2.EXE is a postprocessing program written by the author to read a NEC-2 unity drive output file (CALL_1.OUT) and process the data to calculate the base drive voltages that will create a specified set of field ratios.

It is important to remember that this program (and most other post-processing programs written by the author) expects the wires to be identified using the standard notation defined in the text. The wires are identified using three-digit numbers with the first digit denoting the tower number and the remaining two digits denoting the wire number on that particular tower, for example, wire 3 on tower 2 is identified as 203.

The use of NecDrv2.EXE is quite intuitive. Assuming it is included in the PATH variable, the program is called from the folder containing the file CALL_1.OUT by typing "NecDrv2" and pressing <ENTER>. An input screen appears where the user is asked to identify the subject output file. The file is identified by typing "CALL_1.OUT" in the given box then clicking Enter.

A set of boxes appears into which the user must enter the desired field ratio and phase for each tower then click Continue. If the correct notation has not been used to identify the towers and wires, then the correct number of boxes may not appear.

Once the input data has been entered, NecDrv2.EXE displays a set of boxes containing the normalized base drive voltages that will create the desired field ratios. These drive voltages are displayed in their Real and Imaginary format. When used in a bnec.exe run, they will yield the correct pattern shape but not the correct pattern size. The normalized voltages must be scaled upward, as described in the text to create the correct pattern size.

The output screen also provides the option for a hardcopy printout of the results. It gives the choice of printing the principal and induced moments plus the normalized drive voltages, or printing just the normalized drive voltages.

3.4 NECMOM.EXE

NECMOM.EXE is a postprocessing program written by the author to read a NEC-2 output file (either CALL_N.OUT or CALL.OUT) and calculate both the current moment of each tower, and the field ratios created by the drive voltages used to generate the output file. This is useful to confirm the validity of a calculated set of drive voltages or in any other instance in which it is desired to view the actual current moments.

The program is called in the usual way by typing "NECMOM" from the folder containing the target output file (either CALL_N.OUT or CALL.OUT). The screen asks for the target file identity then <ENTER>. No other effort by the user is required. NECMOM.EXE prints an output screen showing the drive voltages used, the calculated current moments and the calculated field ratios.

The user has the option to obtain a hardcopy printout of the moments and field ratios.

3.5 WJGRAPS.EXE

The WJGRAPS.EXE program is a free public domain program that, at the time of this writing, is available for download from *http://www.si-list. net/swindex.html* under the heading IGRAPS. It reads a NEC-2 output file and makes a rather simplified plot of the radiated pattern as generated by the RP command in the NEC-2 input file. VBRUN200.DLL is a run time file that must be in the same folder as WJGRAPS.EXE or on a path such that the run time file can be located when WJGRAPS.EXE runs.

When the program is called by typing "WJGRAPS <ENTER>", a blank screen appears with a short header at the top giving the choices "File", "Print", and "Exit".

When File is clicked, an Open box drops down and when Open is clicked, a dialog box opens showing all files in the current folder. Highlight the desired file and click OK to create the pattern on the screen. Clicking Print on the header creates a hard copy of the pattern using the default printer. Clicking Exit terminates the program.

Although there are no markings on the graph, it is useful to know that the pattern is normalized to its maximum value and that there are ten rings. Consequently, each ring is 10 percent of the maximum value. Angular markings appear at 10-degree intervals so a little ingenuity allows the reader to get some idea of the numerical details of the pattern.

4.1 Software Support

The software on the CD included with this book is furnished without charge as a convenience to the reader. The author is not able to provide technical support of any kind. No warranty is provided as to the accuracy or capability of the software and neither the author nor the publisher assumes responsibility for the results of its use. (See also Warranty on the envelope of the CD included with this book.)

Index